Religion and Nationalism in Asia

This book re-examines the relationship between religion and nationalism in a contemporary Asian context, with a focus on East, South and South East Asia.

Addressing empirical, analytical, and normative questions, it analyses selected case studies from across Asia, including China, India, Iraq, Japan, Pakistan, the Philippines and Sri Lanka and compares the differences and commonalities between the diverse configurations of nationalism and religion across the continent. It then goes on to explain reasons for the regional religious resurgence and asks, is the nation-state model, aligned with secularism, suitable for the region? Exploring the two interrelated issues of legacies and possibilities, this book also examines the relationship between nationalism and modernity, identifying possible and desirable trajectories which go beyond existing configurations of nationalism and religion.

Bringing together a stellar line up of contributors in the field, *Religion and Nationalism in Asia* will be a valuable resource for students and scholars of Asian religion and politics as well as sociology, ethnicity, nationalism and comparative politics.

Giorgio Shani is Chair in Politics and International Studies and Director of the Rotary Peace Center at International Christian University, Japan. He is author of *Sikh Nationalism and Identity in a Global Age* (Routledge 2008) and *Religion, Identity and Human Security* (Routledge 2014).

Takashi Kibe is Professor of Political Science at International Christian University, Japan. Among his publications are *Martin Luther's Political Thought* (in Japanese, 2000), and *Political Theory of Equality* (in Japanese, 2015).

Political Theories in East Asian Context
Series Editor: Jun-Hyeok Kwak

Political Theories in East Asian Context aims to shed light on the essential theoretical issues spanning East Asia by situating them within cross-cultural frameworks that attend both to the particularity of East Asia as well as the potentially universal patterns arising from East Asia's current issues that can be studied for the global prosperity. It reconsiders issues like historical reconciliation, nationalism, multicultural coexistence, political leadership, republicanism, and regional integration, with a view to opening the discourse of particular issues to a wider theoretical horizon. Including intellectuals in the field of political science, history, ethnic studies, sociology, and regional studies, this interdisciplinary endeavour is a deliberative forum in which we can reflect on ethical problems facing East Asia in the global era.

Inherited Responsibility and Historical Reconciliation in East Asia
Edited by Jun-Hyeok Kwak and Melissa Nobles

Patriotism in East Asia
Edited by Jun-Hyeok Kwak and Koichiro Matsuda

Worlding Multiculturalisms
The Politics of Inter-Asian Dwelling
Edited by Daniel P. S. Goh

Republicanism in Northeast Asia
Edited by Jun-Hyeok Kwak and Leigh Jenco

Religion and Nationalism in Asia
Edited by Giorgio Shani and Takashi Kibe

Leo Strauss in Northeast Asia
Edited by Jun-Hyeok Kwak and Sungwoo Park

Global Justice in East Asia
Edited by Hugo El Kholi and Jun-Hyeok Kwak

Religion and Nationalism in Asia

Edited by Giorgio Shani and Takashi Kibe

LONDON AND NEW YORK

First published 2020 by Routledge

2 Park Square, Milton Park, Abingdon, Oxon, OX14 4RN
605 Third Avenue, New York, NY 10017

Routledge is an imprint of the Taylor & Francis Group, an informa business

First issued in paperback 2020

Copyright © 2020 selection and editorial matter, Giorgio Shani and Takashi Kibe; individual chapters, the contributors

The right of Giorgio Shani and Takashi Kibe to be identified as the authors of the editorial material, and of the authors for their individual chapters, has been asserted in accordance with sections 77 and 78 of the Copyright, Designs and Patents Act 1988.

All rights reserved. No part of this book may be reprinted or reproduced or utilised in any form or by any electronic, mechanical, or other means, now known or hereafter invented, including photocopying and recording, or in any information storage or retrieval system, without permission in writing from the publishers.

Notice:
Product or corporate names may be trademarks or registered trademarks, and are used only for identification and explanation without intent to infringe.

British Library Cataloguing-in-Publication Data
A catalogue record for this book is available from the British Library

Library of Congress Cataloging-in-Publication Data
Names: Shani, Giorgio, 1970– editor.
Title: Religion and nationalism in Asia / edited by Giorgio Shani and Takashi Kibe.
Identifiers: LCCN 2019028279 (print) | LCCN 2019028280 (ebook) | ISBN 9780367183424 (hardback) | ISBN 9780429060922 (ebook) | ISBN 9780429595042 (adobe pdf) | ISBN 9780429592461 (mobi) | ISBN 9780429593758 (epub)
Subjects: LCSH: East Asia—Religion. | South Asia—Religion. | Southeast Asia—Religion. | Nationalism—Religious aspects. | Nationalism—East Asia. | Nationalism—South Asia. | Nationalism—Southeast Asia.
Classification: LCC BL1055 .R424 2019 (print) | LCC BL1055 (ebook) | DDC 322/.1095—dc23
LC record available at https://lccn.loc.gov/2019028279
LC ebook record available at https://lccn.loc.gov/2019028280

ISBN: 978-0-367-18342-4 (hbk)
ISBN: 978-0-367-77742-5 (pbk)

Typeset in Times New Roman
by Apex CoVantage, LLC

Contents

List of contributors	vii
Acknowledgements	x
Introduction: legacies and possibilities GIORGIO SHANI AND TAKASHI KIBE	1
1 **Tagore and the conception of critical nationalism** SUDIPTA KAVIRAJ	13
2 **Midnight's children: religion and nationalism in South Asia** GIORGIO SHANI	32
3 **Articulations of religiously motivated nationalism within Philippine Catholicism: a critical assessment** MANUEL VICTOR J. SAPITULA	47
4 **Reconsidering the relation between 'sectarianism' and nationalism in the Middle East** FANAR HADDAD	62
5 **The irony of secular nation-building in Japanese modernity: Inoue Kowashi and Fukuzawa Yukichi** TAKASHI KIBE	79
6 **Buddhism, cosmology, and Greater East Asian Co-prosperity Sphere: multiculturalism and nationalism in the pre-war period Japan** KOSUKE SHIMIZU	94

7	**Political modernity in East Asia: religion, nationalism and subversion of imperialism** ATSUKO ICHIJO	108
8	**Religious nationalism with non-domination: Ahn Changho's cosmopolitan patriotism** JUN-HYEOK KWAK	124
9	**The structural problem of religious freedom in China: toward a Confucian-Christian synthesis** ZHIBIN XIE	139
10	**Augustine's critique of religious identity and its implications for the Chinese church** WEI HUA	154
11	**Post-Chinese reconnections through religion: Buddhism, Christianity, and Confucianism** CHIH-YU SHIH	168
	Conclusion TAKASHI KIBE AND GIORGIO SHANI	186
	Index	199

Contributors

Fanar Haddad is Senior Research Fellow at the Middle East Institute, National University of Singapore and Non-Resident Senior Fellow at the Middle East Institute, Washington, DC. Prior to obtaining his PhD he was a Research Analyst at the Foreign and Commonwealth Office (2007–2010). He has taught the politics of the modern Middle East at the University of Exeter, Queen Mary University of London, and the National University of Singapore. He is the author of *Sectarianism in Iraq: Antagonistic Visions of Unity* (2011) and of the forthcoming *Understanding "Sectarianism": Sunni-Shi'a Relations in the Modern Arab World*.

Wei Hua (PhD, Peking University) is Associate Professor of philosophy and Christian studies at Yuelu Academy, Hunan University, Changsha, China. His research interests include Augustine's thought, St. Paul's letters, philosophy of late antiquity and Confucian-Christian dialogues. He has published dozens of articles, including "On the Rise of Augustine's Concept of *Voluntas*" (*Sino-Christian Studies* 15 [June 2013]); "*Galatians 2:11–14* and the Exegetical Controversy between Augustine and Jerome" *(Logos & Pneuma: Chinese Journal of Theology* 42 [Spring 2015]); and "Pauline Pneumatology and the Chinese Rites: Spirit and Culture in the Holy See's Missionary Strategy" (in Gene L. Green, Stephen T. Pardue & K. K. Yeo, ed., *The Spirit over the Earth: Pneumatology in the Majority World*, Grand Rapids, William B. Eerdmans Publishing Company, 2016).

Atsuko Ichijo is Associate Professor in the Department of Politics, International Relations and Human Rights, Kingston University, UK. Her research interest is in the field of nationalism studies and is the author of "The Articulation of National Identity in Early Twentieth Century East Asia: Intertwining of Discourses of Modernity and Civilisation" (2018) *Asian Studies Review*, Vol. 42, Issue 2, pp. 342–355; *Food, National Identity and Nationalism* (co-authored with Ronald Ranta, 2016); *Nationalism and Multiple Modernities: Europe and Beyond* (2013). She is a member of the editorial team of *Nations and Nationalism* and a book series editor of 'Identities and Modernities in Europe' series.

Sudipta Kaviraj is Professor of Indian Politics and Intellectual History at the Department of Middle Eastern, South Asian and African Studies at Columbia

University, New York. His main fields of interest are political theory, Indian intellectual history in politics and aesthetics, and the study of the democratic state in India. He has taught previously at the School of Oriental and African Studies, University of London, and Jawaharlal Nehru University, New Delhi, and was a Research Fellow at St. Antony's College, Oxford. His publications include *The Unhappy Consciousness: Bankimchandra Chattopadhyay and the Formation of Nationalist Discourse*; *The Imaginary Institution of India*; *Trajectories of the Indian State*; *The Enchantment of Democracy and India*; *The Invention of Private Life*; and *Civil Society: History and Possibilities* (co-edited with Sunil Khilnani).

Takashi Kibe is Professor of the Department of Politics and International Studies at International Christian University. He received his doctor degree from University of Tübingen. His research interests are egalitarianism, multiculturalism, citizenship, liberalism, philosophy of social sciences, and history of political thought, especially early modern political theory. He is the author of *Frieden und Erziehung in Martin Luthers Drei-Stände-Lehre* (1996); *Luta no Seiji Shiso* (The Political Thought of Martin Luther) (2000); and *Byodo no Seiji Riron* (Political Theory of Equality) (2015). His publications include "Differentiated Citizenship and Ethnocultural Groups," *Citizenship Studies* (2006); "The Relational Approach to Egalitarian Justice," *Critical Review of International Social and Political Philosophy* (2011); and "The 'Multicultural Coexistence': Discourse in Crisis?" in *Social Inequality in Post-Growth Japan*, ed. D. Chiavacci and C. Hommerich (Routledge, 2016).

Jun-Hyeok Kwak is Professor of the Department of Philosophy (Zhuhai), Sun Yat-sen University. He received his PhD from the University of Chicago in 2002. Before joining SYSU in 2016, he taught at various universities including Korea University, Kyungpook National University, University of Bologna, and the University of Chicago. His research interests lie at the crossroads of political philosophy from Socrates to Machiavelli and contemporary sociopolitical theories. Recent works include "Machiavelli and Republican Patriotism," *Australian Journal of Political Science* (2017). He is currently serving as the General Editor of the Routledge Series of Political Theories in East Asian Context.

Manuel Victor J. Sapitula (PhD) is Associate Professor at the Department of Sociology, College of Social Sciences and Philosophy at the University of the Philippines Diliman. He obtained his PhD in Sociology from the National University of Singapore (NUS) in 2013. He is a member of the Philippine Sociological Society and served as member of the board from 2013 to 2015. He is also a member of the Pi Gamma Mu Internal Honor Society for the Social Sciences, the International Sociological Association – Research Committee on the Sociology of Religion (RC 22) and Association for Asian Studies.

Giorgio Shani is Professor and Chair of the Department of Politics and International Studies and Director of the Rotary Peace Center at International Christian University (ICU) in Japan. From 2016 to 2017, he was Visiting Senior

Research Fellow at the Centre for International Studies at the London School of Economics and Political Science (LSE) and recently he served as President of the Asia-Pacific region of the International Studies Association (ISA). His main research interests focus on religion and politics; critical human security; and post-Western international political theory with reference to South Asia and Japan. He is author of *Sikh Nationalism and Identity in a Global Age* (Routledge 2008) and *Religion, Identity and Human Security* (Routledge 2014); and co-editor of *Protecting Human Security in a Post 9/11 World* (2007) and *Rethinking Peace* (2019).

Chih-yu Shih teaches China studies, anthropology of knowledge, and international relations theory in the Department of Political Science of National Taiwan University where he is a professor. Determined to recollect and re-present intellectual heritage in Asia (www.china-studies.taipei/), he has devoted himself throughout his academic career for the past 25 years to researching, teaching, and writing on the cultural and political agency of human society in Asia, especially where the mainstream scholarship in the United States and Western Europe fails to attend. His method is primarily field interview, oral history, and archive research. Professor Shih's publications consistently challenge the mainstream views on the law of human behavior and gather evidence of human agency from ethnic communities, developing countries, people under poverty, and so on.

Kosuke Shimizu is Professor of International Relations at the Department of Global Studies. He is also the director of the Afrasian Research Centre, and the Dean of Research of the Ryukoku University, Kyoto. He received his PhD from the Victoria University of Wellington, and is currently working on critical theories, and philosophy of the Kyoto School. His recent English publications include "Materialising the 'Non-Western," *Cambridge Review of International Affairs*, 28 (1), 2015; "Reflection, the Public, and the Modern Machine," *Japanese Journal of Political Science*, 18 (4), 2018; "Do Time and Language Matter in IR?" *Korean Journal of International Studies*, 16(1), 2018.

Zhibin Xie received his PhD from the University of Hong Kong. He is Professor of philosophy at Tongji University, Shanghai, P. R. China. He is a research fellow at the Institute of Sino-Christian Studies in Hong Kong and a member at the Center of Theological Inquiry in Princeton. His research interests include Christian philosophy and ethics, public theology and its implications in the Chinese context, religion and politics in China. His major publications include *Religious Diversity and Public Religion in China* (in English, 2006); *Public Theology and Globalization: A Study in Christian Ethics of Max L. Stackhouse* (in Chinese, 2008); and *How Public? Why Theological: A Review and Prospect of Sino-Christian Public Theology* (in Chinese, 2016). His articles appear in *Studies in Interreligious Dialogue, Asia Journal of Theology, International Journal of Public Theology*, etc. He serves as one of the general editors for the Public Theology Series published by the Institute of Sino-Christian Studies.

Acknowledgements

This project was first incubated in June 2013, when we met up with Jun-Hyeok Kwak in Nakano, Tokyo. Perhaps aided by the Roman god Bacchus, we heatedly discussed religion and nationalism until the early hours, which led Jun-Hyeok to suggest that we write a volume on this theme for his series. This led to an international symposium "Beyond Nationalism? Peacebuilding and Religion in Asia" on December 20, 2014, at International Christian University, co-sponsored by the Institute of Global Concern, Sophia University and the Peace Research Institute at International Christian University and to a workshop titled "Religion, Nationalism, and Secularism" at Peace Research Institute of ICU, December 22, 2014, to which many of the contributors to the volume were invited, including Sudipta Kaviraj, Atsuko Ichijo, Kosuke Shimizu and Jun-Heok Kwak. Some contributors to this volume (Ichijo, Kibe, Kwak, Shih and Shani) also participated in a panel titled "Beyond Nationalism? Religion and Nationalism in Asia" at the International Studies Association Asia-Pacific Region Conference at City University of Hong Kong, Hong Kong, June 26, 2016. Finally, a symposium entitled the "Routledge Series of *Political Theories in East Asian Context* International Symposium 2016: Religion and Nationalism in Asia" was held at Sun Yat-sen University, November 20, 2016, to which other contributors including Hua Wei, Zhibin Xie and Chih-yu Shih were invited to join the original participants in submitting draft chapters.

We would like to express our enormous gratitude to all participants in the previously mentioned events. We would particularly like to thank Jianhong Chen, Tim Beaumont, Luis Cordeiro Rodrigues (Sun Yat-sen University), Shi-Chi Mike Lan (National Chengchi University), Shin Chiba, Masaki Ina, Katsuhiko Mori, Jae-Jung Suh, Wilhelm Vosse (International Christian University), Nina Hasegawa, Koichi Nakano, Toshiro Terada (Sophia University), Takeshi Deguchi (Tokyo University), Keiko Sakai (Chiba University), and Takahiro Chino (Waseda University) as well as Guoxiang Peng (Zhejiang University) and an enthusiastic supporter, Hayo Krombach (LSE). Our thanks also to staff members of Peace Research Institute and Social Science Research Institute at International Christian University and the Department of Philosophy (Zhuhai) at Sun Yat-sen University, all of whom made the symposia and workshops possible (Kibe owes special thanks to Huang Danping, an SYSU secretary who kindly helped him find his lost luggage at Macau Airport). We are grateful to Routledge and especially to Georgina Bishop for supporting this publication and to three anonymous reviewers for their helpful – and sometimes critical – comments. Finally, we would like to thank our contributors for their patience and cooperation throughout the painstaking process of rewriting and revising their chapters for this volume, and to our friend, Jun-Hyeok Kwak, series editor of "Routledge Series of Political Theories in East Asian Context," who enthusiastically supported this project from the very beginning.

Takashi Kibe and Giorgio Shani

Introduction

Legacies and possibilities

Giorgio Shani and Takashi Kibe

The centenary commemorations of the end of the First World War serve as a stark reminder of the perils of nationalism, which have as yet remained unheeded throughout Asia. In a lecture given in Japan one hundred years ago as the war unfolded, the Bengali poet and Nobel Laureate Rabindranath Tagore criticized the nation-state and the materialist philosophy underpinning it and offered instead a vision of an Asia suffused with indigenous spiritual values. "The political civilization which has sprung from the soil of Europe and is overrunning the whole world," Tagore presciently asserted, "is based on exclusiveness" (Tagore [1917] 1991: 24). Nationalism – or "national patriotism" – was the name he gave to that political civilization. It was based on "science" and not "human" values, unlike "Eastern" civilizations, which were based on "the spiritual idea of man" (Tagore [1917] 1991: 25). "Religion," or more specifically Asian spiritual traditions, was therefore counterposed to the modern ideology of secular nationalism.

This volume seeks to re-examine the relationship between religion and nationalism one hundred years after Tagore's lectures in a contemporary Asian context with a focus on East, South and South East Asia. We do this cognizant of the fact that both "religion" and "nationalism" have their genealogies in the West and as such cannot be translated into an "Asian" context. As Talal Asad (1993) has persuasively argued, there can be no *transhistorical* understanding of religion. Furthermore, Asad asserts that there can be no "universal definition of religion, not because its constituent elements and relationships are historically specific, but that definition itself is the product of discursive processes" (1993: 29). Asad sees the emergence of "religion" as inextricably linked to developments within Christianity and particularly its relationship with political power. Consequently, "religion" is inescapably a "Western" (i.e. Eurocentric) discourse. As Timothy Fitzgerald points out, this insight raises a question about whether the concept of religion presents "a valid analytical category" and "a genuine crosscultural category" (Fitzgerald 2000: 4). Furthermore, it leads us to reconsider secularism. This is because secularism, as Asad (2003) and José Casanova (1994, 2011) among others have pointed out, can only be understood with reference to "religion." The "secular" at one time was "part of a theological discourse (*saeculum*)" denoting the transition from a monastic life to the life of canons. After the Reformation, it signified the "privatization" of Church property, that is, its transfer to laypersons and entry into market circulation. Finally, in the "discourse of modernity, the 'secular' presents itself as the ground from which theological discourse was generated ... and from which it gradually emancipated itself in the mark to freedom" (Asad 2003: 192).

Its genealogy in the Judeo-Christian tradition poses problems for the discussion of "Asian" religious or cultural traditions, blurring the distinction between "religious" and "secular" claims when it comes to discussing "Asian" religio-cultural philosophies such as Buddhism, Confucianism, Daoism, Hinduism, Sikhism and Shintoism which, in some cases, are far older than the concept of "religion" itself. We also acknowledge that the very idea of an "Asia" encompassing China, India and Japan, yet excluding much of the Eurasian land mass, owes much to "Orientalist" scholarship (Said 1978) which developed as a result of the European subjugation and conquest of "Asia." In other words, Asia exists as a category only in the European imagination.

Nevertheless, a century ago many bought into the idea of Asia as an "imagined community" (Anderson 1991). The Japanese victory over Russia in 1905 had acted as a catalyst for an Asian Risorgimento. The first generation of Asian intellectuals had sought, in the words of the Meiji reformer Fukuzawa Yukichi, to "escape from Asia" (*datsua*). The Meiji restoration illustrated how it was possible for Asian societies such as Japan to modernize by selectively appropriating key features of Western modernity under the direction of a strong, centralized state without the tutelage of colonization. Modernization entailed reforming Asian societies along Western lines in order to counter the dominance of the West. However, the wholesale slaughter of the First World War discredited Western civilization in the eyes of many of its most educated subjects. Reflecting the dominant Orientalist narratives of the time, Pan-Asian intellectuals contrasted the materialist, rationalist, militarist West unfavorably with a mystic, spiritual, harmonious East. Thinkers such as the Bengali Nobel laureate Rabindranath Tagore, the Chinese Confucian reformer Liang Qichao and the Japanese scholar Okakura Tenshin sought, through dialogue, to frame a distinctly "Asian" intellectual tradition that provided great sustenance to the various anti-colonial movements of the region (Duara 2001). For Tagore, when the "conflagration" of the First World War, "a European war of retribution," had consumed itself and died down, "leaving its memorial in ashes, the eternal light" of man's spirit "will again shine in the East – the East which has been the birthplace of the morning sun of man's history" (Tagore [1917] 1991: 45). This intellectual tradition drew upon Confucian edicts, the Vedas and most importantly, Buddhist teachings which bridged the Himalayas.

However, "Pan-Asianism" ultimately became subordinated to Japanese Imperial ambitions. The Japanese victory in the Russo-Japanese war convinced many Japanese intellectuals that Japan was the only power capable of leading Asia. Since it both "belonged" to Asia and had mastered Western civilization, Japan was uniquely positioned to modernize Asian civilizations without destroying their traditions. Consequently, Japan had not only a right but a duty to "liberate" East Asia from Western influence and awaken Asian civilizations from the stupor into which they had fallen. Pan-Asian intellectuals such as Okawa Shumei played a key role in legitimizing the Greater East Asia Co-Prosperity Sphere. Okawa saw an underlying unity to Asian civilizations – a spiritual, moral and timeless essence – which could be contrasted to the materialism of the West (Duara 2001: 110–111). But what was this spiritual, moral and timeless essence? And why was Japan, the most Westernized of all the Asian societies, uniquely able to articulate this "essence" and incorporate it in a newly emerging regional order which it helped to fashion through force?

Although the spectacular rise of the People's Republic of China (PRC) and India, along with other members of the BRICS, has constituted a powerful challenge to the hegemony of the West in world politics, the dominant form of political community in contemporary international relations (IR) remains the nation-state. A product of European political history, the nation-state model has been globalized, first coercively through the colonization of much of Asia by European powers, and then subsequently through decolonization. In Japan, the nation-state was adopted after the Meiji Restoration and is widely accepted as a "natural" political community built upon pre-existing ethnic foundations. In recent years, the revival of Japanese "ethno-nationalism," which has remained dormant since the Second World War, and the increasing use of nationalist rhetoric by the People's Republic of China has threatened peace and stability in the region. These have come to a head with the territorial disputes over the Senkaku/Daiyou islands which are also claimed by Taiwan. In many ways, the rise of ethno-nationalism in East Asia mirrors the prior emergence of religious nationalism in South Asia with the added danger posed by the possession of nuclear weapons by both India and Pakistan. But what role does "religion" play in nationalism in East Asia? Is "religion" of limited relevance given the secular nature of East Asian modernity or have "religious" traditions such as Confucianism, Daoism and Shintoism as well as Buddhism and Christianity helped contribute to the construction of a nationalist discourse and the legitimization of the modern nation-state? Furthermore, what role can "religion" play not only in the development of nationalism but also in opposing it?

Rationale for the volume

This volume, which arises out of a symposium and a workshop held at International Christian University, Japan, and a follow-up workshop at Sun-Yat Sen University, PRC, is devoted to the theme of "nationalism and religion in Asia" for contextual and theoretical reasons. A main contextual reason is the fact that nationalism – a decisive factor to understand political issues in this region just like elsewhere – has been accompanied by the issue of "religion" in diverse ways. In some cases, nationalist movements are "secular" attempts to suppress or downplay "religion" to find a basis of national unity; in others, they take on the form of religious nationalism, by appealing to allegedly religious traditions and/or remolding them to fit the cause of national unity. A case in point is India. For example, Jawaharlal Nehru in his Bhopal speech of 1954 stressed the secular nature of nationalism, arguing that "we must not fragment Indian nationalism by bringing religion into it" (Nehru [1954] 2017). This appeared in sharp contrast with the "two-nation" theory put forward by Muhammad Ali Jinnah in 1940. Jinnah claimed that it was "a dream that the Hindus and Muslims can ever evolve a common nationality," since they belonged to "two different religious philosophies, social customs, and literatures" (Jinnah 1940). For Jinnah, the notion of nation appears inseparably intertwined with religion. However, both Nehru and Jinnah founded "secular" states. It was only after Jinnah's death that Pakistan became an Islamic republic. Similarly, Hindu nationalists have sought to redefine the "nation" with reference to India's dominant "religious" tradition: Hinduism. They have sought to do so, however, within the constraints imposed by India's "secular" constitution. In the case of Japan, Imperial Japan was linked with the sacralizing view of the emperor, backed by Shintoism. Even though the post-war Japanese constitution is based on secular political principles, Shinto organizations that exert a certain influence on Japanese politics advocate for a "religious" kind of nationalism. In a pamphlet on Shintoism, for instance, Jinja Honcho (Association of Shinto Shrines) emphasizes the imperial lineage between the current emperor and the goddess Amaterasu. Hence "a symbol of the national character and traditions of Japan" (Jinja Honcho 2013: 34), which the emperor allegedly embodies, has inevitably "religious" ramifications. These examples suggest that it is appropriate to understand nationalist politics in Asian contexts by interrogating relationships between nationalism and religion.

Despite the importance of the relationship between nationalism and religion in Asia, however, it seems safe to say that mainstream political and social theory has not paid sufficient attention to insights deriving from them. There are two reasons for this. One reason is that the scope of mainstream political and social theory is basically defined by the Western context. Thus, discussions on nationalism tend to be based on Western cases, while the potential contribution to political and social theorizing of Asian cases remains unexplored. Another reason is the dominant modernist view of nationalism as represented in the work of Ernest Gellner (1983) and Benedict Anderson (1991) which sees nationalism as a modern phenomenon and secularization is an essential part of modernization. Hence nationalism is understood as a process that detaches itself from religion, marginalizing it: secularism is a hallmark of nationalism as modernization. Integral to this perspective is a view that modernity replaces primordial identity based on kinships, language and religion with civic identity based on citizenship of a nation-state.

But, as the previous examples indicated suggest, this specific, secularist view of nationalism does not do justice to diverse configurations of the relationship between nationalism and religion in Asian countries. Specifically, we have three reasons to critically re-examine this secularist view. First, in the early twenty-first century we witness a resurgence of religion, often in forms of religious nationalism. Mark Juergensmeyer (2006: 184) observes: "By the first decade of the twenty-first century virtually every religious tradition in the world had provided justification for some form of religious nationalism." Second, the so-called secularization thesis that religious life in the modern world is in decline is now called into question. As José Casanova has clearly shown in his work *Public Religions in the Modern World*, the reality is more nuanced: though differentiated from other social spheres, religion is not wholly privatized and does exert significant influence on social life (Casanova 1994). Third, the concept of religion is now regarded as a contested category, far from being self-evident.[1] In a similar vein, the paired concept of the secular is no longer considered a neutral point of view. How we understand religion is framed by our concept of the secular, and vice versa, as Talal Asad (2003) points out. As Peter van der Veer (2014: 64–65) points out, we need to keep in mind that "a concept like religion does not have a transhistorical essence, but that the term is configured and transformed throughout history in relation to a conceptual field." In the field of political theory, the need to re-examine the concept of religion has only recently been recognized. Cécile Laborde (2017: 1–2) claims that the concept of religion, which has remained an "under-theorized" and hence vague notion in liberal political philosophers, is "less than adequate *as a politico-legal category*." All of this means that we cannot properly approach the issue of "religion and nationalism" without critically examining what is meant by key concepts such as "religion," "religious" and "secular."[2]

In the final analysis, the need to re-examine the modernist and hence secularist understanding of nationalism is linked with an alternative, diversified view of modernity. This is what S. N. Eisenstadt calls "multiple modernities." As Eisenstadt (2000: 2) puts it, "the best way to understand the contemporary world – indeed to explain the history of modernity – is to see it as a story of continual constitution and reconstitution of a multiplicity of cultural programs." Expanding on Eisenstadt's seminal idea, van der Veer (2013: 669) points out as follows:

> Nationalism and religion are products of a multiplicity of modernities in different parts of the world. This multiplicity cannot be any longer easily understood in terms of modernization and secularization.

The idea of multiple modernities thus opens up wider and differentiated perspectives on nationalism. In this view, historical trajectories of nationalism and configurations of the relationship between nationalism and religion are diverse attempts to respond to the encounter of imperialism and the universalized concepts of European origin, such as "nation" and "religion." This way of looking into Asian countries help us see not only their differences from the European trajectories and configurations but also differences within themselves.

Our challenges in this volume are to address empirical, analytical and normative questions. Our major empirical question is: What is the relationship between religion and nationalism in Asia with reference to the case studies selected? Another related question is: What are differences and commonalities between the diverse configurations of nationalism and religion in Asian contexts? Finally, we will pose a normative-theoretical question: Is the nation-state model, aligned with secularism, suitable for the region? Another way to raise the third question is to ask under what circumstances secularism is suitable/unsuitable, particularly when paired with the nation-state model. By addressing these questions, we finally attempt to clarify two interrelated issues, epitomized in the subtitle of this volume: *legacies* and *possibilities*. To tackle the first issue, we will examine the relationship between nationalism and modernity, for example, by tracing the legacy of contemporary religiously infused nationalism in the colonial period, or considering the genealogy of secularist aspirations that give rise to specific forms of religious governance. This task is expected to contribute to cultivating a historical sensitivity, thereby providing a basis for the second issue: identifying possible and desirable trajectories that can go beyond current configurations of nationalism and religion. For example, an engagement with "popular" religions may help us think beyond the nation-state to uncover new possibilities for political and religious constellations.

Justification for case studies

To re-examine the relationship between religion and nationalism in East, South and South East Asia, and specifically to respond to the three questions raised previously, this volume is composed of case studies on Iraq, India, Pakistan, Bangladesh, Sri Lanka, the Philippines, People's Republic of China, Republic of China, South Korea and Japan. Although the selection is not exhaustive, we believe it is representative of the region. However, our main aim is *not* to present a complete map of configurations of religion and nationalism in all Asian states. Neither do we believe that it is possible to articulate an essentialist position on a distinctly Asian perspective on religion and nationalism. Furthermore, the volume does not pursue a covering-law position to ask what laws or general propositions explain those configurations. Rather, the aim of our volume is modest but significant. The primary task of the present volume is to find differences and commonalities in configurations of religion and nationalism in various Asian contexts. Since we do not seek generalizations, these differences and commonalities need not be exhaustive. Though limited in numbers, the case studies in this volume suffice. All of them provide significant clues to re-examining the relationship between religion and nationalism in Asia and to reflect on the three questions posed.

Chapter summaries

The main tensions between nationalism as a colonial *legacy* and post-colonial *possibility* are illustrated through an exposition of Tagore's conception of critical nationalism in the opening chapter by Sudipta Kaviraj. For Kaviraj, Tagore's significance for "the urgent political predicaments we face today" lies in his recognition of the *ambivalence* of nationalism. Unlike most intellectuals of his time, Tagore did not *uncritically* embrace anti-imperialist nationalism as the *only* response to European imperialist nationalism but articulated a "critical" conception of nationalism which was cognizant of the inherent violence associated with modern conceptions of the nation-state. Since the colonial state was alien to the people it governed, it needed to be "opposed politically and contested ethically." This, Tagore realized, could only be done through a nationalist popular movement. However, rather than accept the Eurocentric terms upon which the discourse of nationalism is constructed, Kaviraj suggests that Tagore posits the "nation" neither as an object to be liberated by a nationalist movement nor one to be constructed by nationalist elites, but as "a moral imaginary: an ideal of human belonging which no state can historically realize in full, and which, therefore, can be used strategically as a ground from which actual states and their realization of the people-nation can be criticized." Thus, instead of becoming a principle of exclusion, or an idea that serves to legitimize the actions of the state, this idea of the "ideal nation" becomes a principle of criticism. Tagore's reflections on nationalism suggest a larger question which is central to this volume: whether the idea of the nation-state is indeed "the final destiny of mankind" or whether other forms of "imagined community" can fulfill human needs for collective belonging in what was previously considered a globalizing world.

The tragedy wrought by the imposition of the nation-state model in South Asia is central to the next chapter by Giorgio Shani, who traces the rise of contemporary religious nationalism to the colonial construction of the category of "religion." Drawing on the work of the previous contributor, Sudipta Kaviraj, he shows how the introduction of the Census in particular enumerated previously "fuzzy" communities in colonial India, resulting in political mobilization on the basis of religion with catastrophic consequences for the subcontinent. Despite the secular credentials of the nationalist leadership, Shani argues that the "nation" could not help but be imagined on ethno-religious lines. Independence resulted in the formation of two successor states – India and Pakistan – both committed to secularism in theory but in practice made possible by mass ethnic cleansing and acts of genocide. The "spectres of Partition," he argues, continue to haunt contemporary South Asia through periodic communal riots and sectarian conflict. The manipulation of memories of Partition by post-colonial political elites have left South Asian societies in the grip of a nationalist imaginary increasingly articulated in a religious idiom that makes "secular" rule problematic. Of particular importance has been the rise of a Hindu majoritarian nationalism in India mirrored by the emergence of Political Islam and its militant off-shoots in Pakistan and Bangladesh. Although spared the trauma of Partition, colonial categories of religion and nation continue to haunt Sri Lanka in the aftermath of a bloody civil war, making peace and reconciliation difficult.

The inextricable relationship between religion and nationalism is further illustrated by Manuel Sapitula in the case of the Philippines. In his chapter, Sapitula unpacks the mechanisms that allowed the Catholic Church to articulate ideations of a "Catholic Nation" to further religious-based interests. Demonstrated through certain historical events, the appeal to religiously monocultural frames of reference rests on an ambivalent, if not critical, attitude toward actually existing diversity and the need for religious and cultural pluralism. Sapitula also shows how the "Catholic Nation" discourse exposes institutional Catholicism in the Philippines to criticism for its refusal to "play by the rules" of constitutional democracy and its perceived exclusion of alternative frames of reference that cater to the needs of other groups, such as Muslims, Buddhists and Hindus. Sapitula concludes this chapter by pointing to the need of a "postnational track" as a plausible and attractive option that accommodates to religious pluralism of the Philippines.

Fanar Haddad's case study on modern Iraq contributes to bringing to light a modernist bias toward sectarian and religious identities. Haddad argues that common views on sectarianism in the Middle East are premised on a problematic dichotomous view of sectarianism and nationalism. According to this view, sectarian identities – for example, Sunni and Shi'a Muslim identities – and national identities are mutually opposed. Haddad claims that behind this dichotomy lies a modernist bias that regards secularized and territorialized national identities as "modern" and hence "good" in contradistinction with "pre-modern" and hence "bad" religious and transnational sectarian identities. Against this dichotomous view, Haddad compellingly shows that modern sectarian identities are closely linked to nationalism and national identity. In doing so, he makes clear the need to deploy a multi-layered framework to grasp sectarian identities on multiple, interconnected and mutually dialogical fields, which are composed of religious, subnational, national and transnational components.

The dynamic and paradoxical nature of the relationship between secular nationalism and religious nationalism is highlighted by Takashi Kibe in the case of modern Japan. To show this, Kibe focuses on the political thoughts of two key figures in the Meiji era: Inoue Kowashi (1844–1895) and Fukuzawa Yukichi (1835–1901). Unlike the common characterization of prewar Japan as based on religious nationalism, Kibe shows that Inoue and Fukuzawa, though diametrically opposed to each other on important political issues, basically conceived of nationalism as a secularist project. Yet, due to their elitist politics of interpretation that declares Shinto as a non-religion and their instrumental view of religious sentiments, Kibe argues, Inoue and Fukuzawa unwittingly planted the seeds that would develop into religious nationalism in wartime Japan. Kibe concludes this chapter by suggesting that what is religion/non-religion is still an unsettled political question in contemporary Japan – a legacy that Inoue and Fukuzawa's politics of interpretation left behind

Whereas Kibe focuses on the role of Shintoism in modern Japanese nation-building, Kosuke Shimizu focuses on the role played by Buddhist discourses in the legitimization of the Japanese Empire. In Japan, the structural reformation of world political economy appeared in the form of emergence of Romanticism, particularly in the inter-war period. While the Kyoto School philosophy typically exemplifies this phenomenon, some religious organizations – Nishihongwanji temple, the biggest Buddhist organisation of Japan, in particular – also took a leading role to promote the Romantic ideas of Japaneseness. In his chapter, Shimizu strives to reveal the role Nishihongwanji performed to disseminate the Romanticism among ordinary citizens in the era of confrontation against the West, and tries to find out the reason of this incorporation with the Japanese Imperial regime of the time.

Atsuko Ichijo's chapter examines the development of political modernity in East Asia in the early twentieth century through an exploration of the ways in which ideas about political community were produced, used and appropriated by both the imperialists and the colonized. Inspired by the theory of multiple modernities (Eisenstadt 2000) which rejects the teleological assumption of conventional modernization, Ichijo's chapter focuses on the ways in which Asianism, a discourse of resistance to European/Western hegemony, was developed and acted upon by Eastern Asian intellectuals to define modernity in their own terms. In particular, her chapter reviews the ways in which various ideas associated with Asianism, articulated within the context of the philosophy of world history by the Kyoto School, were engaged by colonial intellectuals in Taiwan, Korea and China, which represented an exercise of agency in a broad, sociological sense and subjectivity on the part of the colonized. These ideas include schemes such as the "East Asian Community (東亜協同体)" and the "East Asia League (東亜連盟)." These initiatives clearly were tools of Japanese colonial oppression; but, Ichijo argues, in some instances attempts were made by intellectuals in various parts of the Japanese Empire to make use of these ideas in order to resist, challenge and even subvert Japanese imperialism. Although these attempts were ultimately unsuccessful, by examining the ways in which the oppressed and subjugated tried to mobilize the ideas of the oppressor in order to resist and subvert the oppression, the chapter calls for a more agency-centered investigation of the ideas used by the colonized and the oppressed in the unfolding of modernity.

Jun-Hyeok Kwak explores an important question about how religious nationalism is compatible with universal values, such as human rights. To this end, his chapter examines the thought of Ahn Changho, the Korean independence activist. It identifies the basic principle of Ahn's political thought as non-domination – the very concept central for republican political theory. By juxtaposing Ahn's political thoughts with Giuseppe Mazzini's then-popular thesis on "one's love for humanity," Kwak makes two claims. First, Ahn embraces the politics of non-domination, which gives epistemological coherence to his ideas ranging from the advocacy of the reconstruction of his nation to the assertion of peaceful coexistence in Northeast Asia. Second, Ahn's conception of non-domination, as embodied in his religious aspiration for love for humanity, demonstrates the need for overcoming the simple antinomies between resistance and coexistence on the one hand and between national and cosmopolitan on the other hand. In this way, Kwak shows how Ahn's nationalism, guided by the principle of non-domination, makes it possible to accept other nations as neighbors, thereby ensuring peaceful coexistence among nations. In doing so, he points to a possibility that religion, when guided by a regulative principle of non-domination, can shape a collective commonality without degenerating into a bellicose nationalism.

In his chapter, Zhibin Xie provides a structural analysis of the relationship between the state, religious communities and other social institutions in contemporary China. The central objective is to explain the current religious revival within China despite the state's strict restrictions, growing religious dynamics and the demand for more autonomy. Xie attempts to integrate Confucian ideas of the state and association (including religious communities) with a Christian social theory of the state and social institutions in order to work out a proper philosophical and theological interpretation on the structural problem of religious freedom, focusing on the role of the state in particular, with respect to traditional Chinese cultural and religious resources, political order and the current religious situation.

The relationship between state and religion in China is further examined in an innovative way by Wei Hua, who draws on the experiences of the Donatists to discuss church-state relations in China with reference to the insights of St. Augustine of Hippo. Hua first examines the emergence of the Donatists and their repression by the Roman Empire, before elucidating how Augustine first used the unity of the Catholic church and the national religious identity promoted by the Roman Empire to criticize the Donatists' localized religious identity and, second, argued for the priority of Catholic faith by means of his theory of the two cities. With a continuous reflection on the fall of Rome in 410, Augustine eventually abandoned the early Christian political theology represented by Eusebius and Orosius, as he argued that Christians' identity should be eternal and transcendental, and would not be restrained by time or an earthly state. Finally, with the aid of Augustine's arguments on the political-religious relation, Hua attempts to find possible solutions to religious and political issues in mainland China: the illegitimacy of Protestant house churches and underground Catholic churches, conflicts between those illegitimate churches and officially recognized churches, and a healthy form of the separation between church and state. Interestingly, Hua's attempt is made possible, largely because he finds a considerable similarity between contemporary China and ancient Rome in the fourth and fifth centuries. Hua's chapter suggests that an encounter between Asian modernity and the pre-modern West can contribute to find ways to tackle the political-religious problems.

Whereas the previous two chapters take "China" as a cultural formation as an axiomatic, political category, in his highly innovative chapter Chih-yu Shih provocatively discusses how the category of China is constituted by discourses of what he terms "post-Chineseness." The emerging character of post-Chineseness, Shih argues, informs the cultural function of Chinese religions and the ineffectiveness of statist nationalism in the religious sphere despite a pragmatic policy of the authorities to occasionally enlist the derivatives of cultural power. Post-Chineseness enacts differing epistemological perspectives that engender wide-ranging cultural nationalism for different constituencies because populations at different sites improvise their connection, reconnection or disconnection differently. Such undecidability neutralizes statist nationalism and Orientalism. However, reconnection reproduces post-Chinese identities to make Chineseness ontologically accepted as given and yet epistemologically undefinable, culturally unproductive, or socially unstable. Post-Chineseness, as a process of reconnection between perceived Chinese actors, can rely on religious resources. This chapter discusses three of these religious resources, namely, Buddhism, Christianity and Confucianism. Although they may be considered components of modern Chineseness, these religions have far from being the major resources in the making of political nationalism in China.

Finally, in the concluding chapter, Shani and Kibe examine the *legacies* and *possibilities* opened up by this survey of the relationship between religion and nationalism in Asia before returning to the questions posed in the introduction. The chapter first reviews modernist theories of nationalism before examining how the various contributors to this volume have challenged conventional accounts of the relationship between religion, nationalism and modernity. It then explores the possibilities which religion can bring for going *beyond* nationalism in the region. We will then conclude with our responses to the three questions posed and suggest that a rediscovery of the "human" values to which Tagore referred may help counter the exclusivity of modern Eurocentric conceptions of the nation-state.

Notes

1 We observe an expansive use of religion-related terms in scholarship. Scholars speak of totalitarianism as "political religion" (Voegelin 1996 [1938]; Gregor 2012) and nationalism as "ersatz religion" (Alvis 2005: xv), "surrogate religion" (Smith 2010: 38), or "quasi-religion" (Smith 1994). For instance, Anthony Smith (2010: 154) refers to "political religion" of secular nationalism to highlight "the sacred bases of the nation" that draw on "older religious motifs for its liturgy, symbolism and myth-making." In this way, religious aspects in nationalism are often stressed, as if any sacralized form of politics could be labeled as "religious." Such expansive use of the concept "religion," mainly drawing on the Durkheimian functional view of religion (Smith 2010: 38; cf. Brooker 1991: 318–323), appears to be so far stretched and so comprehensive that at the end of the day we may wonder what is properly religious. For an aptly differentiated view on politicized religion, civil religion, and political religion as totalitarianism, see Gregor 2012: 10, 282–283.

2 For example, Rogers Brubaker (2012) explains different ways of studying the relation between religion and nationalism in a succinct way. But he does not interrogate the very concept of religion but emphasizes the need to distinguish between religion and nationalism as analytical concepts. Another case in point is Joseph Chinyong Liow's excellent study on religion and nationalism in Southeast Asia (Liow 2016). Based on the case studies on Philippines, Thailand, Malaysia and Indonesia, it shows how religious identity and discourses can be vital in framing political conflicts. But this book does not critically interrogate the concept of religion. Another interesting case is Peter van der Veer's study on India and China, entitled *The Modern Spirit of Asia: The Spiritual and the Secular in China and India*. Instead of religion, van der Veer deploys the concept of spirituality in order to avoid the Western concept of religion. But since he uses "spirituality" as a concept paired with "the secular" (van der Veer 2014: 7), one might rightly wonder whether he successfully avoids the aporetic problem of demarcation between "religious" and "secular." A more cautious and more differentiated use of the dyad between religion and the secular is shown in a book edited by Mirjam Künkler and John Madeley, *A Secular Age beyond the West*. This book is a critical engagement with Charles Taylor's book *A Secular Age* (2007), mainly consisting of case studies on China, Japan, Indonesia, India, Pakistan, Iran, Russia, Turkey, Egypt, Morocco and Israel. Even though the book does examine "the link between secularity and nationalism" (Künkler and Madeley 2018: 42) as one of its themes, its main focus is different from that of this volume.

References

Alvis, Robert. 2005. *Religion and the Rise of Nationalism: A Profile of an East-Central European City*. Syracuse, NY: Syracuse University Press.

Anderson, Benedict. 1991. *Imagined Communities: Reflections on the Origin and Spread of Nationalism*. Revised ed. London: Verso.

Asad, Talal. 1993. *Genealogies of Religion: Discipline and Reason of Power in Christianity and Islam*. Baltimore: Johns Hopkins University Press.

——. 2003. *Formations of the Secular: Christianity, Islam, Modernity*. Stanford, CA: Stanford University Press.
Brooker, Paul. 1991. *The Faces of Fraternalism: Nazi Germany, Fascist Italy, and Imperial Japan*. Oxford: Clarendon Press.
Brubaker, Rogers. 2012. 'Religious Nationalism: Four Approaches,' *Nations and Nationalism*, 18(1): 2–20.
Casanova, José. 1994. *Public Religions in the Modern World*. Chicago: Chicago University Press.
——. 2011. 'The Secular, Secularizations, Secularism,' in Craig Calhoun, Mark Jurgensmeyer and Jonathan VanAntwerpen (eds.), *Rethinking Secularism*. New York: Oxford University Press, pp. 54–75.
Duara, Pransenji. 2001. 'The Discourse of Civilization and Pan-Asianism,' *Journal of World History*, 12(1): 99–130.
Eisenstadt, Shmuel Noah. 2000. 'Multiple Modernities,' *Daedalus*, 129(1): 1–29.
Fitzgerald, Timothy. 2000. *The Ideology of Religious Studies*. Oxford: Oxford University Press.
Gellner, Ernest. 1983. *Nations and Nationalism*. Oxford: Blackwell.
Gregor, A. James. 2012. *Totalitarianism and Political Religion: An Intellectual History*. Stanford, CA: Stanford University Press.
Jinja Honcho. 2013. 'Soul of Japan: An Introduction to Shinto and Ise Jingu,' available at: www.jinjahoncho.or.jp/en/image/soul-of-japan.pdf
Jinnah, Muhammad Ali. 1940. 'Presidential Address by Muhammad Ali Jinnah to the Muslim League Lahore, 1940,' available at: www.columbia.edu/itc/mealac/pritchett/00islamlinks/txt_jinnah_lahore_1940.html
Juergensmeyer, Mark. 2006. 'Nationalism and Religion,' in Gerard Delanty and Krishan Kumar (eds.), *The Sage Handbook of Nations and Nationalism*. London: Sage Publications, pp. 182–191.
Künkler, Mirjam and Madeley, John. 2018. *A Secular Age Beyond the West*. Cambridge: Cambridge University Press.
Laborde, Cécile. 2017. *Liberalism's Religion*. Cambridge, MA: Harvard University Press.
Liow, Joseph Chinyong. 2016. *Religion and Nationalism in Southeast Asia*. Cambridge: Cambridge University Press.
Nehru, Jawaharlal. [1954] 2017. 'What Is the Meaning of Nationalism?' Awaam India, available at: http://awaam.net/nationalism-by-jlnehru/
Said, Edward. 1978. *Orientalism*. New York: Vintage Books.
Smith, Anthony. D. 2010. *Nationalism: Theory, Ideology, History*. 2nd ed. Cambridge: Polity Press.
Smith, John. 1994. *Quasi-Religions: Humanism, Marxism and Nationalism*. Basingstoke: Palgrave Macmillan.
Tagore, Rabindranath. [1917] 1991. *Nationalism*. London: Palgrave Macmillan.
van der Veer, Peter. 1999. 'Hindus: A Superior Race,' *Nations and Nationalism*, 5(3): 419–430.
——. 2013. 'Nationalism and Religion,' in John Breuilly (ed.), *The Oxford Handbook of the History of Nationalism*. Oxford: Oxford University Press, pp. 655–671.
——. 2014. *The Modern Spirit of Asia: The Spiritual and the Secular in China and India*. Princeton, NJ: Princeton University Press.
Voegelin, Eric [1938] 1996. *Die Politischen Religionen*. 2nd ed. München: Fink.

1 Tagore and the conception of critical nationalism

Sudipta Kaviraj

In the discipline of conceptual history, few concepts are so hard to tackle as the idea of the nation. This is so because of its variations across two different axes: different stages in history accord different collective valences to the concept; but within each period and each group individuals inflect the term in distinctively different ways. Some political terms like the *state*, despite their own indeterminacies, at least have some elements of material, institutional fixity. The nation, by contrast, is just an idea – one of the most indefinable, intangible and yet emotionally forceful concepts affecting political action in the modern world. Nationalism in its two primary forms – European imperialist nationalism[1] and anti-imperialist nationalism in Europe's colonies – were shaping the world throughout the span of Tagore's life; and he looked at these vast political convulsions with great attention and rare insight. His peculiarity lay in the fact that unlike most intellectuals of his times he did not embrace the simple solution of deciding which side to support; he decided to observe critically the strange impulses that emerged from the diffuse nationalist sentiment, and provided a critique of both sides, not just of imperialist Europe. Nationalist sentiment associated with religious communities has re-emerged as a powerful force in our times as well – though not in forms that were familiar to Tagore. Thus there is a straight connection between the question that fascinated and troubled Tagore and the urgent political predicaments we face today. Because of the detachment, sanity and civility of his thinking on this question, it repays close attention in our troubled world. I am a Bengali, and for a Bengali interested in literature, thinking about Tagore is a fraught and intense experience – not unlike the experience of believers in thinking about God: it is a pleasure to think about him, but it is also a humbling experience. He was the creator of my world, at least the intellectual world inside which I live and think, because he literally created the language through which I think, through which my mind touches every object in my world.

The intellectual world that Tagore's mind/art created is one of great beauty, but one that is not always grasped, also of great intellectual complexity. It is inadequate to honor him simply as a great artist. Apart from a producer of great art, undoubtedly, he was also a producer of social thought of unusual complexity and subtlety – gifted with a strange, unordinary vision. He was able to see much about the world of his times that others who were social thinkers of the more obvious often failed to grasp. I have argued elsewhere that he was an unusually astute analyst of the nature of modern political power; and his complex reflections on nationalism form part of that very unusual corpus of profoundly critical reflection on the nature of the political. In this chapter I shall use material from his essays and writings on nationalism, but supplement them with some readings of his poetry and fiction.

There is a widespread, but to my judgement erroneous, view that accounts for the rise of nationalism in Asian societies like Japan, China and India in a simple diffusionist way. The prejudice that all significant things originate in Europe and circulate to the rest of the world with a lag is so deeply entrenched that we often accept a casual, inattentive, entirely diffusionist theory of the spread of modern nationalism.[2] Through the accumulation of several mutually reinforcing processes of modernity – the rise of capitalist industrialism, of the modern state and its requirement of a form of sociability that transcended the 'unsocial sociality'[3] of bourgeois economies, a new relationship emerged between rulers and their subjects – of an unprecedented connection of intimacy and ownership between political subjects and their state, which was known as nationalism. It was not merely the power of capitalist economic productivity that enabled the expansion of Western power across the world, but its coupling with this entirely new form of collective belonging. Once other societies saw the immensity of the effects of this power – that lay behind the dominance of modern Europe – they started emulating this sentiment. That is simple version of this textbook story of nationalism.

Historically minded people will realize that this story is woefully inadequate and misleading. There is no doubt that many Asian observers thought that the strange fact that a small number of people from a distant island could navigate the world and conquer India could not be simply explained by the power of military technology. After all, military techniques could be easily mastered by Asian peoples; what gave the Europeans an ability to mobilize a superior form of force was a peculiar organization of emotion behind their state apparatus, and the chemistry of an affect that produced an unprecedented figuration of collective intentionality and collective action.[4] This was the invention of the nation-state. The negative experience of European colonization made this sentiment attractive to the elites of colonized societies. Intelligent observers from Asia prefigured in their analysis of European power some of the disciplinary features later examined by Foucault, and this gave rise to an envy for forms of similar techniques for forming collective intention and launching collective action. But it was not easy initially to introduce this new idea, or even to linguistically capture and express it with precision and clarity. In India, Bengal was the first regional culture in which these questions began to be raised, simply because it was the region subjected to British rule earliest, and for the longest time. Bankimchandra Chattopadhyay, a novelist, satirist and political essayist, spoke first of the need for anti-colonial opposition to British rule.[5] But it was not easy to introduce this novel idea that Indians – all the diverse communities who were subjects of the British Indian Empire – should begin to think of themselves as a single people: a *nation*. When he wrote about this theme, Bankim would often signal the awkwardness and absence of an equivalent term in Bengali by using the telling phrase – what the English call 'the nation'. The Bengali word that he was forced to use to capture this sense was the word *jati*, which was heavily freighted with previous semantic weight. It referred to either a bland *logical* class – like the class of cows, the class of tables, the class of pots; or *caste* groups like Brahmins or Kayasthas or Shudras. Eventually, the term settled into a polyvalent use, adding the reference to the nation parallel to its other antecedent semantic denotations: but audiences could unerringly understand its particular valence in a sentence by techniques of contextual reference. *Go-jati*, for instance, will mean the class of cows, *Vaishya-jati* the Vaishya or mercantile caste and *Bharatiya jati* the Indian nation. Clearly although the same term – *jati* – is used, the three meanings are separate; but the only linguistic marker of this semantic difference would be the contextual placement of the term in the syntactic chain. Bankimchandra's works were pioneering in two senses: they showed both the newness and the vagueness of a pioneering idea: though Bankim passionately wrote to persuade his compatriots that they should oppose British power/rule, there remained a fatal ambiguity in his thinking.[6] The *jati* that was to take on the historic task of opposing British rule remained oddly unspecified: at times it seemed this was the historic task of the Bengalis, at others of the Hindus or of the Indians – which had very different implications for the character of subsequent nationalism. Bankim was surely a passionate anti-imperialist; but strangely he had not yet chosen his nation.

By the time Rabindranath Tagore became a young intellectual, a prolific writer of poetry, fiction and serious political commentary, Bankim's literary interventions had made nationalism a familiar idea. His historical novels were immensely popular, and translated widely in numerous other languages – to provide them with vast audience that transcended the boundaries of his native Bengal. Bengalis began viewing with intense interest the dramatic unification processes unfolding in Italy and Germany, and reading Mazzini's works in English translation.[7] But this unfamiliar new sentiment, which could sweep everything before it, took concrete form and expression through a British decision in 1905 to divide the province of Bengal into an eastern and western part.[8] Though the ostensible reason was given as administrative convenience, as Bengal was an unwieldy, large territorial unit, research has convincingly shown that their objectives were less benign.[9] A split in the province would create two administrative regions statistically dominated by two religious communities – likely to fuel discord between their elites, and thus retard Indian demands for self-government. Certainly, this was not the first major uprising against British rule: the 1857 rebellion started by a section of the native soldiers of the British army which spread to much of northern India, was a major upheaval that seriously threatened British dominion in India; but clearly, the organization, ideology, leaders and followers of this uprising were quite different from what we see as a *modern* nationalist movement. The partition of Bengal evoked a massive popular response against the British decision, and it brought about for the first time in Indian history the peculiar convergence of elite-intellectual and mass-popular mobilization against foreign rule. Tagore, a relatively young intellectual, initially enthusiastically supported the growing mass movement. But Tagore practiced a peculiar and rare form of intellectual participation – taking part in action and observing the consequences of one's actions at the same time.[10] In classical Indian philosophy, the mind is sometimes likened to two birds – one of which acts, and the other observes the other acting; this, by implication, is the nature of truly intelligent action, a mark, as the *Gita* would say, of detachment in the process of acting itself

As the Swadeshi movement ended after three years of deep political convulsions, with some success, two divergent views of political action emerged which derived utterly different conclusions from a retrospective analysis of what had happened. For ordinary political activists and intellectuals, the Swadeshi movement showed, first of all, that the power of the British colonial state was not entirely unanswerable. A decision of the British government, even at the highest point of imperialism, could be thwarted by a 'movement' – an entirely new form of political action. Western educated intellectuals knew about the powers of such movements from the history of modern Europe; but this kind of collective action was unprecedented in Indian colonial history. Political intellectuals began thinking about what could be the ways in which such mass mobilizations could be better organized and directed towards larger goals – e.g., extracting more self-governing powers, or eventually, even independence from British rule. After Swadeshi, the central question of Indian political thought changed: from How did India become colonized? to How can India become independent?

Rabindranath's individual reflections took a wholly different and distinctive direction. Tagore closely examined the stages through which the movement had evolved, and what happened inside every stage, and his analytical conclusions were far more complex. Like many other young intellectuals, he was impatient with the strange contentment of the leaders of the moderate, constitutionalist agitation of the early Indian National Congress (INC), chafed at the restraints such leaders accepted; and sought a more rebellious infusion of popular participation in the defiance against British rule. When the Swadeshi movement gathered strength, he exultantly supported its cause. But, like all popular movements, as it expanded in its influence and support, it also became more complex, developing many different strands of mobilization and political action. Two types of development caused him concern. The first was an intensification of activist enthusiasm into terrorist action against individual British officials. The outbreak of terrorism profoundly troubled Tagore's consciousness because of its complex features – its immense heroic attractiveness to youth, its colossal waste of idealistic lives, and its futility as a political technique. As the movement intensified, Tagore observed with unease, mobilizers became more ferocious and desperate to increase the force of popular power. Hindu activists of the Swadeshi movement began to use appeals of Hindu religion, eliciting responses of resistance from Muslim groups opposed to the movement. A movement directed at a political objective became troubled with intense mobilization of two religious communities. For Tagore, this was a strangely frustrating outcome of a popular mobilization which had brought out deep democratic energies of politics, widened participation, but also mobilized the darkest forces of atavism. Associated with this were deeper causes of concern. In mobilizing popular numbers, politicians not merely showed unconcern for religious divisions, and felt happy if they could mobilize large groups of people despite the cost of antagonizing an equally large number – creating a large mobilized popular force, but at the same time threatening to rip apart the fabric of everyday peaceability and neighborliness between Hindus and Muslims. It was a travesty of the dream of a mobilized people: the dream, in parts, had turned into a nightmare.

From the troubled outward field of political life, after the apparent success of the Swadeshi agitation, Tagore retreated into the internal field of his artistic imagination, where his thought was untrammeled by constraints of external reality, and he could depict without hindrance the logic of these different, often contradictory strands of dark populist politics – which, for Tagore, would either make freedom impossible, or it might bring into reality an entirely travestied version of independence. He was not a stranger to the conflicts of political debate – but was an unenthusiastic controversialist.[11] In directly political debates, he appears an unenthusiastic combatant, restrained continually by demands of extreme civility. But inside the world of his artistic fiction, within an interior world under his authorial sovereignty, he was free to create characters and situations that would reveal the logic of disaster which outer social reality did not show with remorseless clarity. His novels were his revenge on reality in that sense.

Fictional reflections

Three of Tagore's novels are concerned with painting artistic pictures of both personal and collective forms of nationalist politics: but their intellectual force consists in the fact that unlike political theory writings, they capture processes at three levels. Fiction offered a profound analysis of the transformation of individual subjectivities as they engage in the business of transforming themselves in transforming their society. Doing politics is a transformative activity in two ways: it seeks to and often succeeds in transforming society. Acting politically also often transforms the acting subject – partly because self-transformation, or self-fashioning, is a purpose of those acts. Politics is not an activity that occurs only at the level of larger social processes: its effects reach deep into the inner recesses of the individual's mind, sensibility and his use of reason. It is only one particular kind of personality that can succeed in the special field of activity we call politics. That is a personality that subjects to instrumental political calculation the consideration of effects in the lives of real people, a personality that sacrifices, at the level of personal rationality, the *wertrational* to the *zweckrational* to use Weber's dichotomy, or ends to means. Instrumental calculation has significant cumulative effects on the life of the political group. Fictional writers often portray a tendency towards natural degeneration in the character of political groups – like small secretive terrorist cells and the large mass movements – as they evolve towards greater power and maturity. Through systematic substitution of the instrumental over the morally rational, they become massive collective instruments of self-aggrandizement of large groups which learn to maneuver and to corner, neutralize and humiliate other large social groups – who are obliged to enter into spiraling exchanges of hostility. Although idealistic individuals join movements through their love of ideals, they are forced into submission to an internal discipline enforced by leaders. Eventually they learn to curb their subjectivity and judgement for the 'greater cause' the movement represents. Starting as forces of liberation, they often degenerate into producing their own pockets of submission. Finally, in their large historical consequence, such movements are likely to damage their societies by polarizing them through the contestation of more lethally organized power than was the condition before. Observing the Swadeshi movement at close proximity, Tagore produced a very interesting diagnosis of modern politics. This 'picture' in fiction was entirely distinct from most of his associates and collaborators who participated in enacting or supporting the agitation. The lesson they took away from the movement was that in future such movements were to be organized on a more expanded scale to be more effective and to pose a serious threat to the power to the colonial state. Tagore went away with a more complex and pessimistic lesson: that such large-scale enterprises of political mobilization – creating a new form of power out of the helpless submission of the atomized masses of ordinary people – were fraught with great dangers and required vigilance and critical monitoring.

Critical reflections of 'movement politics' were expressed in Tagore's writings in two forms – in a series of critical essays, a favorite form of political comment of Indian nationalists and a number of novels exploring human experience and political subjectivities in times of great mobilization. In my view, therefore, to read Tagore's mind on modern politics, we must see his analytic intention distributed between his political writings about the world of political facts and his imaginative work on the fictive world of real but unrealized possibilities. Two of his novels explore the logic of these deformations of modern politics – *Home and the World* (*Ghare Baire*), and *Four Chapters* (*Char Adhyay*).[12]

In the first, which has been turned into a film by the great film auteur Satyajit Ray, Tagore prepares a narrative exploration of an individual political career. Sandip, its main protagonist, begins his political career in genuinely intense idealistic attachment to his nation. Gradually, by exaggerating the importance of this cause over all other ideals and values, he sets in motion two types of manipulative actions – one by exploiting individual relationships and developing an illicit attachment to the wife of his closest friend, subordinating her to his desire; and secondly, he cynically incites a communal religious frenzy in the locality. But when the fire he lights gets out of control and the fight for the motherland degenerates into a war between Hindus and Muslims, the wily politician slinks away with the excuse that, as a leader, he has the supreme obligation to preserve his own life over those of others, so that he can start his noble and unending fight for his country's liberty at some other more propitious time. We get a sense that he will inevitably 'succeed': he will reappear in the same role in some other context, he will affect the lives of others close to himself, and lead other communities which had lived as neighbors for centuries into a bonfire of the peace.[13] The ideal of the nation will burn to ashes in the fire of communal strife. Sandip's degeneration is not a lapse, but a degradation. His act is not an uncharacteristic isolated act of a still idealistic youth. His personality has been changed by politics: it is impossible to reach that earlier self; because that no longer exists.

A second novel, *Char Adhyay*, depicts the life of another youth collapsing into utterly meaningless political sacrifice. His idealism leads the hero, Atin, into a feeling of guilt about his comfortable upper-class life, and draws him towards a group of terrorists vowed to liberate the nation by redemptive acts of violence against the British. Slowly they entice him into acts of violence which he increasingly finds repugnant, and his descent into this vortex of violence inevitably draws with him his woman friend who is an object of lust to other revolutionaries without scruples. Once he is drawn into this closed politics of terror, all his paths to ordinary life are cut off; his life descends into an inescapable route of violence which he finds meaningless and destructive. Eventually, Tagore characteristically ends the narrative by suggestion rather than clear diegetic finality, in which the lives of these two promising young people are destroyed without much benefit to the motherland. They end in pointless, utterly wasted sacrifice

Placing these two narratives together, we can get a sense of Tagore's deepening concern about the temptations in the path of political violence for justice, in some ways quite similar to Gandhi's.[14] In a series of reflections Tagore produced a compelling historical sociology on the question of social power. He saw modernity as a combination of historical forces which irreversibly altered the nature of power; placing political power at the center and at the top of a society in a historically unprecedented fashion.[15] Through endogenous modernity, as in Europe or Japan, or colonial intrusion of modern politics as in colonies like India, politics became the dominant force in modern society: this was entirely unlike pre-modern social structures. But this politics is all powerful, it does not allow people to ignore it, it does not allow any place to hide from its tentacles. Modern people must make political power a principal object of their historical thinking. I shall argue at the end that despite its perceptiveness, there was also a strangely unsatisfactory quality to Tagore's thinking about modern power, and he arrived at conclusions that were finally theoretically antipolitical, and remained caught in a paradox: arguing intellectually that politics could not be marginalized in the social life of modern societies, and yet exhorting people to take a stance that disallowed politics the power to dominate all forms of social life.[16] Although this eventual position maneuvered him into a rather strange location in political theory, he arrived at that conclusion through some rarely insightful reflections on the effects of politics on modern life.

I would like to argue that there are three major innovations in Tagore's political thought, and I shall speak about each of these in turn before concluding with what I think is the real value of Tagore's thinking about political modernity. The first element of great value is Tagore's exploration of the relation between words and the world: his growing perception that new practical ideas were making an entry into Indian social life, altering and breaking the coherence of its categorial language. Second, he slowly developed an unusual and highly interesting theory of power and resistance in modern societies. Finally, he fashioned by consistent critical reflection on the idea of the nation a strangely sophisticated conception of a *critical* nationalism – a strange nationalism critical of itself.

Tagore was particularly perceptive in grasping that the two new concepts that invaded the political-moral imaginary[17] of modern India were the ideas of the 'nation' and the 'state' – both of which were historically entirely new to the preexisting intellectual vocabularies of the subcontinent. Somewhat like Gandhi, Tagore thought that the main problem with colonialism was not subjection in sovereignty, but a subjection to the modern social imaginary which made sovereignty the center of all political attention and collective activity. Introduction of these practical concepts carried the promise – to unrepentant modernists, and a threat to thinkers like him and Gandhi – of re-structuring the most fundamental relations in society in a way that imitated transformations in modern Europe. Colonialism, by denying sovereignty to the indigenous society, made people focus on it perversely, and Indian society was gradually becoming habituated to the idea that all significant initiatives affecting society must come from the power of the state – *rajashakti*, rather than *atmashakti*, associative powers of the society itself. For Tagore, pre-modern Indian society was not state-centric; and the affliction of colonialism was two-fold. The more obvious problem with colonialism was that political sovereignty passed into the hands of alien rulers. But nationalists who saw that as the exclusive problem did not have a deep enough vision of what was really wrong with colonization. In an underlying sense, it was the idea of modern sovereignty itself that Tagore saw as the problem: imposition of a regime of the modern sovereign state which surrendered all other sources of authority in social life to its comprehensive domination. It would be a tragedy, Tagore thought, if this underlying regime became permanent, even though Indians came to acquire this sovereign power. Interestingly, on this particular point, his diagnosis was exactly parallel to Gandhi's in *Hind Swaraj*: dominance by an Indian elite which continued with the regime of modernity would simply be colonization by other means, a permanent historic defeat of the Indian civilization. Tagore's opposition to modernity was not as comprehensive as Gandhi's: he did not view the entire civilization of Western modernity as a degrading force for the world, only some of its constituents. But their similarity lay in the fact that both thought similarly regarding the *logic* of the modern state, and techniques of modern power. Tagore argued passionately that India had never known a concept like the nation whose feeling of community was based on peoples' common link to the political power of the modern state. And, as becomes apparent through the narrative developments of his novel, *Gora*, his major concern was about the homogeneity demanded and celebrated by the ideal of the European nation-state. His novel was meant as a critique of this ideal that was gaining increasing popularity in Indian nationalist opinion. The narrative artfully suggested that the only adequate definition of an Indian should be one that could include in its wide embrace the abandoned son of an Irish soldier of the British army raised by Bengali Hindu mother.[18] A subtler stratum of the argument should not be missed. Tagore's concern was that those who got easily persuaded to this fundamental transformation did not even realize that they were converted to an entirely new optics about the social world, because much of this change occurred at a level of thought that was pre-argumentative. Intellectuals are always self-conscious about putting together arguments forming strings of connection between individual ideas. No intellectual can develop an argument about a significant subject unselfconsciously. But the substitution in this case was not happening through an explicit argument persuading Indians to change their minds about the nature of their society. It was happening through a silent substitution of semantics – shift of the term 'state' from one meaning to another, and a sense of the social community from one meaning to the European meaning of the word 'nation'. European colonization of the Indian mind, especially of its intellectuals, habituated them to having no other community except the 'nation' – which he thought was untenable in India for two reasons. First, it was not a normal outcome of the history of sociality in Indian culture; and second, it was an ideal of unity which always had a seed of profound exclusion at its heart. By taking these two English-European concepts of 'state' and 'nation' for granted, as natural, Indians were assenting to the greatest historical transformation of their social world. That was why it was important to explore the meanings of the two concepts and their implications.[19]

States and oppositional movements

To state his new idea about the untenability of the nation in the European sense, Tagore needed a framing argument about the nature of the modern state. This was, to my judgement, entirely unprecedented in Indian reflection[20] and captured a profound truth about the modern world. His argument consists of two parts, the first of which is rather similar to one found in Tocqueville.[21] Like Tocqueville, Tagore starts from the premise that the modern state is unlike states and regimes of power that had existed in earlier times. In many of his literary essays, he uses effective tropes like the uproar of a storm to refer to the power of rulers who sat on top of societies, but did not involve themselves in their everyday lives, making for a stark distinction between *political* and *social* life. What happened on the top layers of political power was cataclysmic, but did not involve the settled layers of everyday life – which continued undisturbed through such upheaval: 'even in a day of a great storm, the storm is not the most significant truth: the life that occurs wordlessly in the everyday is the greater truth of this life.'[22] Emergence of the modern state irreversibly altered this relation – creating a new type of state which had not merely the practical power to dominate all fields of social life, but also carried the ethical sanction for acting on behalf of society as a whole – which premodern political elites never could. This utterly altered the order and structure of social life, placing the state at the center of everything. Pre-modern states could face two kinds of responses – of either being ignored or being successfully opposed by cliques of powerful dissident aristocracy. The disciplinary power of the modern state could hardly be restrained by such devices. Social conditions of modernity destroyed the aristocracy – which constituted competitive centers of political and military force. Atomized ordinary citizens simply had no hope of successful opposition to the state. To this point Tagore's diagnosis of the modern political predicament runs mainly parallel to Tocqueville's. Given these conditions, Tocqueville believed, the only serious opposition to the power of the state could be a vibrant 'civil society', a lively associational life which did not cede all social initiative to the state. Perception of the modern state's unanswerable power created a deep anxiety – widely shared among political theorists – about its potential misuse. What if the state holding such unprecedented power happened to be unjust or oppressive? One answer to that could be found in constitutionalism and checks and balances – distribution of the state's power among its constituent branches with such institutional ingenuity that one agency restrained the other.[23] Tagore faced a different historical reality from the European thinkers. The colonial state was by nature alien to the people it governed, and therefore there was a constitutive injustice in its nature. How could a crowd of ordinary people, unarmed, unendowed with the power of conventional aristocracy, contest and challenge the state's unanswerable force in a colonial context? European history in recent times showed that the only force which could successfully oppose the state were large popular movements. Tagore thought it was inevitable that in colonial situations popular power would be mobilized through large popular movements. This is why the example of the Swadeshi movement was not contingent, but paradigmatic. The historical field of modern politics opened up between two grand contestants, two collective protagonists of political force: states and popular movements. Not surprisingly the political history of modernity was primarily a story of states and their conflicts with mass popular movements. But this optic about modern political life also leads to a fatal/decisive conclusion about present Indian political life. The colonial state was a typical state of injustice which had to be opposed politically and contested ethically. If in modern times the unanswerable power of the state could only be challenged by the counter-power of a disciplinary political movement – which generated its own power through very similar mechanisms of symmetric collective action of mass-popular collective actors – then it followed that the only prospect of an end to foreign domination was through a nationalist popular movement. But this reading of history contained dismal forebodings of enslavement of free human life to another gigantic incarceration. Prophetically, in his plays often there is a conjunction of political power and the overwhelming forces of technology. Colossal technological mechanisms are always, symbolically, in the hands of the king of the dark chamber.[24]

Although Tagore did not present it as a political program, his solution lay in the patient fashioning of a new theory of collective belonging – for which even he could not find a distinctive name. He developed this idea through descriptive elaboration of the precise nature of this sentiment of collective identity. We face a deep linguistic problem here – because human beings' language, as Mill said, is always poorer than its ideas. As we are habituated to using the term 'nationalism' to refer to such collective sentiments of belonging, or community, people generally use the word 'nationalism' to refer to it. In one sense, that description is apt; in another entirely inappropriate; and without understanding this distinction, we cannot grasp Tagore's utterly innovative thinking about the 'problem' of nationalism. It is generally recognized that the phenomenon termed nationalism has some internal variation: the most well-known distinction is the one between civic and ethnic nationalism – a differentiation suggested by the irrefutable difference between French and German forms. However, even this distinction does not really capture the finer point that concerned Tagore, and we cannot express his distinctions with precision and accuracy by borrowing a terminology fashioned to make sense of European history. It is best to try to illustrate this point by closely reading some of Tagore's celebrated 'patriotic' poems.[25]

Patriotism and nationalism

Ashis Nandy, one of India's distinguished political theorists, has made a cryptic claim in his work *The Illegitimacy of Nationalism* (1994) that it is a mistake to characterize the two great figures of Indian freedom – Tagore and Gandhi – as nationalists; they were not nationalists, but patriots. I think this represents a very significant insight, but I want to look into the logic of this argument more closely. Nandy explains that he views nationalism as a feeling of collective belonging *that is centred on a state* that not merely protects the people, but also gives the people their enveloping sense of identity. He is entirely right in stating that if nationalism is defined in this state-centric fashion, Gandhi and Tagore are certainly not 'nationalists'. The trouble with this line of reasoning is that it accepts without critical demur an entirely Eurocentric conception of nationalism; because although there is a profound difference between civic and ethnic forms of nationalism, they are both undoubtedly centred on the idea that in modern times human beings preemptively base their primary identification with reference to the state. By contrast, if Tagore and Gandhi harbored a sense of nationalism, it sought the foundation of the nation not on the state, but elsewhere. So we have to engage in a double exercise – of analyzing their actual modes of thinking, and of theorizing this form of thinking in the context of academic discussions on nationalism.

Tagore's nationalist poems were written in the context of an emerging literary tradition in Bengali. An entirely innovative form of literary thinking about a nation imagined as Mother had emerged in the preceding decades through the literary works of Bankimchandra Chattopadhyay, whose novel, *Anandamath* inaugurated this literary form. The novel also contained the first poetic composition which could be called patriotic, 'bande mataram' – an inspired, but utterly exceptional digression into poetry by a writer who was a great master of prose fiction. Probably this indicated that there was a deep internal connection between sentiment and poetry: affect is conveyed much more expressively in the language of poetry rather than the unmusical language of prose. But Bankimchandra's initial creation – which he did not follow up at all – spawned an immense literary genre of patriotic poetry and music. Fairly quickly, this genre went in the direction of nationalist sentiment everywhere – towards an unrestrained, excessive adoration of the motherland as the best in the world.[26] Dwijendralal Roy, a talented contemporary poet and musician, composed one of the most famous instances of this genre of enthusiasm and excess:

> In this earth – full of the bounties of wealth, food and flowers –
> There is one land that is the finest of all
> It is made of the stuff of dreams, and bounded by memories
> You will find such a country nowhere else
> She is the queen of all nations, my motherland.

Enthusiasm tends to be infectious and uncontrollable; and Roy's poem continues its cascading descriptions towards sentimental intensity and excess: 'Where do you get such mighty mountains and rivers?' but more interestingly, 'where will one get such affection from brothers and mothers?' The invocation of the motherland soon bursts all bonds of restraint, and the world becomes putatively a vast scene of contending, warring nations – all vying for unequalled glory. This tradition of nationalist self-adoration becomes bolder and more extensive, spreading from the creation of literary word icons to visual ones when the specular elements of iconicity are increasingly drawn from the repertoire of Hindu mythology and iconic devotion – the Mother is viewed as a goddess. She is depicted often with many arms in an iconic suggestion of infinite power, riding the lion, at times holding not bounties in her many arms but weapons, eventually combining contradictory features – beautiful and protective to her children, fearsome to 'others'.[27]

Dissenting nationalism in Tagore

As I have written extensively about these themes in my recent book,[28] I shall focus on aspects not covered in those previous readings. Ostensibly, it might appear that Tagore too wrote some poems that were similar to Roy's or Bankim's songs – for instance, numerous celebrated patriotic poems about Bengal, one of which was turned into the national anthem of independent Bangladesh.[29] But this corpus also contains several distinctive compositions which show subtle redactions and inversions of these raging nationalist sentiments. One song acknowledges a feeling of blessedness in being born in this country, and being blessed in its feeling of love.[30] But in pointed reference to the 'queen of all lands' – a tropic figure invoked by adorers of both Mother India and Britannia – it says, 'I do not know if you have riches worthy of a queen, but I know that my soul finds peace when I rest in your shade'. Both Roy's poem and Tagore's – sung endlessly in modern Bengal – are expressions of patriotic love of one's country conceived as mother; but there is a stark contrast in the structure of feeling that the two poems express. In the first the dominant sentiment is of exultation expressed in a language of majesty, competitiveness and conquest – almost literally drawn from poetry that celebrated European figures of Britannia, or France or Germania. The second poem expresses a sentiment of contentment, peace and intimacy – the calm that descends on the soul in the presence and nearness of the familiar. Inhabitance of the land is in one case exultant, because that nature, that earth is incomparable; in the other calm and cooling because it is the world that is nearest and most familiar. That world enchants us not because it is the best, but because it is our own. It is true that both poems seek to express a form of devotion, but devotion of very different nature, because the devotion is directed at quite different deities.[31] The spirit in one song is of conquest, in the other of contentment.

The strangeness of the affect of Tagore's nationalism is expressed most forcefully in two other poems which are celebrated as patriotic songs, but which, on closer inspection, reveal very unusual features. The first poem – *he more durbhaga desh* – begins with an address to "My unfortunate land" in a tone of sadness that is hardly ever found in this genre of poetic invocation.[32] The whole poem is a litany of sadness at the wrongs that lie at the heart of India's past and present. Its primary theme is expressed in the initial lines: 'those you have wronged/humiliated, you have to be equal in humiliation with them; because those you pushed down would drag you down with them, those who have left behind are dragging you from the back'; on the day of the creator's purifying wrath, at the door of a looming famine, this 'nation' will have to learn the lesson of a putative equal dignity that nationhood confers on every single member of its community.[33] A second poem from the *Gitanjali* celebrates India as a place of pilgrimage where all streams of humanity have arrived to find a common home.[34] The poem repeats the urgings found in the previous one about restitution of honor and love to those dishonored by India's history; but it stresses the openness of India's identity. Those who came down 'the stream of wars' have become part of its soul; and even the West, which brings new gifts in a new age, must find a place in its heart.[35] Tagore's famous novel, *Gora*, pushes the same kind of argument by narrative arrangement. It not merely states the equal belongingness of all India's traditional peoples – Hindus, Muslims and Christians – but the entire narrative operation centers around a character who is the abandoned son of an Irish soldier during the 'mutiny' of 1857 who mistook himself for long as a Hindu Brahmin. At the climactic point of the story, when he has to face the burden of his identity, the novel urges an adoption of a form of belonging – a definition of Indianness in which this complete 'outsider' can be included with complete acceptance – as, interestingly, as it turns out, his illiterate Hindu mother had accepted him all his life. Others had given him acceptance under a mistaken identity; only his mother, who prevailed on his reluctant father to pick up the infant, had given him an acceptance as himself, and really made him her son. He was a man without a father, only a mother – only a mother could give people shelter in her calming shadow. That is the shadow that Tagore believes the nature of Bengal provided her children. What is shown subtly in *Gora* at the level of personal destiny outlines a notion of care and motherhood that we can see transferred to the figure of the iconic mother – who is a figure not of cosmic strife, but of a cosmic tranquillity.

Deferral of celebration: the nation in past and future

I want to finish with reading another layer of poetic operation in these two poems. All patriotic poems are usually celebrations of a collective self; obviously nationalism is a highly political emotion, and it matters deeply who are included in the celebration of the collective entity. For Hindu nationalists like V. D. Savarkar and his followers, who were to strive to impose a Hindu construction on India's anti-colonial nationalism, the collective self is composed only of those for whom India is both the fatherland (*pitrbhumi*) and the holy land (*punyabhumi*), by implication clearly excluding Muslims and Christians. By contrast, Gandhi's collective self was generous and pluralist, embracing in its idea of the nation all who lived in India – whom history had made neighbors and sharers of this world. We are used to such differences in the inclusive and exclusivist definitions of the collective self. In these two poems Tagore makes a more unusual and complex move. Of course, Tagore sided with a definition of the self that worshipped the territory – literally, the land – which meant that its inhabitants shared the bounties and hardships of its nature, its common material culture and were linked to it by the relation of care that the mother had for her children. In that sense, Tagore's nation was the same as Gandhi's. But the actual presentation of the idea is quite different, partly because it unfolds on the terrain of art. What is truly remarkable in these poems is a crucial deferral of the celebratory moment for even this inclusive, plural collective self. Take the first sentence of the first poem:

He mor durbhaga desh jader korecho apaman
Apamane hote habe tahader sabar saman

'O my unfortunate land, those whom you have insulted: you have to become equal to them in humiliation'. The verbs used contain a remarkable signal: the insult, indignity and injury to parts of her own 'people' happened in the past and continue in the present – *korecho* in Bengali grammar connotes a bland generic past 'what you have done' that can arch over past and present time. In the second phrase, '*hate habe*' – 'you have to be', 'to become' – is in the future tense – setting up a deep temporal and practical rupture across time. The time of the 'nation' is marked, tainted by its humiliation of its own members; and Tagore's tone shows that in this present state this collectivity, if you call it the nation, does not deserve any honor. Its celebration is conditional on its realizing what is implicit in its history but still unachieved, in its promise of fusion and internal equality. Celebration of the nation is inappropriate in the present: it can only occur in a perfect, deferred future. The content of the nationalist emotion is startlingly transposed. Feeling for the nation does not mean exultation in its past glory or its incomparable present majesty; it is a grieving over its imperfection. By this move, Tagore does something interesting to the idea of the nation, or Indian collective identity. It is turned into a *moral* imaginary,[36] an ideal of human belonging which no state can historically realize in full, and which, therefore, can be used strategically as a ground from which actual states and their always imperfect realization of the people-nation can be criticized. Instead of becoming a principle of exclusion, or an idea that serves to endorse the acts of the state, this idea of the ideal nation, the ideal sociability of its constituent peoples, becomes a principle of criticism.

In trying to think through Ashis Nandy's interesting paradox – that two of the greatest figures of Indian nationalism are not really nationalists – we are forced to open up a distinction between two notions of nationalism. The first meaning of nationalism is simply an intense sentiment of anti-colonialism: the idea that rule of one people by another is unjust, and must be ended. The second meaning of nationalism is a sense of cohesion among a group of members of a state that they are its 'nation', the people to whom the state belongs, who 'own' the state; which immediately produces the implication that those who cannot crowd into that definition are its internal others, marooned inside its borders but outside its collective self-definition. Tagore was certainly a nationalist in the first sense, and certainly not in the second. But more significantly, from the point of view of political theory, his reflections around the idea of the modern nation – in both political writings and artistic reflection – suggest a larger question: whether the idea of a nation-state in the European model is a final destiny of all mankind, the only viable political form of collective belonging; or should the political imagination of humanity set itself the task of thinking of some fundamentally different ways of organizing ordinary people's relation to political power?

Tagore's political critique of nationalism

Primarily, Tagore was not a political thinker, but an artist. Naturally, his deepest and most profoundly expressive thoughts regarding nationalism can be found in his artistic production – in poems, songs, music and fiction. But he was a deeply engaged inhabitant of his times. Detachment did not mean leaving the world itself without comment. He wrote a substantial amount in direct political commentary on the question of nationalism and modernity; and it is these prose essays which allow us to inspect the larger argumentative frame concerning modernity within which he set his reflections on nationalism. Like many other observers of history, Tagore saw modernity as a vast, contradictory assemblage of ideals and practices. But contradictoriness is a condition that can be interpreted in different ways. Contradiction could mean the simultaneous existence of two conflicting sides none of which can be shaken off. It could also indicate, in a quasi-Buddhist way, to be constructed out of principles which are affirmative in its restrained form, but destructive when it is pushed to extremes. Tagore saw some of the principles of Western modern civilization as valuable: 'higher obligations of public good above those of family and clan', the 'sacredness of law', 'justice to all men of all positions of life', 'above all . . . the banner of liberty . . . liberty of conscience, liberty of thought and action, liberty in the ideals of art and literature'. The central problem with this civilization, Tagore thought, was that it moved the political – the power of the state as a collective agency of the people – to the centre of everything, eclipsing all other fields of social activity. Tagore called this evil 'the nation' and attachment to it the sentiment of nationalism. 'The political civilization which has sprung up from the soil of Europe and is overrunning the whole world, like some prolific weed, is based upon exclusiveness'.[37] To him, its faults are clear: it strives to increase its power to make it unanswerable; it is naturally jealous of other nations, and tries 'to thwart all symptoms of greatness out of its own boundaries'; and consequently, it creates a world of competition and fear amongst all nations. It also does not allow internal diversity of races – by which he meant ethnicities. By developing military technology it forces the creativity of science to serve the ends of state power. It was dependent upon an economic system that created material wealth – which used technology in a predatory way to destroy the earth, and its natural capacity for renewal. Criticisms can be advanced against some of Tagore's arguments. He seems not to see that the ideals he admires in Western modernity are also political, and stem from the primacy of the political in the new civilization. He does not make a distinction between the nation – the intangible idea of a common people – and the state, which is a tangible, insensate machine, though his metaphor of a gigantic octopus seems to point to the state and its technologies of power which subordinate other peoples, but indirectly also its own. Yet, this lack of distinction between the nation and its state also has a forceful appositeness at his historical moment. And it is generally acknowledged today that there was an immense truth in his argument, alongside Gandhi's, that answering European power with a nationalist power in its mirror image was fraught with great danger. The answer to the dangers that European nationalism had created in the modern world was not to generalize that form of political union into a device of collective agency, but to develop a political theory on the basis of what he called, with some awkwardness, the 'no-nation': i.e., the opposite principles. I believe that this awkward locution contains an idea of immense and imminent promise for political theory.[38] In India politicians favoring pluralist nationalism – like Gandhi, Nehru and Ambedkar – produced through their practice a constitution that elaborated some of the implications of this alternative principle; but they neglected the philosophical elaboration of its central ideal. Hindu and Muslim nationalists directly opposed and derided it in favor of a simple adoration of European style ideas of nationhood. Radical theorists, in search of a more equal union, relentlessly criticized it as ambiguous, unpractical and sentimental. The recent rise of the nationalism of the European variety, which Tagore dreaded, not only in India, but across Europe and the United States, reveals the philosophical requirement to think deeply through the implicit irenic promise of the concept of the 'no-nation'. Examined closely, the history of the European state that Tagore had taken for granted from the lyrical narratives of European modernity can be faulted easily. He repeated the idea that European states did not have to contend with the diversity of peoples that an Indian nationalism had to face; yet, this was clearly wrong. The British, as Colley[39] demonstrates, had to be formed as a people through a combination of incentives of colonial expansion, and the threat of French rivalry along with simple cultural coercion. In the nineteenth century the French state had a historic task of turning peasants into Frenchmen.[40] The cultural formation of a nation involved coercion on a large scale even in Europe, even after the initial phase of coercive homogenization following Westphalia. Tagore took for granted a historical narrative that erased the formative violence of the European modern state. But the implication of that fault is not that his analysis was wrong; rather that it was more accurate than he believed. The purist conception of a homogeneous nation was a lyrical but lethal falsehood in European history, as much as in the Indian. Eventually, the Indian experiment successfully squared the circle – by basing a genuine, intensely felt collective sentiment of being an Indian in a way that instead of going for a fatal search after purity, learnt to celebrate its diversity – 'its ocean of humanity'[41]. Today, as much as in his times, a fundamental task of political philosophy is to square this circle, and defend it. Reading his novel *Gora* in our dark times shows that it contains not merely a riveting narrative, a noble sentiment, but surprisingly the only political philosophy of collective belonging that can teach the diverse people of India how to be a 'nation'.[42]

Notes

1 This is not to imply that European nationalism was invariably imperialist. In its initial appearance in European history, nationalism often played an emancipatory role against large imperial formations from the Spanish dominions to the Napoleonic empire. But by the time colonial intellectuals like Tagore encountered this amazing political phenomenon, it was inextricably connected to European imperial expansion. For different trajectories of European nationalism, see Greenfeld (1993).
2 For objections to this simple diffusionist view, see Chatterjee (1993), ch. 1.
3 Kant's phrase: Idea of a Universal History from a Cosmopolitan Point of View, Fourth Thesis, Kant (1991) p. 44.
4 I have discussed this connection in my 'collective intentionality' in Kaviraj (1997: 47–63).
5 Kaviraj (1995), especially chapter 4. For a more detailed argument, Kaviraj (2010).
6 For a detailed discussion of this question, see ibid, ch. 4.
7 Tagore wrote an early comic poem about the effect of such education in European history on college-going Bengali youth. 'Banga Bir' (Heroes of Bengal) in *Manasi*, *RR*, Volume 2, Kolkata: Visvabharati, 1946.
8 For an excellent and exhaustive account of the movement, with considerable attention given to the evolution of Tagore's ideas regarding this momentous event, see Sarkar (1977).
9 Ibid.
10 Sarkar's work provides a detailed analysis of Tagore's understanding of the movement, and its slow transformation. Ibid.
11 He did not enjoy sharp controversy with Leftist radicals; but continued to have very respectful but often profoundly critical exchanges with Gandhi. Bhattacharya (ed) (2005).
12 *Ghare Bairey*, *RR*, Volume 8, English translation, *The Home and the World*, trans. Surendranath Tagore, Madras: Macmillan India, 1992; *Char Adyay*, *RR*, Volume 13, Kolkata: Visvabharati, 1946, English translation, *Four Chapters*, Trans. Rimli Bhattacharya, Kolkata: Srishti Publications, 2003, a shorter novella.
13 See particularly the final sections of *Ghare Bairey*
14 See the continuing exchanges between the two in Bhattacharya (2005).
15 Tagore wrote some profoundly perceptive essays on this theme in Bengali, 'Swadeshi Samaj', *RR, Volume 3*: translation in Dasgupta (2009).
16 *Swadeshi Samaj*.
17 On the use of social imaginaries in the modern world, see Taylor (2004).
18 In reality, Gora – an infant born to Irish parents, probably a soldier of the retreating British army during the confusion of the 1857 uprising in north India – was sheltered and raised by his Bengali mother, the wife of an accountant in the army office. His father always maintained a strict distance from Gora; his mother treated him as God's gift of a child to her.

30 *Sudipta Kaviraj*

19 *Swadeshi Samaj*.
20 In the Bengali tradition, Bhudev Mukhopadhyay, in the generation that immediately preceded Tagore's, had presented a profound critique of 'Westernness' (*paschatya bhav*); but his critique of the modern state was perfunctory, and self-serving – i.e., he simply pretended that all the main features of representative government were already part of the Hindu view of political authority (Mukhopadhyay 2010). This was a complex position: on the one hand it conceded the preferability of representative government, but its historical claim of Hindu democracy was entirely false. Unlike Tagore, Bhudev, by this polemical move, avoided grappling with the major question of the nature of the modern state.
21 De Tocqueville (1994), Volume I, ch. XVI.
22 *Bharatvarsher Itihas*, *RR*, Volume 8. And *Bharatvarsher Itihaser Dhara*, *RR*, Volume 18.
23 This was the tradition of constitutionalist reasoning from Locke to Montesquieu to the Federalist Papers (Taylor 1990).
24 In two of his plays, *Raja* and *Raktakarabi*, it is a deeply self-alienated king who controls the forces of technology which shrivel the lives of his subjects, and his own. In *Muktadhara*, the connection between political authority and technological enslavement is not direct.
25 I deliberately put the term 'patriotic' in quotes, because, as we shall see, some of thinking on this subject are entirely discordant with the usual meaning of this word.
26 For a more detailed analysis of this poetic trend, see 'A strange love of abstractions: Bengali patriotic poetry' in (Kaviraj 2015).
27 As in Bankimchandra's famous poem, *Bande Mataram*.
28 Kaviraj (2015)especially ch. 4.
29 '*Amar sonar bangla, ami tomay bhalobasi*'.
30 '*Sarthaka janama amar, janmechi ei deshe/ sarthaka janama ma go tomay bhalobese*'. (Blessed I am in being born in this land, blessed in loving you, mother.)
31 There is a parallel distinction in the world of figural images of the mother. The first painting of Bharatmata (Mother India) by Tagore's nephew, the artist Abanindranath Tagore, was a gentle, beneficent figure; but it was gradually replaced by figures which exude power and invincibility.
32 Sometimes the land is seen as unfortunate because of its enslavement, but rarely because what it has done to its own people – for which it ought to atone.
33 *Jare tumi nice thela, se tomare taniche je nice*
    Pascate rekhecho jare, se tomare paschate taniche
    Vidhar rudra roshe, durbhiksher dware base
    Bhag kare khete habe sakaler sathe annapan
    Apamane hote habe tahader sabar saman.
    Those whom you push down, they are pulling you downwards
    Those whom have left behind, they are pulling you from behind
    Facing the terrible wrath of the Maker, sitting at the door of famine/catastrophe
    Your will have to learn to share your food and drink with everyone
    You will have to learn to be equal to everybody else in taking insults. (translation mine)
34 Poem 106, *Gitanjali*, *RR*, Volume 11.
35 *Ranadhara bahi, jaygan gahi unmad kalarabe*
    Bhedi marupath giri parvat jara esechilo sabe
    Tara mor majhe sabai biraje keha nahe nahe dur
    Amar sonite royeche dvanite tar- vicitra sur
    He rudravina bajo bajo bajo, ghrna kari dure ache jara ajo
    Bandha nasibe tarao asibe dandabe ghire
    Ei bharater mahamanaber sagaratire
36 See Vajpeyi (2012) for an examination of different versions of this moral imaginary. Chapter 2: 'Viraha: The Self's Longing' discusses Tagore.
37 Tagore, *Nationalism*, London: Macmillan, 1918, 59–60.

38 In a recent paper, James Tully has called for a 'de-parochializing political theory': a major task of contemporary political theory should be look for a new kind of political order, or state based on these no-nation or non-nation principle. See James Tully, 'De-parochializing political theory', *Journal of World Philosophies*, 2017.
39 Linda Colley, *Britons: Forging the Nation, 1707–1837*, New Haven, CT: Yale University Press, 2009.
40 Eugen Weber, *Peasants into Frenchmen: The Modernization of Rural France*, Stanford, CA: Stanford University Press, 1976.
41 In the complex line of his famous poem, *mahamanaber sagara-tire* – on the shores of this sea of great humanity. It is interesting that he found the use of the mere term 'humanity' (*manav*) inadequate, precisely because it found a place within itself of a greater humanity (*mahamanav*).
42 I have attempted to give a more directly conceptual account of this squared circle – how it is possible to think of a non-European conception of a nation, following thinkers like Tagore and Gandhi in a separate paper: 'Nation/nation-state', Workshop on 'Conceptual Itineraries: Routes and Roots of the Political', SOAS, London, June 10, 2017.

References

Bhattacharya, Sabyasachi. 2005. *The Mahatma and the Poet*. New Delhi: National Book Trust.
Chatterjee, Partha. 1993. *The Nation and Its Fragments*. Princeton, NJ: Princeton University Press.
Dasgupta, Uma, 2009. *The Oxford India Tagore: Selected Writings on Education and Nationalism*. New Delhi: Oxford University Press.
De Tocqueville, Alexis. 1994. *Democracy in America*. London: Everyman's Library.
Greenfeld, Liah. 1993. *Nationalism*. Cambridge, MA: Harvard University Press.
Kant, Immanuel. 1991. *Political Writings*. Ed. Hans Reiss. Cambridge: Cambridge University Press.
Kaviraj, Sudipta. 1995. *The Unhappy Consciousness*. New Delhi: Oxford University Press.
———. 1997. 'Collective Forms in Modern Politics,' in Kathryn Dean (ed.), *Politics and the Ends of Identity*. London: Ashgate, pp. 47–63.
———. 2010. 'Indian Nationalism,' in Niraja Gopal Jayal and Pratap Bhanu Mehta (eds.), *Oxford Companion to Indian Politics*. New Delhi: Oxford University Press.
———. 2015. *Invention of Private Life*. New York: Columbia University Press.
———. 2017. 'Nation/Nation-State,' unpublished paper presented at workshop on 'Conceptual Itineraries: Routes and Roots of the Political,' School of Oriental and African Studies, London, 10 June.
Mukhopadhyay, Bhudev. 2010. *Samajik Prabandha in Prabandha Samagra*. Kolkata: Carchapad.
Nandy, Ashis, 1994. *The Illegitimacy of Nationalism*. New Delhi: Oxford University Press.
Sarkar, Sumit. 1977. *The Swadeshi Movement in Bengal*. New Delhi: Peoples' Publishing House.
Tagore, Rabindranath. 1992. *The Home and the World*. Trans. Surendranath Tagore. Madras: Macmillan India.
———. 2003. *Four Chapters*. Trans. Rimli Bhattacharya. Kolkata: Srishti Publications.
Taylor, Charles. 1990. 'Modes of Civil Society,' *Public Culture*, 3(1), Fall: 95–118.
———. 2004. *Modern Social Imaginaries*. Durham, NC: Duke University Press.
Vajpeyi, Ananya. 2012. *Righteous Republic*. Cambridge, MA: Harvard University Press.

2 Midnight's children
Religion and nationalism in South Asia[1]

Giorgio Shani

On February 14, 2019, an Indian Central Reserve Police Force (CRPF) convoy was rammed by an SUV carrying an improvised explosive device in the town of Pulwama in Indian-controlled Kashmir.[2] At least 40 soldiers were killed along with the suicide bomber, Adil Ahmed Dhar, a local Kashmiri militant who belonged to the *jihadi* terror group Jaish-e-Mohammed, based in Pakistan.[3] Within hours, Indian troops had been deployed to the border and the prospect of war between the two nuclear-armed neighbors, South Asia's 'midnight's children' (Rushdie 1981) born over 70 years previously in an orgy of violence, seemed very real.

India and Pakistan became independent states on the stroke of midnight on August 14 (Pakistan) and August 15 (India), 1947. Like South Asia, Kashmir had been partitioned at birth. A Muslim majority state ruled by a Hindu maharajah, it had been incorporated by India at Independence. However, India's claim to Kashmir was contested by Pakistan, which invaded Kashmir shortly after Partition. The United Nations was called in to broker a ceasefire and divided Kashmir along a line of control, but no final border was established. Further attempts were made by Pakistan to redraw the border by force, most notably in 1965 and then in 1999, when nuclear war was barely avoided, but the line of control separating colonial India's midnight's children in the northwest has remained unchanged.

Although nominally secular states, India and Pakistan came into being as a result of political mobilization along religious lines. Both the Indian National Congress (INC) and particularly the Muslim League had, to varying degrees,[4] made use of religious imagery and symbols in the campaign for independence. The partitioning of colonial India on the grounds of religion by the British, it is argued, placed constraints on the secular articulation of nationalism. Although the emergence of religious nationalism in South Asia may be seen as a modern phenomenon, the origins of what are termed 'communal' identities in the subcontinent lie in British colonial rule. In particular, colonial policies of classification and enumeration (Kaviraj 2010) through the Census (Cohn 1996) and subsequently the introduction of separate electorates, facilitated the development of 'communal' consciousness in colonial India (Pandey 1990). This will be discussed in the first section of the chapter that explores the impact of colonial policies on the construction of 'religion' as a category in South Asia.

The genocidal violence unleashed by Partition will subsequently be discussed. It will be argued that the manipulation of the memory of Partition by political elites has left South Asia in the grip of a nationalist imaginary increasingly articulated in a religious idiom that makes 'secular' rule problematic. For, despite the 'secular' credentials of the subcontinent's post-colonial elites, both India and, especially, Pakistan could not help but be imagined by its new citizens primarily in terms of its dominant ethno-religious traditions. Partition cleansed Pakistan of its Hindu and Sikh minorities and transformed Indian Muslims effectively into second-class citizens whose loyalty to the nation-state was continuously questioned in times of conflict with their northern neighbour.

The third section will examine the emergence of the Bharatiya Janata Party (BJP) in post-colonial India. It will be argued that its commitment to *Hindutva* has greatly exacerbated communal tensions and made a distinction between religious and secular nationalism problematic. As a form of cultural nationalism, *Hindutva* interpellates[5] all Indians as belonging to a Hindu civilization based on a common pan-Indian Hindu *national* identity. As the BJP stress, *Hindutva* is a 'nationalist, and not a religious or theocratic, concept' (BJP 2014). The violence which occasionally has been carried out in its name is motivated by a desire to *assimilate* – or, in the words of one of its most important advocates, M. S. Golwalkar, 'digest' (Sharma 2011: 176) – India's ethno-religious 'Others' into the Hindu 'Self'.

It is in its desire to assimilate the 'Other' by violence if necessary that Hindu nationalism closely mirrors the more explicitly religiously based nationalism in Pakistan and Bangladesh. This will be discussed in the section titled 'Linguistic and religious nationalism in Pakistan'. Shorn of its Eastern Wing, Pakistan has turned to Islam to legitimize de facto military rule over a democratic façade since General Zia ul Haq ousted the elected government of Zulfiqar Bhutto, and hung him for good measure! The military have intervened to overthrow elected governments led by his late daughter, Benazir, as well as her rival, Nawaz Sharif, for having the temerity to reduce the role which the military plays in Pakistani politics. The election of their world cup winning cricket captain, Imran Khan, as prime minister in 2018 owed as much to his military backers as to his exploits with bat and ball.[6] Similarly, in Bangladesh, the success of the Awami League of Sheikh Hasina in winning three consecutive elections owed much to support from Islamist parties which compromise its secular credentials.[7]

Although spared the trauma of Partition at birth, Sri Lanka has similarly been haunted by its spectres since Independence, as will be examined in the final section. Colonial policies of divide and rule that favoured the Tamil minority led to a consolidation of a Buddhist-infused communal sentiment among the Sinhala majority. Post-colonial Sri Lankan politics became characterized by 'ethnic outbidding'[8] between two rival Sinhalese political parties (De Votta 2004) resulting in the progressive Sinhalization of the state. The Tamil minority, mainly located in the north and east, were increasingly marginalized and subject to institutionalized linguistic discrimination. The communalization of Sri Lankan politics led to civil war, raising the spectre of a further partition of the subcontinent. Although the eventual victory of the Sri Lankan state after more than a quarter of a century of war appeared to have allayed those fears, the wounds of the civil war remain raw and the spectres of nationalist violence articulated in religious terms continue to haunt the island.

The colonial construction of 'religion'

For Tomoko Masuzawa, the rise of the modern social sciences allowed a distinction to be made between the modern, secular West and a mystical East depicted by Orientalist scholarship and historians of religion. Consequently, 'every region of the non-modern non-West was presumed to be thoroughly in the grip of religion, as all aspects of life were supposedly determined and dictated by an archaic metaphysics of the magical and the supernatural' (Masuzawa 2005: 16). However, in much of the post-colonial world the concept of 'religion' is an alien cultural category which was imposed upon indigenous societies as a result of 'colonial governmentality '(Chatterjee 1993).

Foucault had previously defined governmentality as referring to the following: a form of power which could be differentiated from sovereign power. It was connected to the development in early modern Europe from the fifteenth and sixteenth centuries of a whole series of specific governmental apparatuses (*appareils*) and the development of a whole complex of knowledges (*saviors*) which was increasingly exercised by administrative states over the populations it controlled. Political economy emerged as its principal form of knowledge and security as its primary instrument of control (Foucault 2007: 108–109). However, as Chatterjee has pointed out, there were significant differences between governmentality as it developed in Europe and the governmentality which emerged in the colonies. While governmentality in Britain treated the 'population' as a homogenous, undifferentiated mass of individuals, 'colonial governmentality' recognized and built upon seemingly 'primordial' categories of 'race' and 'religion'. In South Asia, the colonial state facilitated the imagination of collective indigenous identities, through the introduction of modern scientific techniques of classification and enumeration that transformed communities in South Asia and continue to shape its politics today.

The introduction of the Censuses in particular transformed previously 'fuzzy' into 'enumerated' communities facilitating the emergence of *essentialized* identities (Kaviraj 2010). As Bernard Cohn points out, 'what was entailed in the construction of census operations was the creation of social categories by which India was ordered for administrative purposes' (Cohn 1996: 8). Traditional South Asian society was characterized by the co-existence of a plethora of, seen from modern eyes, potentially contradictory identities. Examples include localized *jati*[9] identities and forms of religious affiliation, such as Bhakti and Sufism which cut across religious boundaries. The Census *strengthened* these porous religious boundaries, thereby objectifying religious, social and cultural difference. The categories of caste and religion were, henceforth, to be considered homogenous and mutually exclusive. Furthermore, the colonial state facilitated the enumeration of these communities through the inauguration of a process of statistical counting and spatial mapping. Enumeration facilitated the transformation of *local* caste or ethno-religious into *national* political communities. As local communities were mapped by the Census, the terms 'Hindu' and 'Muslim' lost much of their religious and philosophical significance and became markers of distinct, homogenous and potentially conflictual political identities at an all-India level through the formation of the Muslim League and the Hindu Mahasabha.

Colonialism, in short, contributed to the *thinning* out of religious identities by encouraging identification on the basis of loosely defined yet mutually exclusive categories. Traditionally, religion may be considered 'thick' in the sense that its internal contents are a vast archive of ordered beliefs concerned with determining social conduct and ethical problems (Kaviraj 2011). The traditional religious community in South Asia is narrowly defined and limited to members of the immediate locality who satisfy the stringent criteria for membership, frequently segmented on caste and regional lines. The 'thinning out' of religious traditions opens these identities up to adherents of divergent religious practices and philosophies, such as worshippers of different deities such as Vishnu and Shiva in Hinduism and Shi'ia and Sunni sects in Islam. The enumeration of these categories through the Census further facilitated the *politicization* of religious identities. Before the coming of modern statistical processes associated with the Census, it would not occur to an individual to ask how many other people practiced the same religion outside of their locality. However, after colonialism, *all* Hindus or Muslims could be included in a *nationally* defined and structured religious community irrespective of individual belief and faith. As Kaviraj points out, the primary purpose of the *inclusion* of members of different religious communities in a loosely defined, nationally organized community is ironically to *exclude* other religious communities from the political sphere (Kaviraj 2011). Religion ceased to be, to borrow Nandy's terminology, a 'faith' and became an 'ideology': a 'subnational, national or cross-national identifier of populations contesting for or protecting non-religious, usually political or socio-economic interests' (Nandy 1998: 322). It was religion *as* ideology which fuelled the growth of nationalist movements and constrained its secular iteration, giving rise to the bloodbath of Partition.

Partitions

The partition of South Asia into two new successor states, India and Pakistan, was as one of the most violent processes of ethnic cleansing in history and foreshadowed contemporary genocidal conflict in the Balkans and central Africa. More than 12 million people were dislocated in one of the 'greatest human convulsions of human history' (Brass 2003: 75). In Punjab alone, 5.5 million Muslims and 4.5 million Sikhs and Hindus were forced to move to either side of the Radcliffe line[10] and an estimated half a million[11] died in the organized communal riots that swept like wildfire through the province during the summer and fall of 1947. In Bengal, where 'communal' violence erupted in August 1946 in Calcutta, a similar number died, although it is difficult to establish the final toll given the absence of verifiable figures.

Three different conceptions of partition can be identified (Pandey 2001: 21–44). The first was the Muslim League's demand for a Muslim-majority state in a loose, federal structure. Pakistan's founder, the Quaid-i-Azam, Muhammad Ali Jinnah (1876–1948), believed that South Asia's Muslims constituted a separate 'nation' with a single culture and language. In the Lahore session of the Muslim League in March 1940, Jinnah claimed that Islam and Hinduism were 'not religions in the strict sense of the word' but were 'different and distinct social orders'. Since both communities belonged to 'two different religious philosophies, social customs, and literatures', any attempt to 'yoke together two such nations under a single State, one as a numerical minority and the other as a majority, must lead to a growing discontent and the final destruction of any fabric that may be so built up for the government of such a state' (Jinnah cited in Jaffrelot 2002: 12).

The second conception of partition involved 'partitioning' the Muslim-majority provinces of Punjab and Bengal. Support for this British designed 'partition' came from the main organization of Hindus, the Hindu Mahasabha, and the Sikh leadership under Master Tara Singh.[12] Initially 'partition' was opposed, but then finally accepted by the Muslim League in 1947. With significant pressure from the United Kingdom, this agreement became the basis for the 'official' Partition. By offering Jinnah a 'mutilated and moth-eaten' Pakistan, the borders of which, shorn of non-Muslim populations in East Punjab and West Bengal, were not known until *after* independence, both the British and the Indian National Congress (INC) under Jawaharlal Nehru (1889–1964) were able to achieve their objective of ejecting Jinnah and the 'communal' Muslim League from the centre, clearing the way for a strong, unitary, centralized state as favoured by Nehru. From Nehru's point of view, 'it was better to enjoy an unimpeded monopoly of power in the larger part of India than to be shackled by having to share it in an undivided one' (Anderson 2012: 14).

The final 'partition' was the violence which accompanied the 'official' partition: the massacres, the nightmares, 'those other partitions that people would have to live with for decades to come' (Pandey 2001: 35). Violence was central to Partition and differed from the periodic inter-religious 'communal violence' of the colonial period. It was dominated by national discourses and issues of state formation and bore the imprint of the Westphalian world order of territorialized nation-states. A 'new' national discourse emerged to challenge the 'old' multi-ethnic discourse of co-existence amongst Hindus, Muslims and Sikhs and became a driving force for the violence (Hansen 2002: 29). The violence, in turn, permitted the construction of national boundaries between the two new states and *legitimized* their claims to state sovereignty.

From secular to religious nationalism in post-colonial India

Partition continues to haunt the two 'midnight's children' in the form of periodic communal violence between ethno-religious communities and strained regional relations. Nuclear-armed India and Pakistan have been to war three times since Partition in 1947 and relations have been exacerbated by alleged Pakistani support for militant groups suspected of carrying out terrorist attacks upon Indian soil. In India, the secular settlement imposed upon a deeply 'religious' society by a modernizing nationalist elite under Jawaharlal Nehru appeared to suggest that the state was committed to implementing 'the same civilizing mission that the colonial state had once taken upon itself vis-à-vis the ancient faiths of the subcontinent' (Nandy 1998: 323). The secularization of Indian society by the state led to the exclusion of religion (as faith) from the public sphere. In turn, this created space for the politicization of religious identities by non-state actors alienated by the perceived neo-colonial attitude of the Nehruvian leadership. In particular, it facilitated the development of an explicitly Hindu nationalist discourse articulated through the Rashtriya Swayamsevak Sangh (RSS).

Initially suppressed by the state in the immediate aftermath of the assassination of Mohandas 'Mahatma' Gandhi (1869–1948) by an ex-member, the RSS has since its inception in 1925 provided the institutional mechanism for Hindu nationalism. It has done so through the establishment, first, in 1964, of the Vishwa Hindu Parishad (VHP), which seeks to mobilize Hindus throughout the world; and, second, in 1980 of the Bharatiya Janata Party (BJP), the political wing of the RSS. The BJP has in recent years successfully contested elections at a state and national level through the articulation of an explicitly Hindu nationalist ideology. A middle class, high caste project of 'cultural homogenization' (Appadurai 1996), Hindu nationalism seeks to create a unified, homogenous Hindu political identity out of the multiplicity of different faith, ethnic, regional, linguistic and caste-based identities which characterize multi-ethnic India. Central to the Hindu nationalist project is the concept of Hindutva, first developed by Veer Savarkar (1883–1966), which refers to an *ethnicized* Hindu identity. For Savarkar, the Hindus 'are not only a nation but a *jati* (race), a born brotherhood' (Savarkar 1923: 89). Consequently, *all* Indians, including those professing other religions, are considered Hindus with the exception of Muslims and Christians, since their 'holylands' are outside India. The concept of Hindutva was explicitly adopted by the BJP in its election manifesto of 1996 as 'a unifying principle which alone can preserve the unity and integrity' of India (BJP 1996) and has remained the party's guiding philosophical principle ever since.

Although the BJP appears to dilute its Hindutva ideology once in power, it has retained authoritarian characteristics (Vanaik 2017). Furthermore, it presided over – and was deeply implicated in – one of the worst 'communal' riots of post-Partition India in Gujarat. The mass pogrom of Muslims in Godhra in 2002 seems to offer a tragic illustration of what Paul Brass has termed an 'institutionalized riot system' at work. In Gujarat, over 2,500 were brutally murdered by Hindu mobs and 200,000 families displaced in a state then led by the future BJP leader and Indian prime minister Narendra Modi. Brass has argued that the 'the organizations of militant Hindu nationalism' affiliated to the RSS are 'deeply implicated' in the organization and production of Hindu-Muslim violence (Brass 2006: 4). This can be clearly seen in the RSS instigated 'communal riots' of 1992–1993. Following the destruction by RSS *kar sevaks* (volunteers) of the Babri masjid mosque in Ayodhya, organized pogroms of Muslim communities were carried out by armed mobs of militant Hindu nationalists throughout India leading to an estimated 3,000 deaths (Talbot and Singh 2009: 150). In Bombay, Shiv Sena, a regional party based in Maharashtra espousing a particularly virulent form of Hindu nationalism under the leadership of Bal Thackeray, systematically planned mob attacks upon Muslim individuals and businesses in India's financial capital: Mumbai (Bannerjee 2001). The riots form the backdrop to Danny Boyle's Oscar winning film *Slumdog Millionaire* (2008) based on a 2005 book by former Indian Foreign Service officer Vikas Swarup.

Responsibility for communal violence, however, is not limited to militant Hindu nationalists affiliated to the Sangh Parivar. Arguably, the mass pogrom against Sikhs in Delhi in November 1984 following the assassination of Prime Minister Indira Gandhi provided the template for future attacks upon ethno-religious minorities. An estimated 2,000 Sikhs were killed in organized 'riots' between October 31 and November 4, 1984. The massacres were directed by senior members of the ruling Indian National Congress (INC) and there is evidence to suggest that the then prime minister, Rajiv Gandhi, son of slain Prime Minister Indira, stoked the communal fires with inflammatory comments.[13] However, Muslims appear to have been the target of most communal riots, at least post-9/11, suggesting they have become an 'internal other' to be securitized rather than an integral part of an India increasingly imagined exclusively on Hindu lines. Muslims are, in any case, among the poorest and least represented groups within India. In 2006, the government appointed Sachar Commission estimated the Muslim population to be 13.4% of the population. It concluded that Muslims were the most marginalized community within India in terms of literacy and employment and that 'the abysmally low representation of Muslim OBCs suggests that the benefits of entitlements meant for the backward classes are yet to reach them' (Sachar 2006).

Linguistic and religious nationalism in Pakistan

Purged of significant religious minorities, two competing forms of nationalism emerged in Pakistan: a religious state-based nationalism in the nominally Urdu-speaking west and an ethno-linguistic nationalism in the Bengali-speaking east. The latter resulted in a further partition, no less violent than the one that gave birth to the two 'midnight's children' of the British *raj* in the first place. Jinnah and the Muslim League argued that Muslims in South Asia constituted a distinct nation and laid claim to territorial sovereignty on the basis of religion, yet sought to simultaneously deny its salience to the construction of the new nation. This was evident in his speech of 1947, when he told the Constituent Assembly not only that the citizens of Pakistan were free to belong to any religion and creed, but also that, 'in the course of time Hindus would cease to be Hindus and Muslims would cease to be Muslims, not in the religious sense . . . but in the political sense as citizens of the state'.[14] Constitutionally and legally, Pakistan has subsequently struggled to resolve this fundamental ambiguity: failing either to separate or combine the secular and religious dimensions of the Muslim nationalism that gave birth to the new state. When a constitution was finally agreed upon almost a decade after the establishment of Pakistan, it declared the new state to be an Islamic Republic where no law repugnant to the Qur'an and the Sunnah could be enacted, yet did *not* make Islam the official religion of the state. Indeed, Islam only became the state religion of Pakistan *after* the more populous East Wing (now known as Bangladesh) had seceded.

Bangladesh was established in 1971 following a bloody and intense civil war marked by the use of systematic brutality by the mainly West Pakistan army against Bengali-speaking supporters of the Awami League. The Awami League, led by the charismatic Sheikh Mujibur Rahman (1920–1975), was committed to regional autonomy for East Bengal and won a majority of seats in the Pakistan National Assembly in 1970. Although Bengalis comprised over half of the population of Pakistan, they had been politically and economically marginalized in the West Pakistan–dominated Islamic state. Successive campaigns for linguistic autonomy and for a fair share in the profits accrued from the export of jute had been denied by their rulers in far-off Karachi and later Islamabad, sparking varying degrees of repression. However, the democratic mandate given to the Awami League in 1970 to seek greater autonomy within Pakistan raised the spectre of a second Partition. After all, as Jalal (1985) pointed out, the genesis of Pakistan lay in precisely the same demand for greater autonomy for Muslims within an all-Indian context. Pakistan's military rulers, under General Yahya Khan, decided to crush the Awami League by all means necessary. This included not only launching a military crackdown on the regime's opponents, but also orchestrating systematic ethnic cleansing in East Pakistan targeting its Hindu minority by mobilizing Islamist 'volunteers' (*razakhar*) (Talbot and Singh 2009: 148). An estimated 10 million refugees were thus forcibly displaced from their homes and crossed the border into India, leading the Indian prime minister Indira Gandhi to militarily intervene in December 1971. The third Indo-Pakistani war since Independence resulted in a crushing victory for India and the establishment of Bangladesh. However, the violence that accompanied this second partition was no less traumatic than the official Partition of 1947. As in Partition, there are no reliable casualty figures with estimates varying from 300,000 to 3 million dead in a little over six months of fighting. The difference this time was that the violence was perpetrated by co-religionists in the name of 'national' unity against fellow citizens divided by ethnicity and language. Jinnah's dream of 'two nations' defined by religion living side by side in South Asia was shattered.

Following the secession of East Bengal, Pakistan enjoyed a short-lived experiment with democracy under Zulfiqar Ali Bhutto (1928–1979) that was brought to an end by a military coup. General Zia, who led the coup, selectively imposed Shari'ia laws on what Jinnah had envisaged as a secular state while at the same time supporting the jihad of the Afghan Mujahadeen against the Soviet Union. Relying upon the support of the Jammat-e-Islami (JI), an Islamic political organization, Zia's policies led to an increasing *Islamization* within Pakistan. In the first place, members of the Ahmadiya sect that had been declared 'non-Muslim' by the Bhutto government were prohibited under Ordinance XX from 'posing as Muslims'. This meant that the Ahmadis, who consider themselves to be Muslims, could be arrested for practicing what the state has determined to be a heretical version of Islam preached by a 'false' prophet. Secondly, the institutionalization of Sunni legal codes led to increased insecurity for the Shi'ia minority in Pakistan who found themselves excluded from *their* nation by the majority mainstream Sunni population and subject to increasing attacks by militant groups. Zia's death in a mysterious plane crash and the return to civilian rule under, first, Benazir Bhutto (1953–2007), Zulfiqar Ali Bhutto's daughter and leader of the Pakistan People's Party (PPP), and Nawaz Sharif of the Muslim League, did little to stem the tide of Islamization of Pakistani politics. Indeed, following the withdrawal of Soviet forces from Afghanistan, the ISI recruited and funded the Taliban from the *madrassas* of the Jamiat-e-Ulema-e-Islam (JUI), the more fundamentalist and sectarian of Pakistan's Islamist parties, at a time when the nation was ostensibly returning to democracy.

Since the Taliban were ousted from Afghanistan, the 'War on Terror' has largely been fought in Pakistan. As a frontline state in the war against Jihadis inspired by a Wahabite ideology that is a marked contrast to the syncretic and tolerant Sufi traditions that long prevailed, Pakistan has borne a heavy price with almost 50,000 casualties since 9/11 (Raja 2013). The 'War on Terror' has provided a legitimizing narrative for the use of indiscriminate violence by Sunni Islamic extremists affiliated with the Pakistani Taliban, on the one hand, and state repression by the military, on the other. This makes a separation between 'religious' and 'secular' forms of nationalism problematic since both the military and the Taliban are waging a war in the name of Islam. The election of Imran Khan as prime minister has done much to blur the boundaries between religious and secular nationalism since he appears to derive support from both the military and his pro-Taliban Pashtun base.

In retrospect, Muslim nationalism successfully mobilized the Muslim masses behind the movement for a territorially defined Muslim homeland within South Asia, yet once the goal of Pakistan was achieved and the new state established, it was difficult to maintain a sense of national identity on religious grounds alone. The subsequent disintegration of the 'moth-eaten' state separated by ethnicity, language and over a thousand miles of hostile territory appeared to deprive Pakistan of its legitimacy as the homeland for Muslim South Asians. However, Islam continues to provide South Asians from different ethnic, cultural and linguistic backgrounds with a coherent and cohesive politico-religious identity. Part of the tragedy of the Muslim League's position in seeking to territorialize Muslim identity through the demand for a homeland in Pakistan was that it ostensibly divided the very community it sought to represent, leaving those Muslims most in favour of a separate Muslim state trapped in a Hindu-dominated India as a permanent minority.

Ethno-national conflict in Sri Lanka

In Sri Lanka, the divisive colonial legacy was ethno-linguistic rather than religious between the majority Sinhala and minority Tamil communities. The global 'War on Terror' provided the Sri Lankan government led by former President Mahinda Rajapaksha with the opportunity to seek a military solution to end the intractable thirty-year conflict with the Liberation Tigers of Tamil Eelam (LTTE). As elsewhere in South Asia, the origins of Sri Lanka's civil war lay in the failures of the post-colonial state, dominated by the Buddhist Sinhalese majority, to recognize the ethno-linguistic, religious and cultural distinctiveness of the Tamil minority (Tambiah 1992; De Votta 2004). After Independence, the United National Party (UNP) and the Sri Lanka Freedom Party (SLFP) dominated Sri Lankan politics, with both pandering exclusively to the majority Sinhalese community. The 'ethnic outbidding' (De Votta 2004) between the two parties resulted in the Sinhalization of the main institutions of the Sri Lankan state and marginalization of the Tamil minority. The misrepresentation of legitimate Tamil grievances such as linguistic autonomy as a threat to the territorial integrity of the state, and the instigation of riots against Tamils by militant Sinhala organizations, often with the involvement of Buddhist monks (Tambiah 1992), led to the emergence of LTTE which advocated violent armed struggle in an attempt to create an independent Tamil state in the north and east (Tamil Eelam). The LTTE had fewer than fifty members before the outbreak of the civil war following anti-Tamil riots in 1983, yet extended its control over most of the Tamil majority areas in the north and east after the riots. Although it did so by coercive means, developing into a quasi-fascistic terrorist organization pioneering the use of female suicide bombings and specializing in the recruitment of child soldiers, it enjoyed substantial popular support amongst the Tamil community within Sri Lanka and the diaspora. At its peak, the LTTE constituted a state within a state; it ruled a quarter of Sri Lanka and had a conventional army of twenty thousand militants complete with navy and air force. The LTTE managed to keep the Sri Lankan forces at bay and even withstood the Indian army's intervention between 1987 and 1990 (De Votta 2004). A peace process leading to recognition of the de facto partition of the island along ethnic lines appeared to be the only realistic option for peace and security on the island. However, the SLFP leadership had different ideas. Haunted by the spectre of the official Partition of the subcontinent, Rajapaksha embarked upon his own 'War on Terror' which resulted in an overwhelming victory over the LTTE and decimation of its leadership. The military crushing of the LTTE did help to restore peace and security to the island but at considerable human cost to Tamil civilians. It is estimated that 280,000 people were displaced in the latter stages of the war and at least 7,000 civilians killed, according to UN figures, in a 'no fire' zone in the northeastern tip of the island. Unofficial estimates put the figure far higher at between 30,000 and 40,000. These 'credible allegations' are being investigated by the UN Secretary-General's Panel of Experts on Sri Lanka who have warned that, if proven, they would 'amount to war crimes and crimes against humanity' (United Nations 2011). A US-tabled resolution was subsequently passed in the Human Rights Council asking the government of Sri Lanka to take credible and independent actions to address these alleged violations of international humanitarian law. The fundamental causes of Tamil grievances, and therefore of their insecurity, however, remain unaddressed. In 2015 President Rajapaksa was ousted from power and his successor immediately embarked on various reform and reconciliation initiatives, while promising a full reckoning regarding the alleged war crimes.

However, in 2018, Rajapaksa was briefly back as prime minister, appointed by the president who had defeated him in the 2015 elections. Consequently, the communal divisions between the Sinhalese and Tamils remain volatile, and overcoming the trauma of prolonged civil war remains a daunting challenge. The Easter day bombings of churches by Islamist inspired militants which killed an estimated 300 worshippers served as a tragic reminder that minority religious identities are not immune to inflammation. Consequently, there is a danger that the Muslim community in Sri Lanka will be subject to similar levels of securitization as those experienced by their co-religionists in her giant neighbor to the north.

Conclusion

The re-election of Narendra Modi in May 2019 as Indian Prime Minister with a landslide majority raises the spectre of Hindu majoritarian rule in South Asia's largest state.[15] This brings into question the degree to which religion and nationalism can be separated in South Asia given the legacy of colonialism and Partition. It has been argued that the 'idea of India' (Khilnani 1997) as an inclusive, secular nation as envisaged by Nehru at Independence was compromised by the violence of Partition which rendered his dream stillborn. The BJP have filled the ideological vacuum at the heart of Indian politics since Nehru's death with a militant Hindu nationalism and hastened the demise of the Congress 'one party dominance system' (Kothari 1964). As the 2019 election demonstrates, it remains a formidable political movement with a coherent ideology, support from India's emerging middle class and dedicated cadres belonging to the RSS. Across the border in the other midnight's child, the dream of a secular homeland for Muslims in South Asia has long since died. Jinnah's 'two-nation' theory was disproved by the bloody secession of Pakistan's Eastern Wing on *ethno-linguistic* grounds. The cultural glue of a common religion proved insufficient to unite two peoples divided by ethnicity, language and, most insurmountably, geography. After the establishment of Bangladesh, the 'spectres' of Partition continue to haunt Pakistan and Bangladesh in the form of sectarian violence against religious minorities and a civil war that, in threatening to fragment the state, legitimizes military interference in the political process. In Sri Lanka, the spectre of the partition of the island on ethnic lines strengthened the resolve of the Sinhala-dominated government to use force to eradicate the threat posed by Tamil separatism arising initially from demands for linguistic autonomy and greater representation in government.

Given the difficulty separating religion and nationalism in South Asia, one is forced to conclude that the nation-state model coupled with secularism is no longer suitable for the region, if it ever was. A unified, consociational India with institutionalized representation for caste, ethnic and religious minorities was the only realistic option for a multicultural, multi-ethnic society emerging from the shackles of imperial rule. Colonial policies of 'divide and rule,' part of a colonial 'rule of difference' based as much on the prevalence of Orientalist thinking as on calculation of imperial interest, had contributed to the construction of reified, essentialized 'communal' identities based on a 'thin' conception of religion. However, these identities had their basis in different 'faiths' and cosmologies and could not be merely disregarded as products of the imperial imagination (van der Veer 2004). This makes the adoption of Western notions of secularism premised on the notion of the separation of politics and religion problematic. Rather, the Indian variant of secularism, *Sarva Dharma Sambhava* ('let all religions flourish') could have been the basis for a unified state at the time of independence if it had taken into consideration demands for political representation for minority communities in the electoral system.

Unlike Western understandings of secularism, Sarva Dharma Sambhava does not attempt to banish religion from the public sphere but sees it as an integral part of politics. Secularism in India was neither intended to exclude religious practice or institutions from the domain of politics nor to guarantee state non-interference in religious affairs, but merely to entail equal respect or consideration of all religions (Bhargava 1998). As such, from a Western perspective, it may be considered a form of *post-secularism* (Shani 2014). However, its application in India has preserved the 'epistemic privilege' (Mignolo 2010) of caste-based Hinduism by maintaining the distinction between majority and minority religious communities. This has created space for the construction of a militant majoritarian Hindu discourse which equates India's political traditions with those of its majority community. The other midnight's child forced out of the womb of colonial India serves as its 'constitutive outside', allowing independent India to be imagined along Hindu ethno-religious lines. Nevertheless, had a reworked version of the post-colonial Indian variant of (post)-secularism, purged of its epistemic privilege for the majority community, been applied in a pan-Indian context at the time of Independence, then the trauma of partition whose spectres continue to haunt the sub-continent would have been avoided. Although dreams of reuniting South Asia's 'midnight's children' have faded with the memories of the dwindling number of aging South Asians who experienced Partition, it is hoped that greater regional integration among the states that form the South Asian Association of Regional Cooperation (SAARC) may one day bring about a reimagining of relations between the different political communities which make up the sub-continent along post-secular lines. This may well bring into being a post-national moral imaginary as envisaged by Tagore over a century earlier. The experience of the European Union, however, suggests that the path towards integration is fraught with difficulties and that nation-states are reluctant to cede sovereignty which makes continued conflict between South Asia's 'midnight's children' over Kashmir increasingly likely in the short term.

Notes

1 This chapter is based upon Shani (2016). However, it has been substantially revised, updated and rewritten.
2 www.nytimes.com/2019/02/23/opinion/india-terror-attack-modi-election-politics.html
3 https://foreignpolicy.com/2019/02/19/narendra-modi-should-calm-tensions-in-kashmir-rather-than-inflame-them-india-pakistan-crpf-pulwama/

44 Giorgio Shani

4 The INC led independence struggle under the leadership of Mahatma Gandhi had a 'Hindu nationalist dimension of considerable weight, even as it also had a secular dynamic' (Vanaik 2017: 5).
5 The term 'interpellates' was used by Louis Althusser to explain the process by which ideology constructs subjects through a process of 'hailing'. For Althusser, 'all ideology hails or interpellates concrete individuals as concrete subjects'(Althusser 1971: 115). The use of interpellation here implies that nationalism constructs subjects as belonging to a 'nation'. Therefore, Hindu nationalism constructs 'ethnicized' Hindu subjects in the same way as Indian nationalism creates 'secular' Indian subjects.
6 See Fair (2018) for an analysis of the 2018 elections.
7 See Ganguly (2019).
8 Ethnic outbidding refers to an auction-like process whereby political parties compete to outbid their rivals in adopting anti-minority stances in order to capture the majority vote (de Votta 2004).
9 A *jati* is a localized sub-caste group, usually organized around occupation.
10 The line dividing India and Pakistan was drawn hastily by a civil servant with no experience of South Asia, Cyril Radcliffe, barely five weeks before Partition. Radcliffe was immortalized in W. H. Auden's poem *Partition* (Auden 2003).
11 Basing his figures primarily on British reports, Brass, however, estimates that 'only' between 200,000 and 360,000 died as a direct result of partition violence (Brass 2003: 75). This contrasts with Butalia's higher figure of 1 million (Butalia 2000: 3).
12 The term 'Sikh' refers to the followers of Guru Nanak (1469–1539) and ten subsequent gurus ending with Guru Gobind Singh (1666–1708). Most orthodox (male) Sikhs live in the Punjab and wear external symbols, making them a readily identifiable group (See Shani 2008: 17–40).
13 See Shani (2008: 94–98), for more on the Delhi riots and their impact upon the development of a Sikh 'national' consciousness.
14 Jinnah cited in Alavi (2002).
15 See Election Commission of India (2019) for an analysis of the 2019 elections which resulted in the BJP increasing its majority.

References

Alavi, Hamsa. 2002. 'On Religion and Secularism in the Making of Pakistan,' available at: www.sacw.net/2002/HamzaAlaviNov02.html (accessed 2 November 2012).
Althusser, Louis. 1971. *Lenin and Philosophy*. Trans. B. Brewster. London: New Left Books.
Anderson, Perry. 2012. 'Why Partition?' *London Review of Books*, 19 July: 11–19.
Appadurai, Arjun. 1996. *Modernity at Large: The Cultural Dimensions of Globalization*. Minnesota: University of Minnesota Press.
Auden, W. H. 2003. 'Partition,' available at: www.poemhunter.com/poem/partition-2/ (accessed 17 October 2004).
Bannerjee, Sikata. 2001. *Warriors in Politics: Hindu Nationalism, Violence and Shiv Sena in India*. Cambridge: Cambridge University Press.
Bharatiya Janata Party. 1996. *For a Strong and Prosperous India – Election Manifesto 1996*. New Delhi: Kapoor Press.
———. 2014. 'Philosophy,' available at: www.bjp.org/en/about-the-party/philosophy
Bhargava, Rajiv 1998. 'What Is Secularism for?' in Rajeev Bhargava (ed.), *Secularism and Its Critics*. New Delhi: Oxford University Press, pp. 486–543.
Brass, Paul R. 2003. 'The Partition of India and Retributive Genocide in the Punjab, 1946–47: Means, Methods, and Purposes,' *Journal of Genocide Research*, 5(1): 71–101.

———. 2006. *Forms of Collective Violence: Riots, Pogroms, and Genocide in Modern India*. Gurgaon, HR: Three Essays Collectives.
Butalia, Urvashi. 2000. *The Other Side of Silence: Voices from the Partition of India*. London: Hurst and Company.
Chatterjee, Partha. 1993. *The Nation and It Fragments: Colonial and Postcolonial Histories*, Princeton, NJ: Princeton University Press.
Cohn, Bernard S. 1996. *Colonialism and Its Forms of Knowledge*. Princeton, NJ: Princeton University Press.
De Votta, Neil. 2004. *Blowback: Linguistic Nationalism, Institutional Decay, and Ethnic Conflict in Sri Lanka*. Stanford, CA: Stanford University Press.
Election Commission of India. 2019. 'General Election to Lok Sabha Trends and Results 2019,' 24 May, available at: http://eciresults.nic.in/ (accessed 24 May 2019).
Fair, C. Christine. 2018. 'Pakistan's Sham Election,' *Foreign Affairs*, July 27, available at: www.foreignaffairs.com/articles/pakistan/2018-07-27/pakistans-sham-election (accessed 31 August 2018).
Foucault, Michel. 2007. *Security, Territory, Population: Lectures at the College de France, 1977–1978*. Trans. Graham Burchell. Houndmills, Basingstoke, Hants: Palgrave Macmillan.
Ganguly, Sumit. 2019. 'The World Should Be Watching Bangladesh's Election Debacle,' *Foreign Policy*, available at: https://foreignpolicy.com/2019/01/07/the-world-should-be-watching-bangladeshs-election-debacle-sheikh-hasina/ (accessed 2 February 2019).
Hansen, Anders Bjorn. 2002. *Partition and Genocide: Manifestation of Violence in the Punjab 1937–1947*. New Delhi: India Research Press.
Jalal, Ayesha. 1985. *The Sole Spokesman: Jinnah, the Muslim League and the Demand for Pakistan*. Cambridge: Cambridge University Press.
Jaffrelot, Christophe. 2002. 'Nationalism Without a Nation: Pakistan Searching for Its Identity,' in Christophe Jaffrelot (ed.), *Pakistan: Nationalism Without a Nation?* London: Zed Books, pp. 7–51.
Kaviraj, Sudipta. 2010. *The Imaginary Institution of India: Politics and Ideas*. New York: Columbia University Press.
———. 2011. 'On Thick and Thin Religion: Some Reflections on Religion and Modernity in India,' in Ira Katznelson and Gareth Steadman Jones (eds.), *Religion and the Political Imagination*. Cambridge: Cambridge University Press, pp. 336–356.
Khilnani, Sunil. 1997. *The Idea of India*. Harmondsworth: Penguin Book.
Kothari, Rajni. 1964. 'The Congress "System" in India,' *Asian Survey*, 4(12): 1161–1173. doi:10.2307/2642550
Masuzawa, Tomoko. 2005. *The Invention of World Religions*. Chicago: University of Chicago.
Mignolo, Walter D. 2010. *The Darker Side of the Renaissance: Literacy, Territoriality and Colonization*. 2nd ed. Ann Arbour: University of Michigan Press.
Nandy, Ashis. 1998. 'The Politics of Secularism and the Recovery of Religious Tolerance,' in Rajeev Bhargava (ed.), *Secularism and Its Critics*. New Delhi: Oxford University Press, pp. 321–345.
Pandey, Gyan. 1990. *The Construction of Communalism in Colonial North India*. New Delhi: Oxford University Press.
———. 2001. *Remembering Partition: Violence, Nationalism and History in India*. Cambridge: Cambridge University Press.
Raja, Mudassir. 2013. 'Pakistani Victims: War on Terror Toll Put at 49,000,' *The Express*, 27 March, available at: http://tribune.com.pk/story/527016/pakistani-victims-war-on-terror-toll-put-at- 49000/ (accessed 27 September 2013).

Rushdie, Salman. 1981. *Midnight's Children*. London: Jonathan Cape.
The Sachar Report. 2006. *The Social, Economic and Educational Status of the Muslim Community in India: A Report*. New Delhi, November, available at: http://mhrd.gov.in/sites/upload_files/mhrd/files/sachar_comm.pdf (accessed 1 June 2014).
Savarkar, Vinayak D. 1923. *Hindutva*. Bombay: Veer Savarkar Prakashan.
Shani, Giorgio. 2008. *Sikh Nationalism and Identity in a Global Age*. London and New York: Routledge.
———. 2014. *Religion, Identity and Human Security*. London and New York: Routledge.
———. 2016. 'Spectres of Partition: Religious Nationalism in Post-Colonial South Asia,' in Jeff Kingston (ed.), *Asian Nationalism Reconsidered*. London: Routledge, 2015, pp. 35–47.
Sharma, Jyotirmaya. 2011. *Hindutva: Exploring the Idea of Hindu Nationalism*. 2nd ed. New Delhi: Penguin.
Talbot, Ian, and Singh, Gurharpal. 2009. *The Partition of India*. Cambridge: Cambridge University Press.
Tambiah, Stanley. 1992. *Buddhism Betrayed? Religion, Politics and Violence in Sri Lanka*. Chicago: Chicago University Press.
United Nations. 2011. 'Human Rights: Secretary-General's Panel of Experts on Sri Lanka,' available at: www.un.org/en/rights/srilanka.shtml (accessed 26 July 2018).
Vanaik, Achin. 2017. *The Rise of Hindu Authoritarianism: Secular Claims, Communal Realities*. London: Verso.
van der Veer, Peter. 2004. *Religious Nationalism: Hindus and Muslims in India*. Princeton, NJ: Princeton University Press.

3 Articulations of religiously motivated nationalism within Philippine Catholicism

A critical assessment

Manuel Victor J. Sapitula

At the height of debates regarding the passage of the then–Reproductive Health Bill in 2012, Archbishop Socrates Villegas, president of the Catholic Bishops' Conference of the Philippines (CBCP) issued a pastoral letter condemning artificial contraception as "corruption". The pastoral letter reiterates the Catholic position on the immorality of artificial means of birth control but does not repeat the repertoire of theological arguments; instead, it gives a stark reminder of the impending risk on the nation's moral fiber should this bill be enacted into law. Villegas commended legislators who voted "no" to the proposed bill, calling them "heroes of our nation . . . who care for the *true welfare* of the people" (emphasis supplied). Notwithstanding this campaign, however, the bill was approved by President Benigno S. Aquino III one week after the release of Villegas's pastoral letter on 21 December 2012 as the Responsible Parenthood and Reproductive Health Act of 2012 (Republic Act No. 10354).

This episode is one of many instances wherein the Catholic Church in the Philippines appealed to notions of nationhood and "will of the people" to argue for stances that are congruent with its institutional interests. This has a long and established history, and has seen numerous variations depending on the nature of the issues. The continuing relationship between Catholicism and nationalism is a timely matter for reflection, particularly the possibilities of a "religiously motivated" nationalist discourse. This discourse utilizes aspirations for freedom and self-determination for purposes that are congenial to religious interests. This remains as the underlying narrative of Catholicism in the Philippine experience, and the crafting of religiously motivated nationalist discourses is premised on placing religion at the forefront of identity-formation of citizens and institutional regulation of the public sphere. These mechanisms demonstrate how the Catholic Church as an institution crafts its continuing relevance in the light of new challenges and situations.

The articulation of religiously motivated nationalist discourse by the Catholic Church in the Philippines is the most likely illustration of institutional adaptation because of its conspicuous location in the country's history, culture and politics. Although the country is religiously plural, Catholicism, because of its historic position as the religion of most Filipinos, has displayed prowess in utilizing opportunities afforded by emerging conditions to assert its control over the panoply of public symbolisms. This chapter's contribution toward an assessment of the dynamics of religion and nationalism in the Asian context is premised on an institutional approach that treats the Catholic Church in the Philippines as an "agent of signification". By actively appropriating nationalist discourses to suit its own projects, the Catholic Church in the Philippines challenges the secular-religious divide and resists being relegated to the private sphere. This resonates with José Casanova's (1994) contention that *public religion* is premised on its deprivatization in the modern world. As will be demonstrated in this chapter, the Catholic Church in the Philippines resisted being sidelined from modern nation-building projects by crafting its own version of religious nationalism.

Particularly, this chapter unpacks mechanisms that allowed the Catholic Church to articulate ideations of a "Catholic Nation" to further religious-based interests. As highlighted in Giorgio Shani and Takashi Kibe's introduction, it is viable to conceive of religion and nationalism as intertwined entities, although they can be analytically distinguishable from each other. It will be shown, however, that such intertwining is ambivalent and, in some instances, even fragile, as appeal to monocultural notions of nationalism become increasingly questionable in the face of actually existing religious diversity and the need for pluralist frames of reference. In this sense, the "Catholic Nation" discourse's exclusivism as demonstrated by its ambivalence to "play by the rules" of constitutional democracy shows the limits of religious nationalism as a "viable principle of political order" (see introduction).

Catholicizing Filipino-ness: conflating nation and religion

The engagement of the Catholic Church with Philippine nationalism is long as it is nuanced and complex. This active placing of ecclesiastical interests at the forefront of budding nationalist projects is premised on its well-positioned base in the public sphere, which it worked out since the Spanish colonial administration and continued well after that period. The conflation of nation and Church in the Catholic ecclesiastical imaginary is the product of, on one hand, the privileged position of the Catholic church and, on the other hand, the formation of "nationalisms" that account for Filipinos' aspirations for independence. The tensions between these two forces that aspired to be the centerpiece of the postcolonial order produced this strategy, on the part of the Catholic Church, of conflating nationalist discourse and religious interests.

Religiously motivated nationalist discourses in the Philippines emerged during the late nineteenth century, when Catholicism was already entrenched within Spanish colonial administration. These discourses, however, are premised on the close relationship between Catholic evangelization efforts and the formation of colonial subjects during centuries preceding the nineteenth century. Although conversion to Catholicism was slow and uneven during this time, the eventual congruence of Catholic symbolism with certain dimensions of precolonial beliefs facilitated the "translation" of Christianity to everyday life discourses (see Rafael 1988). The cult of saints and their iconic representations replaced the pre-conquest practice of worshipping household deities or *larawans* (Phelan 1959), and in due course patron saints played a crucial role in the foundational narratives of *pueblos* (Blanco 2009).

As the organizational structures of the Catholic Church were configured more closely into the exercise of colonial administration, issues of pastoral administration were entangled with emerging nationalist consciousness of the Filipino secular clergy[1] who challenged the control of Spanish friars over local ecclesiastical affairs. From its beginnings as a reform movement within the colonial church establishment, the struggle of the Filipino secular clergy took on a more nationalistic tone and erupted forcefully during the revolution against Spain that culminated in 1898 (Schumacher 1981). In the mind of early Filipino priests, the culprit for the degradation of Catholicism in the islands is the unrelenting desire of Spanish friars to control the Philippine church. This view framed the struggle for independence with the granting of equal rights to the Filipino clergy in ecclesiastical administration.

This conflation of Catholicism and national interest, however, was put to the test after the Philippines gained independence from Spanish control. Although the conflation was not clearly articulated at the height of the struggle against Spanish colonial authorities, it took a more definite form when constitutional delegates gathered in Malolos (in Bulacan Province, north of Manila) in 1899. The constitutional delegates debated, among other issues, if Catholicism ought to be recognized as the official state religion of the new republic. This issue deeply divided the delegates, and discussions were intense between those who sought to make Catholicism the official religion and those who held the equality of all religions and the separation of Church and state. Looming in these discussions is the fear of disappointing the Filipino secular clergy, a significant number of whom were ardent supporters of the cause for independence. The voting, which took place on 29 November 1899, upheld the separation of church and state on second voting (the first voting was a tie), and by only *one* vote difference (Agoncillo 1960). During the debates, it was clear that the unease did not involve distrust for the Filipino clergy, but outside control of the affairs of the Philippine church.

This period of budding republicanism is a useful reference point in locating the role of religion in the formation of Filipino nationalism. The struggle for liberation from colonial rule is premised on the multiplicity of partisan interests based on class, ethnicity and political persuasion. Compounding this interplay of diverse interests is the multiplicity of "Catholicisms": the Catholicism of the Spanish friars, the Filipino priests, the regular townspeople, and the revolutionaries, which disagreed with each other on the proper role of religion in the emerging Filipino nationalism. The defeat of the proposal to declare the Catholic church as the official state religion in the Malolos Congress is a strategic loss for the struggle advocated by a sizable number of the Filipino secular clergy, which argued for the congruence between an independent republic and an independent church. The disestablishment of religion enshrined in the 1899 Malolos Constitution signaled the end of this aspiration.

As the United States annexed the Philippines as a colony in 1899, internal instability and division in the postcolonial Catholic Church created a situation of "institutional panic" (Blum 1996), or, in terms of historical periodization, an era of "withdrawal and redeployment" (Schumacher 2009: 248). In this sense, panic and the feeling of wanting to retreat is a "normal social fact" following an experience of severe strain, and it "calls for speed of response and pacification of diversity as the sine qua non of an efficient reply" (Blum 1996: 677). In the context of early twentieth-century Philippines, institutional panic owed to a growing sense of alarm over the rise of Protestantism, disarray in diocesan administration, and the religious revolt of former Catholic priest Gregorio Aglipay, who helped in establishing the Iglesia Filipina Independiente (IFI) in 1902. The core of the institutional panic is the fear that, unless something is done to remedy the situation, the church will lose its footing in the public sphere and will slip into irrelevance. The response, crafted with outside help,[2] sought to recoup existing resources and create a united front to respond to challenges that threaten the church's role in public life. This united front is exemplified in a "fortress-type" Catholicism that operated on survival mode and was generally suspicious of religious diversity.

The strategy employed by this type of response is premised on the conflation of "Filipino" and "Catholic" identities in a seamless cultural and historical narrative. But rather than justifying this response to the aspirations of the Filipino secular clergy for the independence of the Philippine church, American ecclesiastical leaders resorted to "Catholicize Filipino-ness" by buffering perceived negative impacts of religious diversification on the formation of Filipino Catholic identity. The fear faced by US Catholics who succeeded in managing the Philippine Catholic Church is the adverse effect of Protestant missionary activity to the church's interests. This emerging religious diversification is countered through appeals to religiously monocultural frames of understanding Philippine history and culture. This is quite similar to the conflation of Polishness and Catholicism in modern-day Poland, which is premised on the borrowing of "repertoire[s] of actions and symbols that could easily be recognized" by the majority of people (Zubrzycki 2010: 285).

This monocultural variant of nationalism is then deployed on two fronts: Catholic popular religion and the assertion of religious instruction in public schools. Popular religious practices, which already served as important reference points for the formation of local identities, were linked to translocal and unified "Catholic culture" centrally regulated by ecclesiastical authorities. Popular religion is important in the project of fostering a "Catholic culture" because it is public in character; it projects the salience of Catholic symbolism; and it has a strong emotional/non-rational aspect that caters to people's needs for cultural competence. "Catholic culture" was particularly manifested in public displays of fervor that showcase the Philippines as culturally Catholic to the outside world. Examples of such public gatherings are the International Eucharistic Congress in Manila in February 1937 (during the American Commonwealth), and the International Marian Congress, also in Manila, in December 1954 (after the American Commonwealth period). In both instances, ostentatious displays of fervor (Catholic Masses in public parks, processions, formulas of consecration) projected the spectacle of a "Catholic Philippines". The conflation of religion and politics was also quite apparent in these gatherings: in the 1954 Marian Congress, President Ramon Magsaysay attended the ceremonies, and led, on behalf of the Philippine government, the consecration of the entire country to the patronage of Mary.

The Catholic Church's battle for the control of formal education is hinged on the premise that most of the population of the Philippines identifies as Catholic. This battle is foregrounded by the difficulty that schools established by Spanish religious orders faced amidst the fast pace of change that characterized US educational policy in the country (Gutay 2015: 147). As control of formal education was wrested away from the hands of the Catholic Church with the introduction of US-style public schools, Catholics alluded to the incompatibility of secularism with the "deeply Catholic" nature of Filipinos, as stated in the letter of appeal addressed to President Theodore Roosevelt dated 10 July 1902:

> We respectfully submit that the clause of the Constitution which requires the absolute separation of Church and State was intended by the framers of the document to meet the conditions in the United States of America and not those which obtain in the Orient and among a people unanimously of one form of religious belief. Your Excellency, we are profoundly convinced that the Filipino people, deeply Catholic at heart, will deem it an unjust invasion of their rights to be taxed for the maintenance of a system of education which cannot command the free and full approval of their conscience.
>
> (cited in Evangelista 1968)

This appeal, signed by Archbishop William Henry Elder of Cincinnati, Bishop Michael Tierney of Hartford, and the priests of their respective ecclesiastical territories in the United States, rests two claims: first, that the absolute separation of church and state is not applicable to the Philippines because of unanimity in belief; and second, that the educational system should be based on principles that are not harmful to the students' conscience. Both claims unproblematically presuppose that to be Filipino is to be Catholic, and concessions ought to be given because of the privileged status of Catholicism in Philippine culture and history.

The appeal to the statistical superiority of Catholics, and hence the privileged treatment that ought to be given to Catholicism, was also used as a platform to criticize the irregularity of the preponderance of Protestants in public school administration (Raftery 1998). When feeling threatened, Catholics retaliate by accusing the colonial government in the Philippines of favoring Protestant interests. Bishop Rooker of Jaro, Iloilo, in the Visayas, for instance, complained to US president Theodore Roosevelt in 1904 that James Francis Smith, then secretary of the Bureau of Public Instruction, did not properly protect the faith of Filipinos by hiring Protestant teachers (Raftery 1998). Furthermore, religious instruction in public schools was relentlessly demanded by Catholics. It was one of the rallying cries of Catholics gathered during the International Eucharistic Congress in

Manila in 1937, citing a provision in the 1935 Commonwealth Constitution that allowed optional religious instruction in public schools (Gutay 2015).

Thus, from the period immediately prior to the Revolution against Spanish colonialism to the early decades of US colonialism, "Catholicizing Filipino-ness" emerged alongside the ongoing quest for national identity. These are two different, but intertwined, processes, and is premised on the conflation of "Catholic" and "Filipino" identity claims, which allowed religious interests to exert influence on the fabric of nation-building. It must be pointed out, however, that this variant of religiously motivated nationalism is superimposed by individuals and groups that viewed the situation as outsiders (although some of them have lived in the Philippines). The "exceptional" character of the Philippines is deployed in this case to protect the historic role of the Catholic Church as a marker of Filipino identity.

Nevertheless, it is this conflation between Catholicism and nationalism effected by outside agents that enabled the preservation of cultural formations that showcase Catholicism's successful identification with purported Filipino values and aspirations. The strategy of "Catholicizing Filipino-ness" afforded the Catholic Church a voice in public life, especially in the formation of a post-Hispanic generation of Filipinos. Products of Catholic school education formed part of the emerging Filipino elite, which eventually took over important posts in government, various industries and formal education. Catholicism could thus reassert its presence in public life, paving the way for increased visibility of Catholics in local and national politics (Shirley 2004).

Straddling between nationalism and emerging democracy

The formal end of the US occupation of the Philippines in 1946 allowed Filipinos to manage their own domestic affairs and once again paved the way for the rise of nationalist aspirations. Broadly referred to as the period of Filipinization, the period of the 1950s saw the emergence of state-sponsored nationalism and sought to decolonize various facets of Philippine society. Historian Reynaldo Ileto (2017) argued that this post-US turn to nationalism on the part of Filipinos is a manifestation of the desire to revisit the aspirations of the "unfinished revolution" of 1896, which was suppressed (although not fully arrested) by the US colonial regime.

The impetus toward Filipinization at this period profoundly affected the status of the Catholic Church in public life. Since Filipinization was premised on nationalistic pride that Filipinos are neither subservient nor inferior to any other race, high-ranking lawmakers publicly questioned the conspicuous presence of foreigners in Catholic institutions in the country. This insinuated that the Philippine Catholic Church was not fully independent from the interference of foreigners, who may use the institutions they head to dictate their will on Filipinos. Such criticisms also implied that the Catholic Church was unpatriotic, and thus incongruent with efforts to build a "Philippines for Filipinos".

Nowhere has this showdown between the Philippine state and the Catholic Church more poignant than the Rizal Law controversy in 1955. Nationalist senator Claro M. Recto proposed a bill in the Philippine Senate seeking to include the unexpunged version of the novels[3] of national hero Dr. Jose Rizal in high school curriculum. This was not much of a problem for most people except for Catholic bishops, who opposed this move because the novels were perceived as anti-Catholic in content and thus endangered the religious sensibilities of Catholic students. The struggle between bishops and senators (foremost of which was Claro M. Recto) spiraled into other contentious issues, and nationalization of Catholic schools and Filipinization of the leadership of religious orders were discussed in the Senate session hall (Ileto 2017). The Catholic Church eventually suffered defeat in this fight, with Recto's bill enacted into law, although an abridged version of Rizal's novels that toned down criticism of the church could be used in Catholic schools.

This and similar skirmishes with the state betray, among others, the interesting turn of events wherein, from utilizing a variant of nationalism to craft a congenial relationship between Filipino culture and Catholicism, the Philippine bishops had to defend the institutional church from aggressive variants of nationalism (Francisco 2014).

The response of the Philippine bishops to the Filipinization movement betrays Catholicism's long-held ambivalence and misgivings toward nationalism, which was already articulated as early as 1922 by Pope Pius XI:

> Patriotism – the stimulus of so many virtues and of so many noble acts of heroism when kept within the bounds of the law of Christ – becomes merely an occasion, an added incentive to grave injustice when true love of country is debased to the condition of an extreme nationalism, when we forget that all men are our brothers and members of the same great human family, that other nations have an equal right with us both to life and to prosperity.
> (Encyclical *Ubi Arcano Dei Consilio*, no. 25)

The encyclical noted the possibility of abuse in the name of national interests, and thus advocacy for nationalism is contingent upon other relevant moral principles. The acceptance of nationalism, while commendable, ought to be subjected to "higher values" (e.g. universal brotherhood, freedom to conduct missionary work, fidelity to dogma) that are not dictated by nationalist interests. This is the same position adopted by the *Statement of the Philippine Bishops on Nationalism*, signed by Auxiliary Bishop Juan C. Sison and promulgated in 1959. While praising nationalism as an expression of love for neighbor and an impulse for the common good, the bishops warned that

> [w]henever a nationalistic movement propounds that love of one's own country may disregard the Christian moral standards, when it adopts a hostile attitude toward foreigners just because they are foreigners, when it tries to justify the unjust claims of other nations just because our own might thereby gain some material advantage, then the nationalism it advocates is not genuine.

The statement continues by invoking the relative freedom of the Church from nationalist interests because its mandate and mission cannot be restricted to a specific cultural expression:

> Religion, as the primary relation between God and man, and the Catholic Church in particular, as divine in origin, in means, in purpose and in authority, and universal in its mission, is beyond the scope of nationalism.

While the latter portion of the statement lays out the principle upon which the bishops evaluate nationalism, its previous mention of foreigners is reminiscent of criticisms leveled against the preponderance of foreigners among the 1950s clergy (Catholic Welfare Organization (CWO) 1959). As in several instances, the Catholic Church finds itself in a double-bind, and this ambivalence has been exploited by its critics to characterize the church as half-hearted in its commitment to nationalist interests.

As the Catholic Church found itself embattled over nationalistic issues, it found a new strategy to maintain its relevance in public life by staking its claim as the custodian of Philippine democracy. The decade of the 1970s was pivotal for Philippine politics with the imposition of martial law by President Ferdinand Marcos on 21 September 1972. As Marcos eliminated checks and balances in the political system, the Catholic Church became one of the few organizations that wielded significant social and cultural capital to challenge the regime (Youngblood 1978). While the CBCP was slow in wielding its power as an informal check and balance mechanism, it became a critical voice when several priests were detained or deported (if they were foreigners) because they were "instigating civil unrest" (Youngblood 1978).

It was the Marcos regime's heavy-handed treatment of church personnel that provoked the realization that the church's organizational resources afforded a systematic opposition to the state's abuse of power. Drawing from principles of social justice from recent papal pronouncements, the CBCP articulated the relevance of Catholicism as a custodian of democracy against the "immoral" imposition of martial law. This is an important development in Philippine Catholic religious discourse because it spelled a method by which the church as an institution could engage in public life. The Philippine Catholic Church, in this case, mounted a "normative challenge to the authoritarian and totalitarian tendencies of the modern state" (Casanova 1994: 101). In this way, the church engaged the state not from a privileged "Catholic culture" distinct from the rest of society, but from its position as a member of civil society. Its contribution to political discourse is its refusal to accept the relegation of religion in the private sphere, thus linking participation in democratic processes to the principle of freedom of conscience (Casanova 1994: 104).

Owing to the faith-based nature of the church's response to martial law, the EDSA People Power Revolt[4] of 1986 saw the conspicuous use of Catholic piety in public space. The CBCP's *Post-Election Statement* on 13 February 1986 expressed collective withdrawal of support for the Marcos regime and called for non-violent resistance. The plea of Manila Cardinal-Archbishop Jaime Sin for the people to gather at EDSA to protect soldiers who defected from President Marcos was heeded by demonstrators, who brought their rosaries and images of Mary to the streets of EDSA from 22 to 25 February 1986. In this way, the church had become a political actor by mobilizing civil society by utilizing religious symbols (see Moreno 2006). This episode of "peaceful revolt" concluded with the swearing in of Corazon Aquino as president, and Marcos and his family fleeing Malacañang.

Because of the overtly religious nature of the public demonstrations, the transition to democracy was perceived in church circles as the triumph of divine intervention, thus increasing the Catholic Church's moral ascendancy in public life. The CBCP, freed from restrictions imposed by martial law, became an influential commentator of various social issues after 1986. Using pastoral statements, the CBCP commented on issues such as social justice, the death penalty, the foreign debt problem, graft and corruption and human rights violations. The bishops have also collectively spoken about specific issues, for instance about the General Agreement on Tariffs and Trade (GATT) and the Value Added Tax Law (RA 7716) in 1994, the Mining Act of 1995 and Visiting Forces Agreement (VFA) in 1998, and about Small Time Lottery (STL) and constitutional change in 2006. In several instances, church authorities animated civil society movements by leading calls for public demonstrations and mobilizations.

As mentioned at the beginning of this chapter, a bitter dispute between the Catholic Church hierarchy and the government arose in the issue of population control and reproductive health. The opposition of the CBCP to any form of legislation on reproductive health is premised on a fear that secularist values will ruin established Christian principles. In 1990, the CBCP issued *Love Is Life: A Pastoral Letter on the Population Control Activities of the Philippine Government and Planned Parenthood Associations* condemning abortion and artificial family planning methods. From arguments involving correct doctrine about life, family values and family planning in 1990, subsequent CBCP statements also appealed to "authentic cultural values", fidelity to the constitution, respect for democratic processes, freedom of speech and government spending. The bishops' statements did not only stand on theological proofs of the immorality of artificial contraception, but also on an advocacy to preserve democratic institutions and integrity in public office, where they intersect with state and civil society goals (Catholic Bishops' Conference of the Philippines (CBCP) 1990).

Thus, the eventual defeat of the Church's mobilization against reproductive health questions not only the Catholic faithful's adherence to official teaching on artificial contraception, but also their support for the actions taken by their leaders in engaging the state and the public sphere. The party-list Akbayan lauded the passage of the Reproductive Health Law as "victory over religious bigotry" (Claudio 2014). Surveys also show that support for the Reproductive Health (RH) Bill has remained strong despite the Catholic Church hierarchy's opposition: a report by the Social Weather Stations (SWS) in 2008 showed that 76 percent of Catholics support the RH Bill, and that "[s]uch support is high regardless of frequency of church-going, and regardless of trust in the Catholic church" (SWS 2008). Another report published by Pulse Asia in 2010 also revealed that 69 percent support the RH Bill.

An assessment of Catholic nationalism in the Philippines

There are several observations to be made regarding religious nationalism in the case of the Catholic Church in the Philippines. The first is that Catholic nationalism as applied to the Philippines is largely a *postcolonial* project, which distinguishes it from variants emanating from "the West", i.e. in Western Europe, which had no extensive experience with colonialism. Colonial domination in the Philippines is the starting point of inquiry because of significant differences between precolonial and colonial conditions, with Catholicism being a significant, if not the unique, factor defining this difference. Catholicism, both as an institution and a worldview, has no precolonial equivalent and is unique to Spanish colonialism. Thus, the Catholic Church in the Philippines was unable to craft an equivalent precolonial Christian worldview to assert its place in a changing political order. It thus had to make use of emerging forms of nationalism, which were then responding to the continued presence of Spanish colonial power in a supposedly distinct (and supposedly independent) Filipino "nation".

The creative use of Filipino nationalism demonstrated by US and Filipino successors of Spanish friars is a local adaptation of an established Catholic strategy of accommodation to national self-consciousness. The increasingly critical stance of the Catholic Church to nationalism is reminiscent of eighteenth-century developments leading to Gallicanism and Kulturkampf, which are perceived to be extreme forms of nationalism (Grosby 2016). This negative disposition may have influenced papal views on emerging Filipino nationalism in the early twentieth century, owing to reports that reached Rome about the anti-friar character of the revolution against Spain in 1896 (Evangelista 1968).

This does not mean, however, that the Catholic Church is opposed to nationalism per se; in fact, there is ample proof that the Catholic Church recognizes "nations" in the same way that the Jewish people were constituted as a "nation" (Grosby 2016; Villonga 2014). Thus, despite the seeming absence of recognition of Philippine nationalism in Pope Leo XIII's apostolic constitution *Quae mari sinico* in 1902, the Philippine bishops were able to recognize much later certain positive aspects of nationalism (calling it *Filipinism*) in their 1959 statement:

> From this delineation of the idea of Nationalism we may conclude that Filipinism, which is nationalism for Filipinos, means hard work and generous sacrifice for the welfare of the Philippines in the temporal order, genuine love of Filipino culture in its nobler aspects, sincere appreciation of our historic past, honesty in public as well as in private life, mutual cooperation in common endeavors, scrupulous administration of public affairs, faithful compliance with the laws, unselfish acceptance of the burden of services required

by the nation, payment of taxes and sincere love for national symbols and institutions.

This local adaptation of a long-standing ecclesiastical strategy allowed Philippine ecclesiastical authorities to act in accordance with established Catholic principles in engaging with nationalism. In this strategy, nationalism as love for one's country (patriotism) is to be encouraged, but nationalist institutions that are deemed inimical to religious interests are to be resisted. The formation of a localized Catholic brand of nationalism is borne from accumulated experiences of postcolonial Catholicism's adjustment to new ways of exercising political power by the Philippine state.

The third insight that can be gained from observing religious nationalism in the Philippines is that the Catholic imaginary of nationhood is premised on the notion of "one church" than on the notion of "one Filipino people". In the face of the loss of prestige and continuing external threats from US Protestant missionizing and secular modernity, Catholic prelates envisioned a unified front under legitimately appointed leaders. This is demonstrated in political engagements of Catholic institutions since the US Commonwealth period, from Catholic political parties to church-led demonstrations to assert respect for human rights. This "one church" mentality downplays actually existing diversity among Catholics, especially its contentious undertones. This resonates with Benedict Anderson's (2006) notion of imagined community, wherein Catholic leaders were able to operate on a notion of "moral bind" that united all Catholics under the banner of doctrine, practice and identity.

The diversification of "Filipino people", however, would pose problems for the Catholic variant of nationalism discussed here, primarily because of the absence of discourses that bridge the "one church" with the broad spectrum of Filipino identities underlying modern Filipino nationalism. Such bridging is a complex process as it is contentious for both the Catholic Church and various agents of modern Filipino nationalism.

Concluding remarks

The Philippines, together with Timor Leste, are the only countries in Asia where Catholics form the majority of citizens. In the Philippines, however, there is reference, especially in church circles, of the country being a "Catholic Nation" in the Far East. As explained in this chapter, the "Catholic Nation" discourse is a product of the conditions of the nineteenth and early twentieth centuries, as Catholicism was finding new ground amidst an emerging nationalist consciousness. Aspirations for a "Catholic Nation" rely on the active placing of Catholic symbolism on the forefront of public life. During the era of "fortress Catholicism", the church staked its claim on piety and education, two of the most effective means to guarantee successful religious socialization. During the 1970s and thereafter, the church, as a player in civil society, has fluctuated between cooperation with other groups, on one hand, and assertion of its privileged status as the arbiter of moral truth, on the other hand.

The core of the "Catholic Nation" imaginary is the conflation of the "body Catholic" with the country's "body politic" (Francisco 2014), which purports to be nationalistic while at the same time congenial to ecclesiastical interests. This strategic appropriation of nationalist discourse is one variant of Filipino nationalism and is opposed to liberal-secularist variants of European-style nationalism competing for legitimacy in Philippine society and politics. While it is not accurate to speak of a religious resurgence in the Philippine context because there was no significant decline of religion in the first place, what transpired was *institutional panic* on the part of the Catholic Church over impending religious diversity and the rise of liberal democracy, which are perceived to be inimical to ecclesiastical interests (Raffin and Cornelio 2009).

The tenacity of resorting to this strategy, however, rests on certain expectations about the country's ability to steer its own direction for development. Such expectations on the part of institutional Catholicism are being challenged by episodes wherein the rest of society does not conform to the image of the Philippines as a "Catholic Nation". In refusing to relinquish its privileged status, the Philippine Catholic Church is thus exposed to severe questioning and criticism from outside forces. The apparent religious monoculturalism of its responses to social issues misrecognizes actually existing religious diversity, thus alienating non-Catholics (and Catholics) who hold views at variance with the church's stand. This misrecognition also sidelines the historic presence of Islam in the country's history and culture, as well as recent inroads made by other religions like Buddhism and Hinduism. Besides the recognition of two Muslim holidays in the list of public holidays, the governance of public education has increasingly accommodated to specific needs of Muslims, as evidenced by policies that foster respect for their religious and cultural practices in public schools. The insistence on an exclusively Catholic frame of reference thus runs counter to the "turn to pluralism" of the last decades and will become a stumbling block to the adoption of pluralist mindsets and social policies.

The unintended consequence of the "Catholic Nation" discourse is the church's proneness to criticism for unduly influencing public governance to benefit its interests. While self-preservation is an inherent function of social institutions, the "Catholic Nation" discourse operates on "symbolic exclusion" (see Zubrzycki 2010) of alternative viewpoints. From a comparative perspective, the impending untenability of the "Catholic Nation" discourse in the Philippines occasions a deeper reflection on further possibilities of the dynamics of religion and nationalism. This entails due recognition of alternative trajectories of modern transition and the plural bases of national identity. This also means framing and eventually adopting discourses that are premised on the acceptance and integration of differences (Bennett 1986). While religious nationalism may still emphasize understandings that are congenial to faith-based interests, active incorporation of pluralist thinking further aligns it to the trajectory toward social and cultural diversification.

Notes

1 A "secular priest" is one of two types of priests in the Philippines during the Spanish period. A secular priest is not a member of a religious order (e.g. Dominicans, Franciscan, Augustinian, etc.). Filipinos have been granted permission to enter seminaries and be ordained as secular priests after their training; they have, however, not been allowed to enter religious orders as full members. Resentment and suspicion grew between Filipino secular priests and Spanish friars because the former felt that they were marginalized from ecclesiastical administration and were prevented from taking full responsibility of parishes.
2 Outside help came in the form of strengthened control of the Vatican in Philippine ecclesiastical affairs. In 1902 Pope Leo XIII promulgated the apostolic constitution *Quae mari sinico*, which served as the blueprint for the reform of the Philippine Catholic Church after the Spanish colonial period. Another form of outside help was the deployment of members of religious orders of non-Spanish origins (e.g. Divine Word priests, Scheut Fathers [CICM], Sacred heart Missionaries [MSC], etc.) to replace Spanish friars who left the country.
3 During Jose Rizal's time, his novels *Noli Me Tangere* (Touch Me Not, or Social Cancer) and *El Filibusterismo* (The Filibuster) aroused nationalist sentiments among Filipino elites and masses alike. They were instrumental for mounting the resistance movement against Spain, which culminated with the Revolution in 1896. Among other themes touched by Rizal's novels were the corruption in the colonial Catholic Church and immorality of the Spanish friars.
4 EDSA is an acronym for Epifanio delos Santos Avenue, a major thoroughfare in Metro Manila. Owing to its proximity from the central military camp, this was the site of demonstrations against martial law in 1986. This is the reason why the People Power Revolt is also widely known as EDSA Revolution in the Philippines.

References

Agoncillo, Teodoro A. 1960. *Malolos: The Crisis of the Republic*. 1977 ed. Quezon City: University of the Philippines Press.
Anderson, B. [1983] 2006. *Imagined Communities: Reflections on the Origin and Spread of Nationalism*. London: Verso.
Bennett, Milton, 1986. 'Towards Ethnorelativism: A Developmental Model of Intercultural Sensitivity,' in Michael Paige (ed.), *Cross-Cultural Orientation: New Conceptualizations and Applications*. New York: University Press of America, pp. 27–71.
Blanco, John D. 2009. *Frontier Constitutions: Christianity and Colonial Empire in the Nineteenth-Century Philippines*. Berkeley: University of California Press.
Blum, A. 1996. 'Panic and Fear: On the Phenomenology of Desperation,' *The Sociological Quarterly*, 37(4), Autumn: 673–698.
Casanova, Jose. 1994. *Public Religions in the Modern World*. Chicago: University of Chicago Press.
Catholic Bishops' Conference of the Philippines (CBCP). 1990. *Love Is Life: A Pastoral Letter on the Population Control Activities of the Philippine Government and Planned Parenthood Associations*, available at: website http://cbcpwebsite.com/1990s/1990/index.html (accessed 25 July 2017).
Catholic Welfare Organization (CWO). 1959. *Statement of the Philippine Hierarchy on Nationalism*, available at: http://cbcpwebsite.com/1950s/1959/index.html (accessed 17 July 2017).

Claudio, Sylvia. 2014. *RH Law: Victory Over Religious Bigotry*, available at: https://akbayan.org.ph/news/32-specials/429-rh-law-victory-over-religious-bigotry (accessed 30 July 2017).

Evangelista, Oscar L. 1968. 'Religious Problems in the Philippines and the American Catholic Church, 1898–1907,' *Asian Studies*, 6(3), 248–262.

Francisco, Jose Mario C. 2014. 'People of God, People of the Nation: Official Catholic Discourse on Nation and Nationalism,' *Philippine Studies: Historical and Ethnographic Viewpoints*, 63(3–4), September–December: 341–375.

Grosby, Steven. 2016. *National Identity, Nationalism, and the Catholic Church*, available at: www.oxfordhandbooks.com/view/10.1093/oxfordhb/9780199935420.001.0001/oxfordhb-9780199935420-e-61 (accessed 25 January 2019).

Gutay, Jose Femilou D. 2015. 'Catholic Education and Church-State Relations Until the Sixties,' in Daniel Franklin Pilario and Gerardo Vibar (eds.), *Philippine Local Churches After the Spanish Regime: Quae Mari Sinico and Beyond*. Manila: St. Vincent School of Theology – Adamson University, pp. 145–158.

Ileto, Reynaldo Clemeña. 2017. *Knowledge and Pacification: On the US Conquest and the Writing of Philippine History*. Quezon City: Ateneo de Manila University Press.

Moreno, Antonio. 2006. *Church, State, and Civil Society in Postauthoritarian Philippines: Narratives of Engaged Citizenship*. Quezon City: Ateneo de Manila University Press.

Phelan, John Leddy. 1959. *The Hispanization of the Philippines: Spanish Aims and Filipino Responses, 1565–1700*. Madison: University of Wisconsin Press.

Pius XI. 1922. *Ubi Arcano Dei Consilio. An Encyclical Letter on the Peace of Christ in the Kingdom of Christ*, available at: http://w2.vatican.va/content/piusxi/en/encyclicals/documents/hf_pxi_enc_23121922_ubiarcanodeiconsilio.html (accessed 7 June 2017).

Pulse Asia. 2010. *Media Release (30 November 2010): Pulse Asia's October 2010 Nationwide Survey on the Reproductive Health Bill*, available at: https://drive.google.com/file/d/0B3b9qPFV1cRDWkY5NThSa3NXa00/view (accessed 25 July 2017).

Rafael, Vicente. 1988. *Contracting Colonialism: Translation and Christian Conversion in Tagalog Society Under Early Spanish Rule*. Quezon City: Ateneo de Manila University Press.

Raffin, Anne, and Serrano Cornelio, Jayeel. 2009. 'The Catholic Church and Education as Sources of Institutional Panic in the Philippines,' *Asian Journal of Social Sciences*, 37: 778–798.

Raftery, Judith. 1998. 'Textbook Wars: Governor-General James Francis Smith and the Protestant-Catholic Conflict in Public Education in the Philippines, 1904–1907,' *History of Education Quarterly*, 38(2), Summer: 143–164.

Schumacher, John N. 1981. *Revolutionary Clergy: The Filipino Clergy and the Nationalist Movement, 1850–1903*. Quezon City: Ateneo de Manila University Press.

———. 2009. *Growth and Decline: Essays on Philippine Church History*. Quezon City: Ateneo de Manila University Press.

Shirley, Steven. 2004. *Guided by God: The Legacy of the Catholic Church in Philippine Politics*. Singapore: Marshall Cavendish Academic.

Social Weather Stations. 2008. *Third Quarter 2008 Social Weather Survey: 76% Want Family Planning Education in Public Schools; 71% Favor Passage of the Reproductive Health Bill*, available at: www.sws.org.ph/swsmain/artcldisppage/?artcsyscode=ART-20151217135705 (accessed 26 July 2017).

Villegas, Socrates B. 2012. *Contraception is Corruption! A CBCP Pastoral Letter on the Latest Decision on the Reproductive Health Bill*. Dagupan City, Pangasinan, 15 December, available at: www.cbcpnews.com/cbcpnews/?p=9989 (accessed 10 May 2017).

Villonga, Borja. 2014. 'The Theoretical Origins of Catholic Nationalism in Nineteenth-Century Europe,' *Modern Intellectual History*, 11(2): 307–331.

Youngblood, Robert L. 1978. 'Church Opposition to Martial Law in the Philippines,' *Asian Survey*, 18(5), May: 505–520.

Zubrzycki, Geneviéve. 2010. 'What Is Religious Pluralism in a 'Monocultural' Society?' in Courtney Bender and Pamela E. Klassen (eds.), *After Pluralism: Reimagining Religious Engagement*. New York: Columbia University Press, pp. 277–295.

4 Reconsidering the relation between 'sectarianism' and nationalism in the Middle East

Fanar Haddad

The prominence of sectarian (for the purposes of this chapter, Sunni-Shi'a) division in the Middle East since 2003 has been accompanied by the reification of a number of misplaced normative assumptions regarding the Middle Eastern nation-state. Chief amongst these relates to the presumed mutual exclusivity of sectarian and national identities: the rise of 'sectarianism' supposedly signifies a weakness or absence of nationalism and hence a normatively 'good', 'modern', secularized and territorialized national identity is framed as the antidote to a normatively 'bad', 'pre-modern', religious and transnational sectarian identity. This chapter seeks to offer a corrective to these assumptions and in so doing makes three interrelated claims:

1 The term 'sectarianism' has distorted our understanding of sectarian relations and sectarian identity in the Middle East. As such, rather than continuing with the circuitous debates as to what 'sectarianism' *is*, a more fruitful approach would be to abandon the term and shift the focus to sectarian *identity* and its workings (including its interaction with national identity).
2 Viewing sectarian identity as any one thing (a religious identity *or* a social identity *or* a political construct) is inherently flawed. The complexity and ambiguity of sectarian identity mandates a multi-layered framework that acknowledges the fact that these identities operate simultaneously on multiple, interconnected and mutually dialogical fields: religion, subnational, national and transnational.
3 The oft-presumed polarity between sectarian identity and national identity rests on unfounded normative assumptions regarding the content of nationalism and on problematic reductions of sectarian identity to its religious/doctrinal component. The fact is that sectarian identity in the age of the nation-state is as much a function of competing *national* truths and contested claims to the nation-state as it is a function of competing religious truths and exclusivist claims to overarching religious categories. Rather than secessionist movements or fantasies of sectarian homogeneity, the more common pattern is for modern sectarian competition to take place within, and in the name of, the nation-state.

It is hoped that this will provide a corrective to common framings of sectarian identity as a sui generis concept with unique powers of causation and explanation. The chapter's main case study is modern Iraq but, as will be seen, the Iraqi example is significantly echoed in the cases of Bahrain, Syria and Lebanon. What these countries have in common is their high levels of sectarian heterogeneity and, secondly, they are ostensibly civic states where religious/sectarian identity is not an official criterion for political inclusion. As such, the ideal that is consistently looked to, but seldom achieved, is a sect-neutral pluralistic state based on concepts of citizenship. This has a profound impact on how sectarian relations and sectarian plurality are framed. The counter-examples would be Saudi Arabia, Iran and Israel, where there is little pretence to state neutrality regarding sect/religious identity.

From 'sectarianism' to sectarian identity

The many facets and manifestations of sectarian dynamics are simply too numerous and complex to be subsumed under one politically charged, value-laden, elastic and irredeemably negative term such as 'sectarianism'. Even a cursory survey of the literature – let alone mass media and public commentary – reveals a bewildering array of ways in which the concept is understood. In the vast majority of cases the phrase is left undefined (Haddad 2017b). This is particularly problematic given how the phrase's elasticity and presumed negativity have sharpened its utility as a political tool with which to delegitimise political opposition and stigmatize non-conformity – as evidenced in how mass protests in Bahrain and Syria in 2011 were effectively vilified with the undefined charge of 'sectarianism' (Wimmen 2014; al-Rasheed 2017). As such, and considering the policy relevance and social salience of the term 'sectarianism' in the contemporary Middle East, defining or abandoning it is a matter of practical consequence.

While there are several broad approaches to how the term 'sectarianism' is understood, the most popular of these focuses on the intersection of sectarian identity and politics.[1] One of the merits of this approach is that it highlights the fact that much of what is referred to as 'sectarianism' is indeed a function of modern politics rather than ancient religions, thereby pre-empting primordialization and 'medievalization' of the subject (Makdisi 2017: 25). Nevertheless, this approach can only partially unpack the many meanings of 'sectarianism'. For one thing, political behaviour can be sect-centric (hence regarded as evidence of 'sectarianism') even while standing militantly against the deployment of religious identities in politics. This is vividly illustrated in the case of both the Syrian and Iraqi Ba'th regimes where political identity was not overtly linked to religious identity, nor were conceptions of religious orthodoxy especially relevant to questions of political inclusion. Nevertheless, both regimes are associated with 'sectarianism' but less because they have asserted a particular sectarian identity and more because they sustained a set of power relations that revolved around a nexus of tribal, regional and party networks that only partially overlapped with sectarian identity (Van Dam 1979; Hinnebusch 2015: 114–115; Batatu 1978: 1078–1093).

Other weaknesses in this approach include its inherent top-down view of sectarian dynamics and its exclusion of belief/doctrine as a potential driver of sectarian relations/antagonisms.

In practice the phrase 'sectarianism' is hazy enough to act as an all-purpose explainer thereby hampering sound analysis by the suspension of cause and effect. This recalls how the concept of race has been problematized by critical race theorists, something that scholars would do well to emulate when it comes to 'sectarianism': like 'pure race', 'sectarianism' is a product of thought and language, '[h]aving no material existence, they cannot have material causation.' (Fields and Fields 2014: 22–23). Be it race or 'sectarianism', these concepts are presumed to objectively exist and are falsely taken as an analytical starting point with a cascading trail of distortions; hence the prevalent mystification of sectarian identity whereby it is accorded far more causality than is necessary. For example, commentary on Iraq and Lebanon often credits ethno-sectarian identities with *causality* when trying to understand the corruption and dysfunction that so characterize the two political systems. In the process, this overlooks the far more central role of structural drivers such as the absence of robust institutions and weak rule of law. After all, self-styled secular or sect-blind parties are no less capable of and culpable for corruption in such environments. Likewise the apportionment of political offices does not have to follow the logic of sect and would operate in near-identical ways were it based on the logic of region or tribe as opposed to sect. More relevant to our purposes, the incoherence of the term 'sectarianism' has led to a widespread mischaracterization of the relation between sectarian identity and national identity as necessarily Manichean rather than potentially complementary.

The dimensions of sectarian identity

At heart, what is actually being discussed in the rapidly expanding literature on 'sectarianism' is in fact sectarian identity and its many facets and dimensions. Hence, identity is where we should locate our conceptual starting point. How is sectarian identity constructed? What drives its salience? And, for our purposes, how does it relate to and interact with nationalism?

Identity can be understood as the ever-evolving and never-ending process of subject formation as it relates to an individual's sense of belonging to, and shifting relationship with, a set of collectives (the content, relevance and meanings of which are subject to context-dependent change). The dynamic nature of identity is well captured by Lawler's description of it as something that is 'achieved' through social relations rather than statically held by individuals (Lawler 2014: 2). This inherent fluidity of belonging means that identity is best imagined as a mode of cognition. As one study argues, collective identities are 'not things in the world but ways of seeing the world' (Brubaker et al. 2004: 47). Identities, sectarian or otherwise, are reproduced through processes of social and political practice both from above and from below: by individual reliance on identity categories to create meaning and make sense of the world and by political actors and social/political institutions seeking to reproduce the group and order society by persuading members to deepen their belief in, and attachment to, group-specific narratives, symbols, boundaries and fellow members. It is through these practices that the prerequisite personal and social meanings of identity are generated and reproduced. Whether through performativity, narrative or dialogical practice, constructing meaning is essential to turning something into an element of identity. As one study put it: 'having a British passport does not automatically give someone a British identity' (Vignoles et al. 2011: 2).

With this basic starting point, we can frame sectarian identity as belonging (not necessarily voluntarily or actively) to a collective that is marked by sectarian (here meaning major, institutionalized, intra-religious) cleavages:[2] Hanbali, Zaidi, Protestant, Catholic – for our purposes, specifically Sunni and Shi'a. Further, it is crucial to recognize that, rather than being any one thing, sectarian identities are inherently layered and are perceived and experienced through multiple frames. For example, sectarian identity as an a-national signifier of religious truths is very different to sectarian identity as a form of intra-national group solidarity or as a frame for competing claims to state resources. Likewise, at the level of the nation-state, sectarian identity and sectarian relations amongst compatriots are imagined, perceived and experienced differently from one national setting to another. The fact that these are, in one sense, transnational identities amounts to little in terms of commonalities in sectarian relations within different national settings (consider Protestant-Catholic relations in Northern Ireland with those in Brazil or Sunni-Shi'a relations in Lebanon with those in Qatar).

The point here is not to argue for the precedence or relevance of one frame to the exclusion of others – be it the intersection of sectarian categories with class structures (Rahimah 2016; Joseph 1983) or the utilization of sectarian identity in regional geopolitics (Salloukh 2017; Gause III 2014). Rather, analytical precision is better attained by viewing sectarian identity as a composite, multi-layered identity thereby moving beyond narrow approaches that view the subject through a single prism. This follows the lead of earlier studies of identity (Abdelal et al. 2006; Brubaker and Cooper 2000; Yuval-Davis 1999) that found the concept problematic absent a multi-layered framework. Likewise, our conception of sectarian identity and sectarian relations is best served by a similarly segmented approach.

In practice, modern sectarian identity is imagined, formulated, expressed, felt and experienced simultaneously on four interdependent, mutually informing and reinforcing fields or dimensions:

Religion/religious doctrine: On the level of religion and religious truths. In other words as an identity organized around a set of religious truths and as a global or a-national identity.

Subnational: As a frame through which to mediate social and power relations *within* a given national setting.

National: At the level of the nation-state and as a prism through which national identity is mediated.

Transnational: As a prism for international relations, inter/transnational solidarities and geostrategic competition.

Sectarian identity is formed and reproduced by the constant interplay between these four dimensions. As such, the parameters of sectarian identity and sectarian relations will differ depending on which of these dimensions is more relevant to a given context. For example, the religious truths that mark sectarian competition at the religious level are often absent in sectarian competition at the subnational level where tribal, regional and class dynamics are far more likely to animate sectarian relations (Hinnebusch 2018). A recurring example of this is discriminatory association of a particular sect with lower socio-economic categories of class (Shaery-Eisenlohr 2011: 44–45; al-Wardi 1965: 135–136; Salamandra 2013: 305; Owen Jones 2018: 95). It is important to note that, rather than separate concepts, these four dimensions are in constant dialogue – for example, the national dimension impacts on sectarian identity at the religious dimension in the form of personal status laws and national curricula. As such, these four dimensions should not be viewed in a hierarchical way nor is it possible to establish a fixed causal relationship between them. Rather than onion-like with differently sized layers encasing a core, this approach frames sectarian identity as the sum of these four constituent parts.

With 'sectarianism' discarded and sectarian identity thus conceptualized, we can develop a more targeted approach to the study of sectarian dynamics by shifting our theoretical focus in accordance with our dimensional focus: international relations theory can help us decipher the transnational dimension of sectarian identity, critical race theory is useful when thinking about sectarian identity at the subnational level, religious traditions are needed when considering the religious dimension and so forth. For our purposes, an examination of the relationship between sectarian and national identities is best located in the study of nationalism. With a multi-layered framework we can pursue this without denying or underplaying the other dimensions of sectarian identity. This allows us to better contextualize modern sectarian identity and to dispense with the common fallacy that posits it as the negation of national identity and vice versa.

Sectarian identity in the era of the nation-state

One of the most common and misplaced assumptions is the supposed polarity between sectarian identity and national identity. This line of thinking frames a normatively positive nationalism as the antidote to the ills of 'sectarianism' based on a narrow reading of national and sectarian identities that uncritically assumes a synergy between the former and secularism and between the latter and religious dogma. Yet religious truths, as already seen in the multidimensional framework presented previously, are only one aspect of sectarian identity and they are an aspect that seldom drives modern sect-coded political contestation. More to the point, there is nothing to suggest that sectarian identities are an inherently centrifugal driver in national politics. On the contrary, sect-centric actors in pluralistic contexts often internalize the discourse of citizenship and nationalism thereby creating considerable overlap between perceived national and subnational group-interest (Henley 2017; Sayej 2018). This highlights one of the chief characteristics of modern sectarian identity, namely its interaction with, and refraction through, the nation-state, national identity and nationalism. Most commonly, this is manifested in sect-centric visions regarding the form, meaning and content of a given national identity and the management of national resources – symbolic and material. In this way 'Sunni' and 'Shi'a' become potential (though by no means inevitable) frames for national inclusion and exclusion and potential vehicles for claiming ownership of the state and access to its resources. This is abundantly illustrated in the sect-coded conflicts of Syria, Iraq, Lebanon and Bahrain, none of which were concerned with matters of religious orthodoxy or the pursuit of sectarian homogeneity.

Several observations regarding sectarian identity's relation to nationalism can be made at this point. Firstly, the role of religion-as-doctrine (as opposed to religion-as-identity) is often marginal in sect-coded political contestation in the era of the nation-state. Secondly, by extension, far from being a negation of nationalism, the national dimension of sectarian identity allows sectarian competition to act as a function of nationalism. Rather than artificial nations breaking up into supposedly more resonant lines of identity, modern sect-coded conflict is more often the product of a contested, but nevertheless singular, nationalism. Unlike ethnic identities (Amazigh, Kurdish, Baloch, Arab), transnational sectarian solidarities have not developed into sect-coded secessionist/nationalist movements in the Middle East (with the far from straightforward and far from clearly *secessionist* exception of the Islamic State/ISIS). Sectarian identity's transnational dimension and the existence of sect-specific transnational public spheres do not equate to the erosion of national boundaries or the de-nationalization of national issues. Rather, it is an example of the cross-pollination between the transnational and the national dimensions of sectarian identity. In that sense, a transnational public sphere connects different national settings without blurring the boundaries between them.[3] This recalls Shaery-Eisenlohr's argument for a more synergetic conception of national and transnational solidarities: 'transnationalism always operates locally and . . . transnational solidarities . . . need to be studied in their national contexts . . . transnational ties can help the production of nationalism and appeals to transnational solidarities are often rooted in nationalist agendas' (Shaery-Eisenlohr 2011: 3).

Thirdly, it follows that what is at stake in modern sectarian conflict in places like Iraq, Syria, Lebanon and Bahrain is not the survival of the nation-state but the nature of its governing order: hierarchies of power, access to and distribution of political/economic resources, the identity of the nation-state and the symbolic content of national identity. Through it all, the nation-state itself is not challenged; indeed, it is the prize of the contest. Moreover, the nation-state provides the anchor, the legitimacy and popular resonance for competing sect-coded claims. Again, with the exception of the likes of the Islamic State and transnational militants, domestic protagonists in sect-coded conflict almost always frame their stance with reference to the nation-state. This is well illustrated by the Iraqi, Lebanese and Bahraini political classes: all are obliged to denounce 'sectarianism', all must voice their commitment to the nation-state, and political messaging (even at times of civil war) has consistently framed sect-centric claims in national terms. Even a document as unabashedly sect-centric as *The Declaration of the Shi'a of Iraq* (Haddad 2011: 148–150) is one that is inescapably anchored in national claims. In that sense, modern sectarian competition and sectarian conflict happen for, within and in the name of the nation-state.

Fourthly, another recurring theme – one that is again contradicted by the exceptional example of the Islamic State – is that though competing, sect-centric visions of the nation-state can drive political competition to the point of civil war, the concept and reality of sectarian plurality is seldom challenged. Demographic engineering may occur in particular locations for strategic reasons but national sectarian homogeneity is never the goal. Rather than a rejection of coexistence, sectarian conflict in contexts of high sectarian heterogeneity is more often about who gets to define the terms of coexistence (Shaery-Eisenlohr 2011: 9). This is neatly illustrated in a survey that found that Sunnis in the Middle East are more likely to view Shi'as as non-Muslims in countries with few if any Shi'as. In fact, of the Middle Eastern countries that were surveyed, the most accepting of sectarian plurality were those that had gone through sect-coded civil wars – Lebanon and Iraq (Pew Research Center 2012: chapter 5).

Finally, an overlooked fact that explains the often symbiotic rather than antagonistic relation between sectarian and national identities is that the former are, by definition, secondary identities that act as subsidiaries to larger ones (religion, nationality, ethnicity) and that have thus far been incapable of creating sect-based nationalist movements. Even a sectarian minority living in a sect-coded theocracy – Iranian Sunnis – have mobilized primarily along ethnic lines (Baloch, Kurdish, Arab) (Sabahi 2013; Dudoignon 2017: chapter 6). The subordination of sectarian identities to the greater national/religious good can be traced to the 19th century and the rise of Islamic modernism in response to the challenges of Western imperialism (Brunner 2004: 34–43; Enayat 2005: chapter 1). This placed a premium on Islamic unity that was later to be replicated in the prioritization of national unity in confronting colonial interests. This negatively impacted on the acceptability of sect-centricity as it has long been framed, sometimes cynically, as detrimental to the greater good of national unity. Indeed it has created a persistent awkwardness in how sectarian identities are imagined by people in the region. This was perceptively noted by Henry Mack, British ambassador to Iraq, who wrote in 1950, 'the struggle [between the two sects] remains a partially hidden one, of which both sides are vaguely ashamed and which both would like to see resolved without an open political clash' (Kedourie 1988: 253).

Sectarian identity and narratives of nationalism

If competing groups share a single nation-state and lack secessionist ambitions or alternate national consciousness, they will define their national identity according to myth-symbol complexes (Kaufman 2001: chapter 2) rooted both in what may be termed a generic view of the nation-state that is relatively sect-neutral alongside group-specific inflections of the same nation-state.[4] In this way, the nationalist myth-symbol complex can potentially be refracted through subsidiary sect-specific filters: a Shi'a-centric Lebanese nationalism or a Sunni-centric Iraqi nationalism each incorporating sect-specific symbols and narratives into how the nation-state is framed. As such, our understanding of nationalism in the Middle East must be mindful of the competing reservoirs of symbolic and mythological capital that nevertheless have too much overlap for clear and total separation.[5] To illustrate, an overarching Bahraini national identity does not preclude divergences between Sunni-specific and Shi'a-specific tropes and symbols of Bahraini nationalism. For instance, the narrative of conquest surrounding the rise of the ruling family would be one such divergence in the Bahraini case as would the memory of the mass demonstrations of 2011 and their suppression (Strobl 2018: chapter 1; Gengler 2015: chapter 2).

Precisely because sectarian competition in places like Bahrain, Syria, Iraq and Lebanon takes place within, and in the name of, an ostensibly sect-neutral nation-state, sect-specific myth-symbol complexes in such places will locate Sunnis/Shi'as within the nation-state. This further binds Sunnis and Shi'as of a particular country by enhancing the national dimension of their sectarian identity through the creation of added country-specific commonality and contestation. In this way national hyphenation serves to territorialize sectarian relations, anchoring them in a set of issues specific to a particular nation-state; hence the limited utility of doctrinal rapprochement in addressing sect-coded political conflicts.[6] To illustrate, a Lebanese Shi'a debating sectarian issues with an Indonesian Sunni is likely to focus on religious truths because that is the primary site of commonality and hence of contestation between the two. Conversely, the same Lebanese Shi'a debating sectarian issues with a Lebanese Sunni will likely see the discussion shift towards national truths: demographics, national narratives and, generally speaking, entitlement and access to the national pie. In other words, the contestation in this case would be between *Lebanese* Shi'ism and *Lebanese* Sunnism. This dialectic interplay between commonality and contestation is hardly unique to the Middle East or to sectarian relations; coexistence and conflict are seldom absolutes and long-term coexistence can be episodically punctured by instances of tension, even violence, amongst otherwise deeply interconnected communities (Blok 1998: 37; Kolsto 2007: 161).

The idea that there is a national dimension to how modern sectarian identities are imagined, practiced and contested becomes fairly unremarkable if we discard the misplaced normative assumption that national identities are an inherently more benevolent and more secular force than sectarian identities or that the two are completely separable. An older body of literature approached the relationship between national and religious identities in a manner precluding the unrealistic binaries that proliferate in recent treatments of 'sectarianism' in the Middle East – such as the orientalist maximalist view and the equally unhelpful nationalist minimalist view (Makdisi 2008: 560). For example, Brubaker rejects the dichotomization of nationalism and religion by challenging the assumption that the former is an inherently secular phenomenon – something eloquently echoed in the late Saba Mahmood's work (2016). Instead he proposes several ways of viewing religion and nationalism as separate but intertwined concepts (Brubaker 2012). Similarly, Kinnvall (2004) has argued that identity constructs *combining* religion and nationalism are especially common responses to crises of ontological insecurity. Likewise, and as echoed by Smith (2003), Azar Gat (2013: 223) notes that, while religion on its own is rarely able to provide the basis for nationhood, national and religious sources of identity have, more often than not, acted in complementary and mutually reinforcing ways. We see elements of this across the Middle East in the special place reserved for Islam in nominally secular polities (and of Judaism in Israel) thereby recalling Friedland and Moss's observation that it is 'difficult to make a clean separation between religion and nationalism in history, whether nationalism is religionized or religion nationalized' (Friedland and Moss 2016: 434).

In an earlier study Friedland made an important point that is key to understanding the interaction between nationalism and religious/sectarian identity: 'Nationalism offers a form of representation – the joining of state, territoriality, and culture. It has *nothing* to say about the *content* of representation, the *identity* of that collective subject, or its *values*' (Friedland 2001: 138). This insight highlights how all manner of identities, histories, mythologies, and so forth, come to compete for position in the national narrative. In that sense, under certain circumstances and in certain contexts of heightened political relevance, sectarian identity may be asserted by sect-centric actors in an effort to have it furnish the props of nationalism thereby achieving a closer alignment between the symbols of state and those of sect. In the process, a group's belief that they embody the nation-state and vice-versa, or a minority group's sense of themselves as an integral part of the nation-state is validated and feelings of existential/ontological insecurity are allayed. However, given the already mentioned acceptance of the reality of sectarian plurality in countries of high sectarian heterogeneity, the congruence between symbols of sect and symbols of nationalism is never absolute; rather, when relevant, it is a question of relative advantage within a context of acknowledged plurality.[7]

Viewing sectarian dynamics as a displacement of nationalism overlooks the multidimensionality of sectarian identity and baselessly suggests that nationalism has a fixed content that is necessarily positive and inclusive. Friedland's point regarding the undetermined content of nationalism allows us to view sectarian identity as one potential ingredient amongst many in the mix that can supply nationalism with its emotional, symbolic and discursive content. The interaction between religious/sectarian and national identities is self-evident in places like India, Poland, Israel, Ireland and several other contexts; likewise, contestation over the content of nationalism and competition over the place of various identity groups within the national narrative is hardly remarkable – consider European debates regarding multiculturalism or America's 'culture wars' between conservatives and progressives. In a similar vein, in Middle Eastern contexts of high sectarian heterogeneity the essence of sectarian competition on the level of the nation-state is not about denying the nation-state or sectarian plurality within it but about centring a particular sectarian identity at the heart of the national narrative (Shaery-Eisenlohr 2011: introduction; Gengler 2015: chapter 2; Haddad 2017a).

Sectarian competition and nationalism in Arab Iraq

The false juxtaposition of a supposedly secular, political and territorialized nationalism/national identity against a religious, doctrinal and transnational 'sectarianism'/sectarian identity is a common theme in analysis (scholarly and popular) of Iraq, Syria and other cases of sect-coded conflict. For example, one study argues that, whatever the objective drivers of conflict, 'a nationalist politician may consider conflict to be the result of the failure to achieve nationhood . . . and a sectarian [politician] the failure to establish the "true religion"' (Dixon 2017: 13). This counterfactually negates any overlap between the two and restricts sectarian identity to its religious dimension thereby ignoring the reality that matters of religious orthodoxy seldom drive modern sect-coded conflict. Nor is this an isolated example; on the contrary, the dichotomization of 'sectarianism' and nationalism and the presumed polarity between sectarian and national identities are something of a conventional wisdom. In another study, nationalism (*wataniyya*) and pan-Arab ethno-nationalism (*qawmiyya*) are explicitly and normatively framed as integrative processes as opposed to 'sectarianism' which is described as a, 'violation of national unity.' (Bishara 2015: 7). In this way nationalism (including pan-Arab ethno-nationalism) is framed as an uncontested and uniting concept while a loosely defined 'sectarianism' is presented as inevitably leading to fragmentation. These assumptions reduce national and sectarian identities to caricatures that fail to capture their fluidity and their interaction.

Likewise, in introducing a special edition on sectarian identities in Iraq, the editor stresses the 'centrality of sectarian identities to Iraq's future because such identities undermine a key prerequisite for political stability and democratic governance in all nation states, namely the need for a strong sense of national identity' (Davis 2010: 229–230). Such arguments presuppose the incompatibility of sectarian and national identities and accord them causal attributes while ignoring the role of state policy, economic distribution, relations of power and the social and political practices that animate sectarian dynamics. In the case of Iraq, Kurdish separatism and alienation from Iraqi nationalism may have a long pedigree, but there is no Sunni/Shi'a equivalent. There was an abortive plan for a Shi'a federal region but this federalist, not secessionist, project failed to gather momentum or popular support when it was first floated in 2005. A more serious attempt to redraw borders is the Basra separatist (at times autonomist) project (Visser 2005); however, this is clearly driven by regional rather than sectarian considerations (Visser 2007). In short, whatever problems sectarian identity may cause for Iraq's political development, the negation of Iraqi nationalism is not one of them. Indeed, Arab Iraq's 'sectarian issue' (unlike its 'ethnic issue') was never about secession or the redrawing of borders – hence the redundancy of the national(ism)-versus-sectarian(ism) binary. Yet that very binary continues to misinform analysis.

For instance, it is generally accepted that in 2008–2010 there was a significant retreat in the political relevance of sectarian identity. Amongst several indicators of this was electoral behaviour: whereas electoral coalitions and voting patterns of Iraq's first elections in 2005 were overwhelmingly based on ethnic and sectarian identities with only a handful of broad sect-centric and ethno-centric coalitions dominating the field (Dodge 2012: 44–48), sectarian (Sunni and Shi'a) identities were markedly less relevant in the elections of 2009 and 2010 (International Crisis Group 2010: 2–12; Katzman 2011: 9–19, 25). The standard narrative regarding this shift mistakenly posits it as a case of primordial loyalties receding in favour of nationalism thereby repeating the flawed dichotomization of sectarian and national identities and misreading both in the process. For example, in describing the shifting electoral landscape, a study in the *Journal of Democracy* in the election year of 2010 mistakenly looks to the nationalism-versus-'sectarianism' dichotomy in search of causality (Dawisha 2010). Hence, incumbent prime minister Nouri al-Maliki is portrayed as breaking away from the grand Shi'a alliance of 2005, 'denigrating its sectarianism and running on a strict Iraqi nationalist platform' (Dawisha 2010: 27). Yet the grand Shi'a alliance, like all electoral coalitions in Arab Iraq, consistently employed the vocabulary of Iraqi nationalism – including the mandatory denunciations of 'sectarianism'. Doing otherwise is politically costly. In the same article, Maliki's coalition is portrayed as adopting 'an Iraqi nationalist orientation which set it apart from other heavily Shi'a groupings'. (Dawisha 2010: 30). Here we see how the dichotomization of national and sectarian can end up stigmatizing sectarian identity. After all, why should a lack of diversity ('heavily Shi'a') be contrasted against nationalism? The divergence in question is between different visions of Iraqi nationalism rather than between national and anti-national/non-national positions. As such, the shift in electoral behaviour is not one from sectarian to national; rather, it is one of decreasing sect-centricity. Political mobilization on a less inclusive subnational platform (in this case sect-centricity) can be contrasted against a pan-national approach (or a more sect-neutral approach) but it does not necessarily equate with an anti/non-nationalist stance. Whether or not an electoral coalition is cross-sectarian says little about its nationalist credentials. The US Republican party under Donald Trump's presidency is far less inclusive or diverse than their Democratic rivals, yet we would not think of describing them as *less nationalist*.

Not only is the polarity of sectarian and national identities inaccurate, it can obscure causality in political development. The reason that Arab Iraq was torn by sectarian identity after 2003 was not due to an absence of nationalism but due to the empowerment of sect-centric political actors and the rise in political uncertainty that created the conditions in which a zero-sum contestation of political power and of the meaning of Iraq, Iraqi identity and Iraqi nationalism could take place. Crucial in that regard is the rise of existential fear in the form of a security dilemma between sect-coded camps. The easing of sectarian entrenchment in 2008–2010 reflects the easing of these dynamics rather than the rise of nationalism – which though contested was never in short supply. Likewise, the re-emergence of civil war in 2013 and its decline around 2015 were the results of identifiable factors that cannot be understood by falsely dichotomizing 'sectarianism' and nationalism. Rather, surveying the past 15 years, the drivers of sectarian conflict in Iraq were ultimately the international, regional and domestic ramifications of the destruction of the Iraqi state and the political empowerment of Shi'a-centric actors. With the stabilization of the post-2003 order and with existential contestation of the state subsiding, sect-centricity dropped. As such, the recent shift from identity politics to issue politics (Jabar 2018) does not reflect a shift to nationalism any more than the example of 2008–2010 does; rather, it signals the end, for now, of serious contestation of the balance of power between sect-centric actors and hence the loss of sect-centricity's primary raison d'être.

Rather than a rejection of the nation-state or of sectarian plurality, the goal of Iraqi Shi'a-centric political actors has been to ensure that Iraqi Shi'as are reified as the senior partner, or the big brother, in Iraq's multi-communal framework. This political vision is perfectly encapsulated in an internal document that was circulated within the grand Shi'a political alliance of 2005 and that outlined a vision for Iraq in which Iraqi Shi'as would form the core of the Iraqi nation-state: 'Iraq is the Shi'a ... And the Shi'a are Iraq'. Describing the document, former minister Ali Allawi writes that it envisaged an Iraq composed of 'a constellation of lesser sects and ethnicities revolving around a Shi'a sun' (Allawi 2007: 438). This vision relegates rather than negates non-Shi'a Iraqis and redefines rather than abrogates Iraqi nationalism by unapologetically framing Iraqi Shi'as as Iraq's *staatsvolk*. Nor was this an isolated case: whether framed arrogantly as a sense of entitlement or paternalistically as a duty or burden, the idea that they are the major component and hence the big brother in Iraq enjoys considerable currency amongst Iraqi Shi'as. For example, commenting on the 'historic settlement' that was mooted in late 2016 and that was to create a sustainable framework for 'post-Islamic State Iraq', Shi'a populist TV personality and member of parliament Wagih Abbas stated that Shi'a political factions had a set of unofficial preconditions for any such settlement, one of which was that 'the junior partner must recognise the Shi'a as the senior partner' (Interview 2016). In another example we find Iraqi cleric and political leader Muqtada al-Sadr writing: 'It is known that the clear majority in Iraq are the Shi'a. This requires Shi'as to be the big brother [*al-akh al-akbar*] to all and it falls to them to ensure unity and to show kindness' (al-Sadr 2013: 58).

These examples show the essence of sect-centricity in Arab Iraq: competing sect-centric visions of the nation-state within a shared national and territorial framework. Even if we look to more militant examples of sect-centric actors, we still find that the vast majority of these anchor their politics and their violence in the prism of the nation-state. This is clearly evident in the anthems and poetry associated with the Sadrists and the Mahdi Army – one of the chief protagonists in the sectarian violence that engulfed Baghdad in 2006–2007 (Haddad 2013). It is also evident in the messaging of non-Islamic state and non–Al Qaeda Sunni armed groups. More recently, the Popular Mobilization Units (PMU) – an umbrella formation of mostly Shi'a armed groups that were mobilized to confront the Islamic State in 2014 – have centred their messaging around a core narrative of Iraqi patriotism defined by a cross-confessional (but unambiguously Shi'a-led) fight against the Islamic state (Garrison 2017). Whether framed in an arrogant/ condescending way or a paternalistic/patronizing one, the point to note here is that these conflicting narratives are nevertheless grounded in different conceptions of Iraqi nationalism rather than its negation.

Conclusion

The nation-state and the concept of representative government (not to be confused with democracy) created state-centred societies with a novel, bottom-up sense of ownership of, and entitlement to, the state. As argued by Eriksen, 'While [modern] states clearly seek to govern societies, they are at the same time claiming to represent society as a whole, acting on behalf of "the people" . . . the actions of the state are seen as identical to the actions of society' (Eriksen 2017: 774–775). In this way, a national public sphere is created in which sectarian identities become one amongst many potential frames through which competing claims to the nation-state – material, symbolic and ideational – can be made. Once the premise of representative government is reified in the form of the nation-state, the question of *how* 'the people' are to be represented and governed becomes an all-important one and a site of permanent contestation (White 2011: 151). This contestation, particularly when sect-coded, is often misread as a negation of the nation-state. This ignores the layered nature of modern sectarian identities that includes a national dimension to sectarian relations. As with earlier studies of religion and nationalism, the purpose here is not to deny that the two are distinct phenomena but rather to debunk the notion that they are antagonistic, mutually exclusive opposites.

The national dimension of sectarian identity sees modern sectarian competition revolving around the construct of the nation-state, be it in terms of contested access to national institutions, or the need to have influence on and a presence in the national narrative, or the need to be included in dominant conceptions of the *staatsvolk*. More often than not these issues play out in far more subtle ways than the sledgehammer bluntness of the post-2003 era's sect-centricity. A more common manifestation of modern sectarian competition involves differential access to the state and state resources, for example in housing, policing or public services (Gengler 2015: chapter 5). This is often rooted in deeper sources of modern Sunni-Shi'a contestation relating to competing national narratives that variously include, exclude, privilege and marginalize – even if only through omission – certain sectarian identities at the expense of others. Similarly, myths of national authenticity and ethnic purity are used to elevate or demote people within the national framework (Matthiesen 2015: 30–32; Gengler 2015: chapter 2; Haddad 2011: 40–51). Ultimately such examples are sect-coded contests for position in the national narrative.

Notes

1 Other approaches include using 'sectarianism' as a catch-all for all that is related to sectarian identity; as a catch-all for all that is related to intergroup antagonisms; as the

sect-based equivalent of racism; and as a term denoting sect-centricity. See Haddad (2017b).
2 This is not a normative definition: in some contexts (Egypt) sectarian identity denotes religious identities (Muslim, Copt). In Lebanon sectarian identity refers to both inter- and intra-religious identities.
3 A loose parallel would be Irish-American sympathy and support for Republican Irish militancy. This transnational dimension did not make Irish Republicans any less Irish nor did it make Irish-American sympathizers any less American.
4 Similar and equally helpful is Bell's notion of mythscapes – the discursive realm in which myths of the nation are forged, transmitted and constantly reconstructed (Bell 2003: 63–81). Here again we can imagine a national mythscape being composed of, and interacting with, several subnational mythscapes.
5 A common mistake in this regard is drawing too clear a line and assuming too clear a practical separation between pan-Arab nationalism and individual state nationalism or assuming too rigid a binary between a transnational Muslim *ummah* and individual nation-states – for example Armstrong (2007). This overlooks the fluidity and ambiguity of symbols and underestimates the potential for overlap.
6 As evidenced by the inability of the Amman Message of 2005 and the Mecca Declaration of 2006 to ameliorate sect-coded conflict in Iraq. For details see http://ammanmessage.com/; Glenewinkel (2006).
7 In explaining 'religious nationalism' (a state nationalism furnished with religious props of identity), Friedland (2001) argues that it can only exist in countries that are religiously near-homogenous. Using Iraq as an example, he argues that, absent near-homogeneity, religious nationalism will lead to territorial separatism as in the example of the Tamils in Sri Lanka. I would argue that Friedland's framework is perfectly applicable to Iraq provided we acknowledge that nationalism is an internally contested concept and that competing, even antagonistic, non-separatist visions of a singular nationalism are possible.

References

Abdelal, R. et al. 2006. 'Identity as Variable,' *Perspectives on Politics*, 4(4): 695–711.
Allawi, A. A. 2007. *The Occupation of Iraq: Winning the War, Losing the Peace*. London: Yale University Press.
Al-Rasheed, M. 2017. 'Sectarianism as Counter-Revolution: Saudi Responses to the Arab Spring,' in N. Hashemi and D. Postel (eds.), *Sectarianization: Mapping the New Politics of the Middle East*. London: Hurst & Co.
Al-Sadr, M., with commentary. 2013. *Al-Ta'fiyya fi Nadhar al-Islam* [Islam's view on Sectarianism]. Beirut: Al-Basa'ir.
Al-Wardi, A. 1965. *Dirasa fi-Tabi'at al-Mugtama' al-Iraqi* [A Study in the Nature of Iraqi Society]. Baghdad: Matba'at al-Ani.
Armstrong, J. A. 2007. 'Dilemmas of Middle East Politics,' in A. S. Leoussi and S. Grosby (eds.), *Nationalism and Ethnosymbolism: History, Culture and Ethnicity in the Formation of Nations*. Edinburgh: Edinburgh University Press.
Batatu, H. 1978. *The Old Social Classes and the Revolutionary Movements of Iraq: A Study of Iraq's Old Landed and Commercial Classes*. Princeton, NJ: Princeton University Press.
Bell, D. S. A. 2003. 'Mythscapes: Memory, Mythology and National Identity,' *British Journal of Sociology*, 54(1): 63–81.
Bishara, A. 2015. 'Madkhal li-Fahm al-Mas'ala al-Tai'fiyya wa Sina'at al-Aqaliyat fi-l-Mashriq al-Arabi al-Kabir' [An Introduction to Understanding the Sectarian Question and the Creation of Minorities in the Greater Arab Mashriq], *Omran*, 11: 7–18.

Blok, A. 1998. 'The Narcissism of Minor Differences,' *European Journal of Social Theory*, 1(1): 33–56.
Brubaker, R. 2012. 'Religion and Nationalism: Four Approaches,' *Nations and Nationalism*, 18(1): 2–20.
Brubaker, R., and Cooper, F. 2000. 'Beyond "Identity",' *Theory and Society*, 29(1): 1–47.
Brubaker, R. et al. 2004. 'Ethnicity as Cognition,' *Theory and Society*, 33(1): 31–64.
Brunner, R. 2004. *Islamic Ecumenism in the 20th Century: The Azhar and Shiism Between Rapprochement and Restraint*. Leiden: Brill.
Davis, E. 2010. 'Introduction: The Question of Sectarian Identities in Iraq,' *International Journal of Contemporary Iraqi Studies*, 4(3): 229–242.
Dawisha, A. 2010. 'Iraq: A Vote Against Sectarianism,' *Journal of Democracy*, 21(3): 26–40.
Dixon, P. 2017. 'Beyond Sectarianism in the Middle East? Comparative Perspectives on Group Conflict,' in F. Wehrey (ed.), *Beyond Sunni and Shia: Sectarianism in a Changing Middle East*. London: Hurst & Co.
Dodge, T. 2012. *Iraq: From War to a New Authoritarianism*. London: Routledge.
Dudoignon, S. A. 2017. *The Baluch, Sunnism and the State in Iran*. London: Hurst & Co.
Enayat, H. 2005. *Modern Islamic Political Thought*. New York: I. B. Tauris.
Eriksen, S. S. 2017. 'State Effects and the Effects of State Building: Institution Building and the Formation of State-Centered Societies,' *Third World Quarterly*, 38(4): 771–786.
Fields, K. E., and Fields, B. J. 2014. *Racecraft: The Soul of Inequality in American Life*. London: Verso.
Friedland, R. 2001. 'Religious Nationalism and the Problem of Collective Representation,' *Annual Review of Sociology*, 27: 125–152.
Friedland, R., and Moss, K. B. 2016. 'Thinking Through Religious Nationalism,' in E. van den Hemel and A. Szafraniec (eds.), *Words: Religious Language Matters*. New York: Fordham University Press.
Garrison, J. 2017. 'Popular Mobilization Messaging,' *International Centre for Counter-Terrorism – The Hague*, available at: https://icct.nl/publication/popular-mobilization-messaging/
Gat, A. 2013. *Nations: The Long Roots and Deep History of Political Ethnicity and Nationalism*. Cambridge: Cambridge University Press.
Gause III, G. 2014. 'Beyond Sectarianism: The New Middle East Cold War,' *Brookings Doha Center*, Analysis Paper 11.
Gengler, G. 2015. *Group Conflict and Political Mobilization in Bahrain and the Arab Gulf: Rethinking the Rentier State*. Bloomington: Indiana University Press.
Glenewinkel, K. 2006. 'Mecca Declaration on the Iraq Issue,' *Niqash*, available at: www.niqash.org/en/articles/society/1645/.
Haddad, F. 2011. *Sectarianism in Iraq: Antagonistic Visions of Unity*. London: Hurst & Co.
———. 2013. 'Sectarian Relations in Arab Iraq: Contextualizing the Civil War of 2006–2007,' *British Journal of Middle Eastern Studies*, 40(2): 115–138.
———. 2017a. 'Shi'a-Centric State-Building in post-2003 Iraq,' in F. Wehrey (ed.), *Beyond Sunni and Shia: Sectarianism in a Changing Middle East*. London: Hurst & Co.
———. 2017b. '"Sectarianism" and Its Discontents in the Study of the Middle East,' *The Middle East Journal*, 71(3): 363–382.
Henley, A. 2017. 'Religious Authority and Sectarianism in Lebanon,' in F. Wehrey (ed.), *Beyond Sunni and Shia: Sectarianism in a Changing Middle East*. London: Hurst & Co.
Hinnebusch, R. 2015. 'Syria's Alawis and the Ba'ath Party,' in M. Kerr and C. Larkin (eds.), *The Alawis of Syria: War, Faith and Politics in the Levant*. New York: Oxford University Press.

———. 2018. 'Eclectic Approaches to Understanding the Sectarian Surge: The Syrian case,' Paper presented at *BRISMES 2018: New Approaches to Studying the Middle East*, King's College London.
International Crisis Group. 2010. 'Iraq's Uncertain Future: Elections and Beyond,' Middle East Report No. 94.
Interview, Wagih Abbas, Baghdad, December 2016.
Jabar, F. A. 2018. 'The Iraqi Protest Movement: From Identity Politics to Issue Politics,' *LSE Middle East Centre*, 25.
Joseph, S. 1983. 'Working-Class Women's Networks in a Sectarian State: A Political Paradox,' *American Ethnologist*, 10(1): 1–22.
Katzman, K. 2011. 'Iraq: Politics, Elections and Benchmarks,' *Congressional Research Service*, 1 March.
Kaufman, S. J. 2001. *Modern Hatreds: The Symbolic Politics of Ethnic War*. Ithaca: Cornell University Press.
Kedourie, E. 1988. 'Anti-Shiism in Iraq Under the Monarchy,' *Middle Eastern Studies*, 24(2): 249–253.
Kinnvall, C. 2004. 'Globalization and Religious Nationalism: Self, Identity and the Search for Ontological Security,' *Political Psychology*, 25(5): 741–767.
Kolsto, K. 2007. 'The "Narcissism of Minor Differences" Theory: Can It Explain Ethnic Conflict?' *Filozofija I Drustvo*, 2: 153–171.
Lawler, S. 2014. *Identity: Sociological Perspectives*. 2nd ed. Cambridge: Polity Press.
Mahmood, S. 2016. *Religious Difference in a Secular Age: A Minority Report*. Princeton, NJ: Princeton University Press.
Makdisi, U. 2008. 'Pensee 4: Moving Beyond Orientalist Fantasy, Sectarian Polemic and Nationalist Denial,' *International Journal of Middle East Studies*, 40(4): 559–560.
———. 2017. 'The Problem of Sectarianism in the Middle East in an Age of Western Hegemony,' in N. Hashemi and D. Postel (eds.), *Sectarianization: Mapping the New Politics of the Middle East*. London: Hurst & Co.
Matthiesen, T. 2015. 'Shi'i Historians in a Wahhabi State: Identity Entrepreneurs and the Politics of Local Historiography in Saudi Arabia,' *International Journal of Middle East Studies*, 47(1): 25–45.
Owen Jones, M. 2018. 'Contesting the Iranian Revolution as a Turning-Point Discourse in Bahraini Contentious Politics,' in M. Owen Jones, R. Porter and M. Valeri (eds.), *Gulfization of the Arab World*. Berlin: Gerlach Press.
Pew Research Center. 2012. 'The World's Muslims: Unity and Diversity,' available at: www.pewforum.org/2012/08/09/the-worlds-muslims-unity-and-diversity-executive-summary/ (accessed 17 August 2018).
Rahimah, B. E. 2016. 'The Class Oriented Rationale: Uncovering the Sources of the Syrian Civil War,' *The Muslim World*, 106(1): 169–186.
Sabahi, F. 2013. 'Iran, Iranian Media and Sunnite Islam,' in B. Marechal and S. Zemni (eds.), *The Dynamics of Sunni-Shia Relationships: Doctrine, Transnationalism, Intellectuals and the Media*. London: Hurst & Co.
Salamandra, C. 2013. 'Sectarianism in Syria: Anthropological Reflections,' *Middle East Critique*, 22(3): 303–306.
Salloukh, S. 2017. 'The Sectarianization of Geopolitics in the Middle East,' in N. Hashemi and D. Postel (eds.), *Sectarianization: Mapping the New Politics of the Middle East*. London: Hurst & Co.
Sayej, C. M. 2018. *Patriotic Ayatollahs: Nationalism in Post-Saddam Iraq*. Ithaca: Cornell University Press.

Shaery-Eisenlohr, R. 2011. *Shi'ite Lebanon: Transnational Religion and the Making of National Identities.* New York: Columbia University Press.

Smith, A. D. 2003. *Chosen Peoples: Sacred Sources of National Identity.* Oxford: Oxford University Press.

Strobl, S. 2018. *Sectarian Order in Bahrain: The Social and Colonial Origins of Criminal Justice.* New York: Lexington Books.

Van Dam, N. 1979. 'Middle Eastern Political Clichés: Takriti and Sunni Rule in Iraq; Alawi Rule in Syria. A Critical Appraisal,' Lecture Delivered at the University of Durham.

Vignoles, V. L. et al. 2011. 'Introduction: Towards an Integrative View of Identity,' in S. Schwartz et al. (eds.), *Handbook of Identity Theory and Research.* New York: Springer.

Visser, R. 2005. *Basra, the Failed Gulf State: Separatism and Nationalism in Southern Iraq.* Munster: Lit Verlag.

———. 2007. 'Suffering, Oil and Ideals of Coexistence: Non-Sectarian Federal Trends in the Far South of Iraq,' *historiae.org*, available at: http://historiae.org/south.asp

White, B. T. 2011. *The Emergence of Minorities in the Middle East: The Politics of Community in French Mandate Syria.* Edinburgh: Edinburgh University Press.

Wimmen, H. 2014. 'Divisive Rule: Sectarianism, and Power Maintenance in the Arab Spring: Bahrain, Iraq, Lebanon and Syria,' *German Institute for International and Security Affairs*, SWP Research Paper 4.

Yuval-Davis, N. 1999. 'The "Multi-Layered Citizen",' *International Feminist Journal of Politics*, 1(1): 119–136.

5 The irony of secular nation-building in Japanese modernity
Inoue Kowashi and Fukuzawa Yukichi

Takashi Kibe

It is a widely shared view that a state religion called State Shinto played a significant role in shaping Japanese political modernity. For example, Mark Juergensmeyer (1993: 199) categorizes Japan as a case of "religious nationalism," because "religion has a role to play in defining a nation and in stating its basic values." Such religious view of Japanese nationalism, often coupled with the implication of a deviant case from the normal course of modernization, has been widely shared among scholars of Japan studies.[1]

Yet, important questions about the nature of the Meiji regime arise. Did political and intellectual leaders of Meiji Japan intend to establish a modern state based on religious nationalism? How could most oligarchs of the Meiji government, often characterized as Machiavellian (Fujita 1997: 20–21; Yasumaru 2001: 144–153; Tsushiro 2005: 133–134), be theocrats? Were intellectuals of the early years of the Meiji period not engaged in the task of enlightening and hence modernizing Japanese society to hastily catch up to Western countries, in which theocracy was already deemed politically bankrupt? Is fanatic ultranationalism from the 1930s to the mid 1940s – as is depicted by Ichijo and Shimizu in this volume – identical with, or at least a natural consequence of, the type of nationalism pursued in the beginning of the Meiji regime? Or is the religiously focused view of Japanese nationalism not an anachronistic projection from the experience of the religiously tinged fanaticism of the 1930s and 1940s onto the Meiji era?

My chapter attempts to respond to these questions, by critically examining the conventional view of modern Japan as based on religious nationalism. In doing so, I will show *first* that political and intellectual elites of the Meiji regime share aspiration for a secular type of nationalism, and *second* that their secular nationalism is not robust enough to prevent religious nationalism from dominating the regime in the course of time, mainly due to their elitist politics of interpretation and their instrumental view of religious sentiments for their secular nationalist project.

To this end, I will focus on the political thoughts of two key figures in the Meiji era: Inoue Kowashi (1844–1895) and Fukuzawa Yukichi (1835–1901). I focus on these figures for three reasons. First, both of them exerted influence on the formation of the Meiji regime. Inoue is an intellectual statesman who drafted the Meiji constitution; Fukuzawa is the most influential enlightenment thinker in modern

Japan. Second, each of them is self-consciously engaged with the task of nation-building. Third and most importantly, Inoue and Fukuzawa have a basic position on the issue of nationalism in common. To be sure, they are diametrically opposed to each other on important political issues and orientation. For example, concerning a desirable constitutional framework, Fukuzawa stood for the British model in which "the king reigns but does not govern," whereas Inoue opted for the Prussian type that gives the emperor more prerogatives; Inoue is a statist conservative bureaucrat, whereas Fukuzawa is an ant-statist pluralist thinker (cf. Ito 1999). Yet, at stake here is not their difference but commonality. Their commonality is twofold: aspirations for the secular type of nationalism and an instrumentalist attitude towards religion.

To characterize their secular nationalism, as I will show presently, we need a differentiated framework of nationalism in relation with religion. For example, Juergensmeyer's original definition of religious nationalism is so broad that any types of nationalism in which "religion has a role in defining a nation and in stating its basic values" fall under this category (Juergensmeyer 1993: 199; for a critique, see Fitzgerald 2000: 106–117). It is necessary to ask whether the role religion plays in defining a nation and its fundamental values is primary or auxiliary. In order to make this distinction, I will deploy the concept of religious nationalism to denote the type of nationalism in which religion is a primary identity marker. By secular nationalism I understand such type of nationalism in which a primary identity marker is non-religious in nature. As to secular nationalism, I would like to introduce a further distinction between a strictly secularist type and a moderately secularist type. The strictly secularist type of nationalism, being essentially anti-religious, admits no role of religion for a nation-building project; the moderately secularist type is open to an auxiliary role of religion. In my view, nationalism embraced by Inoue and Fukuzawa is moderately secularist in, when deemed expedient, utilizing religion for political purposes.

In order to establish my arguments mentioned previously, this chapter is structured as follows. In the first section, I will present common religiously based views of Japanese political modernity to set the stage for my considerations on Inoue and Fukuzawa. In the second section, I will highlight some common grounds between Inoue and Fukuzawa, thereby showing that their political thoughts basically revolve around secular nationalism. In the third section, I will consider how their secularist project with its instrumentalist attitude towards religion planted within itself the seeds that would develop into religious nationalism and irrational fanaticism culminating in wartime Japan. Finally, I will conclude with implications deriving from my considerations.

Conventional wisdom

The Meiji Restoration in 1868 proclaimed a return to the original form of the Japanese polity, which allegedly started with the first emperor of Jinmu, a descendent of Shinto gods. The return to the beginning means a return to *saisei icchi* (祭政一致), denoting the unity of politics and rituals – allegedly the original form of polity. A theocratic form of politics was thus energetically pursued in the first years of the Meiji era. In the course of time, however, it turned out that this goal was difficult to achieve, mainly for these reasons: first, there were unsettled disputes over fundamental questions over deities among Shinto groups; second, any theocracy ran counter to the urgent task of building a constitutional monarchy. In this way, the theocratic project was finally given up altogether (Hashikawa 2005 [1968]: 129–139).

The nature of the problem emerging from this situation was clearly stated in June 1888 at the first session of the Privy Council (Sumitsuin), in the mouth of Ito Hirobumi.

> What is the cornerstone (機軸) of our country? This is the problem we have to solve. If there is no cornerstone, politics will fall into the hands of the uncontrollable masses; and then the government will become powerless. . . . In Europe . . . there is religion that constitutes a cornerstone and has permeated and hence united the hearts of people. In Japan, however, religion does not play such an important role and cannot become the foundation of constitutional government. Though Buddhism once flourished and was the bond of union between all classes, high and low, today its influence has declined. Though Shintoism is based on the traditions of our ancestors, as a religion it is not powerful enough to become the center of the country. Thus, in our country the one institution which can become the cornerstone of our constitution is the Imperial house.
>
> (Pye 1989: 700)[2]

As is well known, Ito's solution to the problem of establishing the core of political cohesion was to place at this core the emperor as a sacralized monarch, who would rule on the basis of the unbroken imperial line down from the mythic origin of the Japanese polity to present. At this point, a religiously based view steps in: the Meiji leaders endeavored to institutionalize Shinto as a state religion. This is a view not only in line with Juergensmeyer's view mentioned previously but also shared by many scholars.[3] All of these views suggest that the nature of nationalism as pursued by the Meiji regime was religious or, more vaguely, pseudo-religious.

Though being widely shared, these religiously based views face a serious question. How does the view of Shinto as a state religion underlying the Meiji regime cohere with the Meiji government's official stance on Shinto as non-religion? One might reply that the Meiji government unwittingly established a state religion, while sincerely believing in the non-religious nature of Shinto rituals underlying the emperor cult. Yet, this interpretation is problematic in tacitly adopting a functional concept of religion (cf. Fitzgerald 2000). In my view, such approach can be effectively deployed, only after solving difficult questions about the nature of religion and objective criteria of it in a non-arbitrary manner. This chapter, therefore, focuses on the self-understanding of the Meiji elites concerning the religion/non-religion distinction, instead of deploying a functional approach.

82 *Takashi Kibe*

There would be another reply to my critical question. It claims that the Meiji government, albeit knowing that it was religion, officially declared Shinto a non-religion, thereby keeping a façade of a secular modern state and hence deceiving the nation and foreign countries. Yet, this reply begs a crucial question concerning whether political as well as intellectual leaders of the Meiji era self-consciously attempted to establish a state religion and hence to strive for religious nationalism. In the following section, by showing that the thoughts of Inoue and Fukuzawa revolve around not religious but secular nationalism, I will attempt to refute this argument or, at least, to show that it is not the whole story.

Inoue and Fukuzawa for secular nationalism

There is a tendency in the literature to pay more attention to differences than to commonalities between Inoue and Fukuzawa, as I suggested at the outset. On the contrary, I will shed light on an important commonality beyond all of their differences: their aspiration for secularist nationalism. To show this, in this section I will highlight their views with respect to atheism, Shinto, and the emperor.[4]

Atheism

Inoue and Fukuzawa are avowedly atheist thinkers.[5] Inoue (1969a [1872]: 499) claims that only a non-theistic philosophy can claim to be a true moral teaching, saying that "if in a remote future after thousands years a morally and intellectually perfect human being establishes a teaching based on nature, this must be non-theistic." This is, he believes, why Confucian moral teaching is superior to religiously oriented teachings. He is thus dismissive of any irrational, supernatural belief, and even those parts of Confucian canons that deal with augur and supernatural beings – the texts which Inoue claims do not belong to properly Confucian teaching (Inoue 1969b [1905]: 685). In his view, religions are the products of human nature, which, facing defects and evils of this world, is led to imagine that there exist elsewhere perfectly good human beings and a perfectly good society (ibid., 650).

Fukuzawa is another atheist thinker on a par with Inoue. In his major work on civilization, Fukuzawa (2008 [1875]: 48) attacks credulity or blind belief (*wakudeki*) as the main obstacle to civilizing process, which consists in "the progress of man's knowledge and virtue." Seen from this perspective, religious belief is thus a form of credulity that a civilized person would not embrace. In his *Autobiography*, he tells his boyhood experience of dismantling credulity. One day, he opened a small shrine and discovered that it was a little stone that was worshipped as a "holy body"; throwing it away and replacing it with another stone, he was amused to observe that people continued to worship the stone, without later incurring any misfortunes on them (Fukuzawa 1959 [1899]: 18–19).[6]

At this juncture, one may wonder why religions continue to exist despite their backwardness. In reply, Inoue and Fukuzawa agree on a view that religion exists for "the ignorant masses" – the view that reveals a typical samurai's prejudice towards religion as common people's opium. Inoue (1969b [1864]: 4–5) regards the absurdity of religious beliefs as the main reason why religion gains people's hearts. The more absurd and the more deceptive religious teaching is, the easier people are seduced; they prefer sermons by Buddhist monks to a lecture on Confucian's *Analects*. In this way, Inoue links religion with class distinction: non-religion for elites and religion for the masses. A similar distinction is observable in Fukuzawa. According to him, whereas men and women of upper classes can endeavor to grasp what is good and wrong by themselves, people of lower classes, being little more than "benighted men and women," need moral guidance by religion (Fukuzawa 1981 [1897]: 42); there accordingly continues to be the need for religion, as long as there exist such people lacking in moral and intellectual independence (Fukuzawa 1963 [ca. 1881]: 232). Fukuzawa recognizes only an instrumental value of religion as moral guidance for "the ignorant masses." In Fukuzawa's view (1981 [1897]: 42–45), many mysterious stories in religious teachings are "the powerful means" to teach common people morality. All of this suggests that, at least with respect to common people, he gives up or loosens the imperative of civilization to emancipate people from credulity.

Inoue as well as Fukuzawa objects to political regimes based on a close link between religion and politics, such as theocracy and church establishment. Inoue (1977 [1883]: 163) vehemently opposes theocracy and the establishment of church and state religion. In his view, theocratic regimes have disappeared in civilized countries, whereas the established church continues only in Britain and Russia, both of which present "the extreme point of conservatism" – a model that deserves no emulation (Inoue 1966 [1884]: 389). Fukuzawa is similarly averse to theocracy. For him, any government based on divine revelation is nothing but "a temporary device employed in the dark age of the ancient past," which has lost its value as human intelligence has developed (Fukuzawa 2008 [1875]: 40). Put differently, theocracy is a clear manifestation of credulity, in which people obey political authority "in awe of its external forms" (ibid., 39); it thus presents "the height of credulity" to "lead men further down the path of stupidity" and to "make the people ignorant" in order to establish political authority (ibid., 40). Therefore, he is opposed to Shinto scholars who require the unity of politics and religion to be embodied in the emperor (ibid., 29). For Fukuzawa as well as Inoue, religions thus must stay within their own sphere: there is no room for radically politicized religion, which is nothing but irrational fanaticism for them.

Shinto

Where the common view regards Shinto as the main religious pillar of Japanese nationalism, Inoue and Fukuzawa share a non-religious view of Shinto. According to Inoue (1975 [1888]: 383), a religious view of Shinto is a wrong view that was propagated by recent Kokugaku or National Learning scholars and notably Hirata Atsutane and later accepted by Western scholars, who then coined the word "Shintoism" – denoting a religion.[7] Fukuzawa (1960 [1881]: 80) welcomes government's decisions that distance from theocracy towards the non-religious view of Shinto. In his view, Shinto is non-religion, since it is characterized not so much by otherworldliness, which he thinks is the hallmark of religion, as by "this-worldliness" (Fukuzawa 1962 [1883]: 710). It seems safe to say that Inoue and Fukuzawa tacitly deploy the Western concept of religion that places emphasis on doctrine and belief.[8] In the light of this belief-based understanding, Shinto, which originally lacks any systematized doctrine, appears to be non-religious practice of rituals.

One may wonder what Shinto *is*, if it is not a religion. In Inoue's view (1968 [1903]: 604), the essence of Shinto consists in National or Nativists Learning (国学), a body of knowledge concerning "state rituals" and "general education." He stresses the importance of National Learning as general education, saying that the canons of National Learning serve as the basis for the study of national history and language, both of which nurture "a national character." Inoue (1975 [1888]: 384) elsewhere calls such general education "national education" that cultivates "people's patriotic feeling." Simply speaking, by *de-religionizing* Shinto into a set of national classics and history, Inoue attempts to make it serviceable to the secularist project of nation-building.

In a similar way, Fukuzawa de-religionizes Shinto to make it a means for secular nationalism. For him, Shinto priests are in reality "a kind of historians" about Japanese ancient history. This history centers around the unbroken line of emperors that presents "a unique polity unlike any other in the world" (Fukuzawa 1961 [1886]: 433); it provides a moral teaching that "attaches great importance to the country" (Fukuzawa 1960 [1881]: 81). In his view, learning national history is important, because it nurtures "nostalgia for the past" (ibid.) – the very affection that Fukuzawa, following J. S. Mill's argument in *Considerations on Representative Government*, includes among decisive factors in forming nationality in his *An Outline of a Theory of Civilization*. Although his expression of "a unique polity unlike any other in the world" sounds like a typical view of National Learning scholars, Fukuzawa decisively differs from them in recommending that "absurd tales of the age of Gods" be skipped in history teaching (ibid., 82). In this way, Fukuzawa pursues, like Inoue, the nation-building project on a non-religious secular ground.

The emperor

Looking into the views of Inoue and Fukuzawa on the emperor, it becomes clear that their secularist project of nationalism is their guiding principle. Concerning Inoue, however, one might argue that the Meiji constitution, which was drafted by him, presents a serious problem from a secularist interpretation, because the first article of it declares that Japan is governed by "a line of Emperors unbroken for ages eternal." If, as Shinto scholars insist, the allegedly unbroken line of emperors traces back to mythic deities, the view of Shinto as non-religion is undermined: the legitimacy of imperial rule is theocratic in character. Inoue is fully conscious of this difficulty and shows his solution. His solution is to present a secular view of imperial legitimacy, while not publicly denying the theocratic view. Indeed, in the official commentary on the Meiji constitution – penned by himself – as well as in an essay on the nature of imperial rule, Inoue seeks to base the legitimacy of imperial rule not on the divine origin but on a principle of public-orientedness, allegedly inherited from the first emperor Jinmu onward (Ito 1906: 4; Inoue 1969b [1905]: 644). Inoue presents a similar secular interpretation in connection with the Imperial Rescript on Education of 1890 – the emperor's instruction on basic morality, which was drafted by him. Facing a question concerning what is meant by the phrase "imperial ancestor" at the beginning of the Rescript, Inoue (1969b [1905]: 691–692) explains that it denotes an emperor – either Jinmu or Sujin – but not the goddess Amaterasu, who is "heaven's ancestor" distinct from "imperial ancestor." This account is clearly aimed at bringing home the non-religious nature of the Rescript. In this way, Inoue cautiously avoids religionizing and hence theocratizing the emperor, whereas sacralizing him as the highest political authority (see Yamamuro 1985: 130–137).

Unlike Inoue, Fukuzawa does not explicitly develop arguments on the mythic origin of the Meiji constitution and the Rescript on Education. Yet, he sometimes shows his view of the emperor, which is openly expediency-focused. In his essay *On the Imperial House*, Fukuzawa (1981 [1882]: 67) suggests that the imperial house assumes multiple roles to unify the people's hearts in order to fend off possible disintegrating conflicts of future parliamentary politics. For example, the emperor is expected to maintain moral sentiments of the people – say, by giving charities and honors – and to promote arts and sciences. In *Fukuo hyakuwa*, Fukuzawa (1981 [1897]: 217) presents a far more radical view on monarchy, claiming that a civilized country having a monarch is a sign of the low-level intellect of people as a whole. Constitutional monarchy, which normally takes recourse to majestic appearance, is "a temporary expedient means" or "the last resort" to gain the hearts of "the ignorant masses" and thereby to control them (ibid., 222–223). Fukuzawa goes so far as to say that loyalty to a constitutional monarch needs to be strengthened, "as if one were eager at religious as well as secular worship" (ibid., 223). In a sequel to *Fukuo hyakuwa*, he claims that people should worship and respect the emperor, "as if he were a god, as if he were their father and mother" (1981 [1901]: 196). His point is that the emperor system is an expedient means to unite people and particularly "the ignorant masses," because it appeals to their natural and semi-religious emotions of awe and respect towards time-honored things. For him, it is not intellectual persons but "the ignorant masses" that may worship the emperor with emotions comparable to religious ones.

In this section, we have considered the views that Inoue and Fukuzawa hold on atheism, Shinto, and the emperor. All of them suggest that their project of nationalism is primarily secular in nature. Thus, our considerations show that the conventional view does not hold true of the two influential persons in the formation of the Meiji regime.

The irony of secular aspiration for nationalism

In claiming that Shinto is non-religion and that the nature of the Meiji regime is not theocratic, Inoue and Fukuzawa are deeply involved in a politics of interpretation – an act to decide on a right interpretation in the face of alternative interpretations to bring about a desirable situation. This interpretative and hence discursive act has two features: conceptual fluidity and political nature.

First, the distinction between religious and secular nationalism is inherently fluid, because it depends on how people conceives of religion. Inoue's and Fukuzawa's statements that Shinto is non-religion in contradistinction to Buddhism and Christianity presents a belief-based view of religion for which a relatively systematized doctrine is decisive – the very element lacking in Shinto rituals. If Inoue and Fukuzawa adopted a practice-based view of religion, they would duly consider Shinto rituals religious practices. The distinction between religion and non-religion is thus variable, depending on how to conceptualize religion. This suggests that an act to demarcate between religion and non-religion is discursive and interpretative in character.

Second, their discourse over religion and non-religion is political in nature, for it provides justification for specific political positions. Their non-religious view of Shinto is in line with, and in support of, Japanese government's governance over Shinto shrines: officially declared public facilities for national rites, but not for religious practice, they are put under the control of the Home Ministry (Ama 2005: ch. 4). Their non-religious view of Shinto thus presents a discourse that supports government's claim that the governance over Shinto shrines as non-religious public facilities does not violate the secular political principle of the separation between the state and religion. Moreover, this governance policy brought grave consequences to popular religion. Those shrines which were of diverse origins other than Shintoism were incorporated into the hierarchy of Shinto shrines; popular practice and belief connected with them, such as worship of local deities, are now regarded simply as non-religious, customary, and national rites. Hence popular religion, which a practice-based view of religion would consider religious, is de-religionized and nationalized – effecting the self-understanding of ordinary Japanese people as non-religious (cf. Ama 2005: ch. 4). In this way, their discourse over religion and non-religion has political implications. In demarcating between religion and non-religion, Inoue and Fukuzawa engage in a politics of interpretation, a discursive and political act.

At this juncture, it is appropriate to turn to a notion of *religion-making*, coined by Markus Dressler and Arvind-Pal Mandair. Religion-making refers to "the ways in which religion(s) is conceptualized and institutionalized within the matrix of a globalized world-religions discourse in which ideas, social formations, and social/cultural practices are discursively reified as 'religious' ones" (Mandair and Dressler 2011: 21). This notion thus emphasizes "how religion is produced discursively rather than objectively found" (ibid., 19). Drawing on their terminology, we can invent a paired term *non-religion-making* to characterize Inoue's and Fukuzawa's politics of interpretation. It suggests that not only religion but also non-religion is discursively produced through acts of interpretation, thereby relegating them to specific configurations.

In this context, questions of a Hobbesian and Schmittian kind arise. Who judges? Who decides on a right interpretation among others? As Talal Asad (1999:

192) puts it, we need to ask a question, "How, when, and by whom are the categories of religion and the secular defined?" The answer would be clear for Inoue and Fukuzawa: it is elites who decide – statesmen for Inoue and intellectuals for Fukuzawa. Then, more difficult practical questions arise. How effective is the decision? Does interpretation as such command broad acceptance? Do Inoue and Fukuzawa believe that they can knock theocratic and religious notions concerning the Japanese polity out of people's heads, by declaring Shinto to be non-religion?

At least, it is evident that Inoue and Fukuzawa firmly believe that their politics of interpretation should be effective. Moreover, it seems probable that they are not pessimistic about the political prospect of the non-theocratic view of Shinto and the Meiji regime. But in the light of the religiously tinged ultranationalism in the 1930s and 1940s, it inevitably seems that they were overly sanguine about their secularist project – triumphalist secularists. Triumphalist secularism of Inoue and Fukuzawa probably prevents them from being attentive to the dynamic nature inherent in the politics of religion and non-religion. Their triumphalist secularism turns out to be groundless, if "there is no once-and-for-all triumph over theocracy on the part of liberal society," as Ronald Beiner (2011: 415) puts it. Their triumphalist attitude towards religion prevents them from seriously considering a possibility that "a retheocratization of politics continues to look attractive from certain theoretically extreme points of view" (ibid.). Indeed, popular religion is a case in point. According to Toshimaro Ama (2017: ch. 3), popular religion, which was de-religionized and nationalized by the incorporation into the hierarchy of Shinto deities, played an important role in providing a support for religious nationalism with the notion of the emperor as "a deity incarnate" during wartime and the de-deified emperor of post-war Japan.

The vulnerability inherent in the politics of interpretation is further aggravated by a pragmatic, instrumentalist attitude that Inoue and Fukuzawa take towards religion. This attitude is clear, if we recall Inoue's commentary on the Meiji constitution that refers to mythic deities as well as Fukuzawa's instrumentalist-minded demand that the emperor be worshipped "as if he were a god." Based on their assumption of the two-layered view of society consisting of the minority of intelligent, non-religious upper classes and the majority of "the ignorant masses" gravitating towards religion, it is useful to mobilize religious beliefs and feelings in order to support the nation-building. Therefore, their secularist nationalism is *moderately secularist* in admitting the need to utilize religion. To borrow a term coined by John Rawls (1987), it is a situation in which an "overlapping consensus" emerges in support of the imperial legitimacy between secular and religious nationalists.[9] The ambivalent nature of the mythic origin of the Japanese polity, which can be interpreted in both religious and secular ways, makes the overlapping consensus between proponents of the secular reading and those of the religious reading possible.

Ironically, however, it is the very instrumentalist character underlying their moderate secularism that decisively opens the way for future religiously inspired ultranationalism to permeate the Meiji regime and to overwhelm secularist nationalists. This is because the success of their secularist nationalism is premised on a decisive condition: the politics of overlapping consensus does not yield to religious nationalism but in the control of secular-minded elites. As modern Japanese history has shown, the politics of overlapping consensus is unstable und not perfectly controllable. A main reason is that, as Mark Lilla (2008: 398) claims, "[t]he river separating political philosophy and political theology is narrow and deep; those who try to ride the waters will be swept away by spiritual forces beyond their control." Indeed, the secularist project of Inoue and Fukuzawa was swept away by ultranationalist forces with the mantras of "deity incarnate" (現人神) and "divine country" (神国); their project was an attempt to "ride waters" separating secular and religious nationalism. This seems a consequence from an unstable and contradictory nature of their project in deploying the politics of overlapping consensus to utilize religious beliefs and practices to gain a wide support for the Meiji regime, whereas subscribing to the politics of interpretation that triumphantly declares Shinto as non-religion.

Conclusion

This chapter has attempted to show that Inoue and Fukuzawa, two influential figures in Japanese political modernity, share aspiration for the secular type of nationalism. In doing so, it has demonstrated that the hitherto dominant religiously based view of Japanese political modernity is too simplistic. Japanese modernity is more multifaceted and open to paradoxes and ironies. Moreover, my chapter has highlighted the irony of their secularist nationalism: it unintentionally opened the way for religious nationalism culminating in wartime Japan. This politics is ultimately premised on a secularist optimism or even hubris. As mentioned in the introduction, there are in contemporary Japan those forces that seek to return to religious nationalism in wartime Japan. This suggests that even today Japan struggles with what Inoue and Fukuzawa hoped to solve – the dialectical and tension-ridden relationship between politics and religion.

We are now in a position to conclude this chapter by relating it to the three questions posed in the introduction of this volume: (1) What is the relationship between religion and nationalism in Asia with reference to the case studies selected? (2) What are differences and commonalities between the diverse configurations of nationalism and religion in Asian contexts? (3) Is the nation-state model, aligned with secularism, suitable for the region? After relating to the first two questions by clarifying some characteristics in the configuration of religion and nationalism in Japan, I will then respond to the third question.

We can point out at least four features of the configuration of religion and nationalism in Japanese political modernity. *First*, our analysis suggests that the demarcation between religion and non-religion plays a decisive role in determining the relationship between religion and nationalism. Indeed, based on the non-religious view of Shinto, Inoue and Fukuzawa regard their version of nationalism as a secular project.

Second, the politics of interpretation is deeply involved in forming this configuration. In presenting their non-religious understanding of Shinto, Inoue and

Fukuzawa engage in this politics. Considering that this understanding depends tacitly on a specific view of religion, that is, the belief-based view, we can see that what is religion and non-religion respectively is a matter of interpretation, far from being a priori determined; a practice-based view would give rise to a different, religious view of Shinto. This suggests that the distinction between religious and secular nationalism is fluid. Importantly, their interpretative practice is not merely discursive but also political in nature: it has political implications, presenting specific positions on how to politically organize the society. Their interpretative act is thus a political act that subordinates religion and non-religion to specific political configurations.

Third, the configuration of religion and nationalism is not static but dynamic: it changes over time. As the foregoing consideration showed, the original project of secularist nationalism, as conceived of by Inoue and Fukuzawa, eventually yielded to what is normally regarded as religious nationalism. This is clear evidence that the politics of interpretation, which is important in establishing religious and political configurations, is by no means able to fix them permanently. *Fourth*, popular religion is deeply affected by the secularist project: it is de-religionized and nationalized. Those practices linked with Shinto shrines were regarded as not religious but customary, hence relegated to national rituals. Although it was de-religionized popular religion provided a strong support for the transformation of secular nationalism into religious nationalism in wartime Japan.

What can be said about the third question about whether the nation-state together with secularism presents a suitable political principle? Considerations in this chapter suggest that the nation-state coupled with secularism faces serious problems. This is largely because secularism does not function in a stable manner. First of all, secularism is premised on the distinction between religion and non-religion. But as our considerations on Inoue and Fukuzawa show, it is not only a matter of interpretation but also dynamic and hence open to transformation. Furthermore, this unstable character looms large, particularly when the nation-state seeks to de-religionize what can be regarded as religious and thereby to mobilize it in order to buttress nationalism. As the case of fanatic ultra-nationalism in wartime Japan, coupled with the worship of the emperor as a "deity incarnate," clearly shows, beliefs and practices, though officially declared non-religious, might take on a religious character in the course of time. Thus the demarcation between religion and non-religion is not immune from dynamic transformation. Furthermore, secularism functions only when this demarcation is not controversial. A case in point is the Tsu City Shinto Groundbreaking Ceremony Case. In 1977, the Nagoya High Court ruled that "a city-sponsored groundbreaking ceremony for a municipal gymnasium conducted under Shinto rites" does not violate the separation between government and religion, since it is "in accordance with general social custom," far from intentionally promoting Shinto (Supreme Court of Japan 1977; Ama 2005: 211–212). In this way, post-war Japan still faces a demarcation problem of religion and non-religion. All of this suggests that contrary to the widespread view, nationalism of modern Japan has been a problem. At the heart of the issue is not so much a problem of a disguised religious nationalism as a problem of the nation-state coupled with secularism.

Notes

1 For example, Peter van der Veer and Hartmut Lehmann (1999: 11) argue that "the modernization of the state in Japan was instrumental not to the secularization of society but its sacralization," drawing on Harootunian (1999: 148). For State Shinto, see Holtom (1963 [1947]) and Murakami (1970). Basil Hall Chamberlain (1927) dubs State Shinto "a new Japanese religion." For a critical review of the scholarship on State Shinto, see Yasumaru (2001: 193–196) and Shimazono (2008, 2010).
2 Based on the Japanese original text in Shimizu (1974: 104–105), I supplemented the quotation by adding a translated sentence where it is omitted in the English translation. For the process of constitution-making in which Inoue played a decisive role, see Beasley (1989: 651–663).
3 For example, see James Gregor (2012: 276–277) and Mitsuo Miyata (1981: 101). For a view that the emperor system was conceived of as "a functional equivalent of Christianity," see Mitani (1997: 200) and Buruma and Margalit (2005: 63).
4 My considerations in this section basically draw on what I argued elsewhere (Kibe 2014, Forthcoming). As to Fukuzawa's view on religion, see Koizumi (2002), and as to Inoue's view on religion and religious governance, see Saito (2006).
5 As for their skeptical stance towards religion, largely due to the social and intellectual tradition of the samurai class, see Koizumi (2002) and Watanabe (2005). Émile Acollas, a French scholar who was familiar personally with some Japanese elites studying in France, refers in his *Philosophie de la science politique* to "the upper classes" or the former samurai as an example of "peoples without religion" (Acollas 1877: 461).
6 We observe that Fukuzawa evaluates religion and particularly Christianity positively. But he does so only because of its positive effects of enhancing morality of people, far from being interested in religious truth claims.
7 As to the then emerging new, more academic type of Kokugaku in line with Inoue's non-religious view of Kokugaku or Shinto, see Fujita (2007), Inoue (2011), and Josephson (2012: ch. 5).
8 Concerning the acceptance of the Western concept of religion, see Isomae (2003: ch. 1).
9 To characterize the nature of Shinto dominant in the Meiji era, Josephson (2012: 160–161) uses the same concept of "overlapping consensus" to denote a consensus concerning the non-religious view of Shinto and the emperor. In contrast, I apply the term to a wider agreement between secular and religious views concerning them.

References

Acollas, Émile. 1877. *Philosophie de la Science politique*. Paris: Marescq.
Ama, Toshinmaro. 2005. *Shukyo wa kokka o koerareruka* [*Can Religion Transcend the State?*]. Tokyo: Chikuma Shobo.
———. 2017. *Nihon seishinshi* [*Japanese Spiritual History*]. Tokyo: Chikuma Shobo.
Asad, Talal. 1999. 'Religion, Nation-State, Secularism,' in Peter van der Veer and Hartmut Lehmann (eds.), *Nation and Religion*. Princeton, NJ: Princeton University Press, pp. 178–196.
Beasley, W. G. 1989. 'Meiji Political Institutions,' in Marius Jansen (ed.), *The Nineteenth Century* vol. 5 of *The Cambridge History of Japan*. Cambridge: Cambridge University Press, pp. 618–673.
Beiner, Ronald. 2011. *Civil Religion*. Cambridge: Cambridge University Press.

Buruma, Ian, and Margalit, Avishai. 2005. *Occidentalism*. London: Atlantic Books.
Chamberlain, Basil Hall. 1927. 'The Invention of a New Religion,' in *Things Japanese*. 5th ed. London: Kegan Paul, pp. 559–572.
Fitzgerald, Timothy. 2000. *The Ideology of Religious Studies*. Oxford: Oxford University Press.
Fujita, Shozo. 1997. *Ishin no seishin* [*The Spirit of Renovation*]. Tokyo: Misuzu Shobo.
Fujita, Hiromasa. 2007. *Kindai kokugaku no kenkyu* [*Studies on Modern National Learning*]. Tokyo: Kobundo.
Fukuzawa, Yukichi. 1959 [1899]. 'Fukuo Jiden [Fukuzawa's Autobiography],' in *Fukuzawa Yukichi Zenshu* [*Collected Works of Fukuzawa Yukichi*], vol. 7. Tokyo: Iwanami Shoten.
———. 1960 [1881]. 'Shinkan no shokumu [The Office of Shinto Priest],' in *Fukuzawa Yukichi Zenshu*, vol. 8. Tokyo: Iwanami Shoten, pp. 80–83.
———. 1961 [1886]. 'Shinkan muyo narazu [Shinto Priests Are not Useless],' in *Fukuzawa Yukichi Zenshu*, vol. 15. Tokyo: Iwanami Shoten, pp. 432–435.
———. 1962 [1883]. 'Shukyo no setsu [On Religion],' in *Fukuzawa Yukichi Zenshu*, vol. 19. Tokyo: Iwanami Shoten, pp. 710–712.
———. 1963 [ca. 1881]. 'Shukyo no setsu [On Religion],' in *Fukuzawa Yukichi Zenshu*, vol. 20. Tokyo: Iwanami Shoten, pp. 230–232.
———. 1981 [1882]. 'Teishitsu ron [On the Imperial House],' in *Fukuzawa Yukichi Senshu*, vol. 6. Tokyo: Iwanami Shoten, pp. 31–70.
———. 1981 [1897]. 'Fukuo hyakuwa [One Hundred Stories by the Revered Old Mr. Fukuzawa],' in *Fukuzawa Yukichi Senshu* [*Selected Works of Fukuzawa Yukichi*], vol. 11. Tokyo: Iwanami Shoten, pp. 5–244.
———. 1981 [1901]. 'Fukuo hyaku yowa [A Sequel to One Hundred Stories by the Revered Old Mr. Fukuzawa],' in *Fukuzawa Yukichi Senshu*, vol. 11. Tokyo: Iwanami Shoten, pp. 245–304.
———. 2008 [1875]. *An Outline of a Theory of Civilization*. New York: Columbia University Press.
Gregor, A. James. 2012. *Totalitarianism and Political Religion: An Intellectual History*. Stanford, CA: Stanford University Press.
Harootunian, Harry. 1999. 'Memory, Mourning, and National Morality: Yasukuni Shrine and the Reunion of State and Religion,' in Peter van der Veer and Hartmut Lehmann (eds.), *Nation and Religion*. Princeton, NJ: Princeton University Press, pp. 144–160.
Hashikawa, Bunzo. 2005 [1968]. *Nashionarizumu: sono shinwa to ronri* [*Nationalism: Its Myth and Logic*]. Tokyo. Kinonuniya Shoten.
Holtom, Daniel. 1963 [1947]. *Modern Japan and Shinto Nationalism*. 3rd ed. New York: Arno Press.
Inoue, Hiroshi. 2011. *Shinto no kyozo to jitsuzo* [*False and Real Images of Shinto*]. Tokyo: Kodansha.
Inoue, Kowashi. 1966 [1884]. 'Kyodoshoku haishi an [Proposal on Abolishing Evangelists],' in *Inoue Kowashi Den* [*Collected Works of Inoue Kowashi*], vol. 1. Tokyo: Kokugakuin Daigaku Toshokan, pp. 386–392.
———. 1968 [1903]. 'Kyoiku iken [Opinion on Education],' in *Inoue Kowashi Den*, vol. 2. Tokyo: Kokugakuin Daigaku Toshokan, pp. 602–606.
———. 1969a [1872]. 'Jukyo o sonsu [Holding on to Confucianism],' in *Inoue Kowashi Den*, vol. 3. Tokyo: Kokugakuin Daigaku Toshokan, pp. 497–500.
———. 1969b [1905]. 'Goinsonko [Collected Essays],' in *Inoue Kowashi De*n, vol. 3. Tokyo: Kokugakuin Daigaku Toshokan, pp. 637–709.

———. 1969c [1864]. 'Yokoi nuyama mondo kakitome [Notes on the Nuyama Dialogue with Yokoi],' in *Inoue Kowashi Den*, vol. 3. Tokyo: Kokugakuin Daigaku Toshokan, pp. 1–13.

———. 1975 [1888]. 'Kokuten kokyu ni kansuru enzetsu [Lecture on the Study of National Canon],' in *Inoue Kowashi Den*, vol. 5. Tokyo: Kokugakuin Daigaku Toshokan, pp. 383–386.

———. 1977 [1883]. 'Shukyo shobun iken [Proposal on Religion Policy],' in *Inoue Kowashi Den*, vol. 6. Tokyo: Kokugakuin Daigaku Toshokan, pp. 162–171.

Isomae, Junichi. 2003. *Kindainihon no shukyo gensetsu to sono keifu [Religious discourse and Its Genealogy in Modern Japan]*. Tokyo: Iwanami Shoten.

Ito, Hirobumi. 1906. *Commentaries on the Constitution of the Empire of Japan*. Trans. Ito Miyoji. 2nd ed. Tokyo: Chuodaigaku.

Ito, Yahiko. 1999. *Ishin to jinshin [Renovation and the People's Heart]*. Tokyo: Tokyo University Press.

Josephson, Jason. 2012. *The Invention of Religion in Japan*. Chicago: IL: University of Chicago Press.

Juergensmeyer, Mark. 1993. *The New Cold War? Religious Nationalism Confronts the Secular State*. Berkley, CA: University of California Press.

Kibe, Takashi. Forthcoming. 'Civilization, Morality, and Pluralism: A Straussian Perspective on Japanese Modernity,' in Jun-Hyeok Kwak (ed.), *Leo Strauss in Northeast Asia*. London: Routledge.

———. 2014. 'The Theologico-Political Problem and Secular Rationalism in Non-Western Modernity: Inoue Kowashi on Morality, Religion, and Constitution-Making,' Unpublished manuscript.

Koizumi, Takashi. 2002. *Fukuzawa Yukichi no shukyo kan [Fukuzawa Yukichi's View on Religion]*. Tokyo: Keio University Press.

Lilla, Mark. 2008. *The Stillborn God: Religion, Politics, and the Modern West*. New York: Vintage Books.

Mandair, Arvind-Pal S., and Dressler, Markus. 2011. 'Introduction: Modernity, Religion-Making, and the Postsecular,' in Markus Dressler and Arvind-Pal S. Mandair (eds.), *Secularism and Religion-Making*. Oxford: Oxford University Press, pp. 3–36.

Mitani, Taichiro. 1997. *Kindai nihon no senso to seiji [War and Politics of Modern Japan]*. Tokyo: Iwanami.

Miyata, Mitsuo. 1981. *Nihon no seiji shukyo [Japan's Political Religion]*. Tokyo: Asahi Shimbunsha.

Murakami, Shigeyoshi. 1970. *Kokka shinto [State Shinto]*. Tokyo: Iwanami Shoten.

Pye, Kenneth. 1989. 'Meiji Conservatism,' in Marius Jansen (ed.), *The Nineteenth Century*, vol. 5 of *The Cambridge History of Japan*. Cambridge: Cambridge University Press, pp. 674–720.

Rawls, John. 1987. 'The Idea of an Overlapping Consensus,' *Oxford Journal of Legal Studies*, 7: 1–25.

Saito, Tomoo. 2006. *Inoue Kowashi to Shukyo [Inoue Kowashi and Religion]*. Tokyo: Kobundo.

Shimazono, Susumu. 2008. 'State Shinto and Emperor Veneration,' in Ben-Ami Shillony (ed.), *The Emperors of Modern Japan*. Leiden: Brill, pp. 53–78.

———. 2010. *Kokka shinto to nihonjin [State Shinto and the Japanese]*. Tokyo: Iwanami Shoten.

Shimizu, Shin. 1974. *Meiji Kenpo Seiteishi [History of the Formation of the Meiji Constitution]*, vol. 2. Tokyo: Hara Shobo.

Supreme Court of Japan. 1977. 'Case 34. Kakunaga. v. Sekiguchil (1977). The Shinto Groundbreaking Ceremony Case,' available at: www.courts.go.jp/app/hanrei_en/detail?id=51

Tsushiro, Hirofumi. 2005. *'Kokyo shukyo' no hikari to kage* [*The Light and Shade of 'Public Religion'*]. Tokyo: Shunjusha.

van der Veer, Peter, and Lehmann, Hartmut. 1999. 'Introduction,' in Peter van der Veer and Hartmut Lehmann (eds.), *Nation and Religion*. Princeton, NJ: Princeton University Press, pp. 3–14.

Watanabe, Hiroshi. 2005. ' "Kyo" to inbo ["Teaching" and Intrigue],' in Hiroshi Watanabe and Park Choong Seok (eds.), *Kankoku, Nihon, 'West'* [*Korea, Japan, 'West'*]. Tokyo: Keio University Press, pp. 373–411.

Yasumaru, Yoshio. 2001. *Kindai tennozo no keisei* [*The Formation of the Modern View on the Emperor*]. Tokyo: Iwanami Shoten.

Yamamuro, Shinichi. 1985. *Kindai nihon no chi to seiji* [*Knowledge and Politics of Modern Japan*]. Tokyo: Bokutakusha.

6 Buddhism, cosmology, and Greater East Asian Co-prosperity Sphere
Multiculturalism and nationalism in the pre-war period Japan

Kosuke Shimizu

The simultaneous emergence of exclusionism in hegemonic and Romanticism in non-hegemonic areas of the world characterizes the contemporary international political economy. While immigration is a primary concern for the US president Donald Trump and the European Union, China accuses the West of exclusionism and claims a new order with itself at the centre of the world. Consequently, there seems to be a possibility of a clash between the West and a rising China. However, this confrontation between big powers in the West and East is not new. It took place in the inter-war period, and led to a devastating clash between them. E. H. Carr thoroughly analysed the confrontation in Europe and concluded that the reason why the clash took place was the total lack of attention to power relations which were undergoing a substantive structural reformation (Carr 1946). In Japan, the structural reformation of world political economy appeared in the form of emergence of Romanticism. Romanticism here refers to what Carl Schmitt criticised in his *Political Romanticism*, and defines as 'subjectified occasionalism' (Schmitt, [1919] 2011). While the Kyoto School philosophy typically exemplifies this phenomenon (Shimizu 2015), some religious organisations – Nishihongwanji temple, the biggest Buddhist organisation of Japan, in particular – also took a leading role to promote the romantic ideas of Japaneseness. This chapter strives to reveal the role Nishihongwanji performed to disseminate the Romanticism among ordinary citizens, and tries to find out the reason of this incorporation with the Japanese Imperial regime of the time in order to draw a cautionary tale for contemporary politics.

In doing so, the chapter starts with a brief explanation of general background of the Nishihongwanji's involvement with the wartime regime by focusing on the world structural reformation and successive emergence of discourse of Romanticism in Japan in the first half of 20th century. Secondly, it explicates Japanese Buddhism in general, and the positionality of Jodo Shinshu or Shin-Buddhism to which the temple subscribes. Thirdly, I will cast a specific light to the possible reasons why the incorporation was brought about. Here I will focus on a specific dimension of Japanese Buddhism, pragmatism and its total lack of the ethical concern. This will be followed by a brief concluding remark.

Hegemonic transition and confrontation of reason and sensibility

The discourses found in the inter-war period were a reflection of the dichotomy between reason and sensibility. The prevalent liberal order was regarded in the 'non-Western' areas as the cause of the irrational reactions of exclusionism and Romanticism. While both of them can be seen as irrational, thus more relying on emotions and feelings, both sides claimed that they were on the side of reason and blamed the other for being too irrational. If we assume that the dominant order of the time was supposed to be based on reason, in fact the advocates of it claimed so, reactions on the both sides were logically on sensibility. In this sense, the initial cause of the confrontation of the divided world was the transition of the driving ideas of world affairs from reason to sensibility in both hegemonic and non-hegemonic areas. The nations where the romantic ideas emerged in the non-hegemonic areas were by no means limited to Germany, Italy and Japan, but include Korea, China, India and Turkey (Aydin 2007).

For those non-Western nations aiming at catching up with the 'West', nationalism, even if it is based on a romantic idea, is imperative in constructing a new state. As a nation-state is a political construct on the basis of the legal equality among citizens, it must be logically open to different ethnicities as far as they obtain the nationality. However, the contradiction between romantic ideas of particularism and the construction of the universalised modern nation-state is evident in many cases in Asia. In this context, nationalism often functioned in easing the contradiction, and particularism of culture, history and religion were all mobilised in constructing a nation-state.

However, the easing process of the contradiction with the mobilisation of culture, history and religion was not an easy task in the case of Japan. This became evident when it comes to the territorial expansion and colonisation of the Asian continent. It is well known that despite the widespread understanding of Japan as unified and homogeneous, the society of the nation of the pre-war period can be characterized by its multicultural political orientation (Oguma 1995). This does not necessarily mean that Japan was actively engaged in accepting diversity of races or encouraging diversity among nationals, but it was an inevitable consequence of the imperialist expansion of its political territory, which naturally brought diverse races under the control of the Japanese Empire. Multiculturalising Japan was not an easy task of course, and Japanese leaders certainly needed the core of the national political body against which one can ensure his/her identity in the unity of the expanding imperial body in the multiculturalist disguise. In this context, investigation of the role religion and philosophy performed in relation to Japan's imperialism and Romanticism, and introduction of retrospective religious and philosophical self-reflections in the post-war period are imperative as these will certainly bring us a cautionary tale in engaging in contemporary international politics.

Buddhism is one of the most prominent and salient religions in Japan. There are some Buddhist sects in Japan, and I deliberately focus on one sect called

Nishihongwanji, the biggest Buddhist organization of Shin-Buddhism, in this chapter. This is partly because it is the most influential Buddhist organization past and present, and partly because it self-critically published its involvement with the imperialism. In a similar vein, the Kyoto School philosophy was guilty in terms of their incorporation with imperial Japan. They provided apologetic discourses for the confrontational foreign policies of Japanese Empire against the West, and ended up with justifying the expansionist policy of Japanese military.

Japanese Buddhism and its pragmatic orientation

From the fifth century BCE to the present, Buddhism has a long history, and now is widely spread out not only in East Asia, but also Europe and the American continent. Usually Buddhism is regarded as a religion comparing to Islam or Christianity, and it has a variety of dimensions almost encompassing every aspect of everyday life. As it encourages questioning and critical engagement in everyday practice, Buddhism is sometimes regarded as philosophy rather than pure religion. It is also characterised by its diverse forms of religious practices. It is also often said that the contemporary Japanese Buddhism, mainly Mahayana Buddhism, is far from the original form of the early ancient Indian Buddhism, and there are some other variations such as the Hinayana Buddhism in South East Asian countries and Tibetan Buddhism in Tibet. Some researchers indeed claimed that these variants of Buddhism are too diverse to regard them as a consistent, unified religion (Sueki 2006).

Japanese Buddhism is said to have peculiar characteristics. One of those is its salient orientation towards practice rather than theory or philosophy. Shin-Buddhism, for instance, has developed in order to save the ordinary population rather than encouraging religious austerities. In the ancient time, Buddhism was for elites. They were supposed to go through pre-set or advised austerities in order to get out of the vicious circle of painful reincarnation. There, the world the people were actually living in was seen as full of sufferings. Thus the death was regarded as a possible way out. However, all creatures were destined to reincarnation as pre-given fact. Only through austerities were people supposed to achieve the deliverance from the painfulness and anxieties in the present life. However, as those practicing were only a limited number of elites, the ordinary population was completely left out from the possibility. Shinran, the founder of Shin-Buddhism, argued that Buddhism must be open to ordinary citizens, and he devoted himself to propagate his understanding of Buddhism, which claims that all we have to do is to pray to Amida Buddha. As this did not require understanding of complex sutra or harsh austerities, Shin-Buddhism swiftly spread out nationally (Sueki 2006).

For Shinran, the role of Buddhism was not to understand ancient sutra or find a way for the Nirvana through austerities. It was to save ordinary people and emancipate them with prayer to Amida Buddha. It was more about practice than theoretical development. Ever since the commencement of Nishihongwanji, the main temple of Shin-Buddhism and its organizational body, the purpose of their version of Buddhism was to save people from worldly sufferings (Shinran and Kaneko 1957).

Pragmatism is a penetrating feature of Japanese Buddhism. Among those, Zen Buddhism is said to be another typical example of Japanese Buddhism's pragmatic orientation. Originally Zen Buddhism was from China, but it was substantially transformed into an original form when it was brought into Japan. While Shin-Buddhism's pragmatism was to focus on the practice of saving ordinary people's lives, Zen Buddhism of Japan emphasizes austerities of Buddhist practice. It was to transcend the world by attaining the state of awakening. In order to reach such state of mind, Zen Buddhist monks use meditation and a peculiar form of dialogue called *koan*. Koan appears to be a dialogue, which does not make sense, but practitioners are supposed to get meanings out of it (Chan and Mandaville 2001). It is now focused upon in international relations (IR) as it disturbs the pre-given logic of Westphalia and questions the prevailing acceptance of ontology (Huang 2001; Ling 2013).

In either case, Shin-Buddhism or Zen Buddhism, liberation is supposed to take place in this life, not in the next. It is not after the death, but before the death one can achieve the state of nirvana. It seems that this pragmatist orientation of Japanese Buddhism supposedly provides the background for the Nishihongwanji's involvement with imperialism, which will be explained in detail in the next section.

The involvement of religion and philosophy with the wartime regime

Pre-war Japan was, despite the widespread impression of the dark age, very much enjoying the economic boom and consumer society (Inoue 2011). This was particularly so in the case of 1920s. Economic development was going hand in hand with democratization; the civil society was consequently growing. However, the Manchurian incident in 1931 was the turning point and Japan swiftly moving into the era of the total mobilisation. This mobilisation was rather easy because of the dichotomised comprehension of the divided world of the West and East, and the incident was regarded as a part of this confrontation. A particular incident intensified the confrontation in 1937. It was the Sino-Japanese War that Japan started, full-scale war against China. As the war was not legally declared by the either side of the East China sea, the war was not called a war but an 'incident' until December 1941, the outbreak of the Pacific War.

When Japan dived into the war against China and later against the United States, Japanese government promoted emergency policies in order to continue the struggle for maintaining its ascendancy in East Asia. The most famous, or infamous, policy was the mobilisation law in 1937, which I will analyse shortly. In the sense, the government of the time was already domestically regarded as fascist by some intellectuals (Tansman 2009: loc 101/6331). The most acute critique was Tosaka Jun, a Kyoto School Marxist, and he analysed the state of political economy of the nation as an inevitable consequence of capitalism. Although, unlike the fascism in Germany and Italy, Japanese fascism was rather top-down in its dominative control, Tosaka regarded Japanese fascism as a part of a global trend of capitalist expansion (Harootunian 2000; Tosaka 1966). Apparently, the outbreak of the Sino-Japanese War disseminated the fascist domination everywhere in the nation in 1937; all the civil society organizations became expected to promote the principles of Kokutai, national polity.

The power of domination over individuals was excised through all the aspects of everyday life including arts and literature. Tosaka argued that forcing artists to produce works to praise the national polity made fascism look palatable to liberal-thinking citizens who formerly regarded fascism as unacceptable (Tosaka 1966 82). This was because the artists used such words which liberals were familiar with as 'love', 'art' and 'tradition (Tansman 2009, loc.117/6331). As a result, there was an atmosphere where language of everyday life became bound to that of national polity even though the officials denied that (Tansman 2009, loc.117/6331).

The permeation of discourses of national polity took two different paths. One is through books and magazines published under the strict censorship of government. In this path, the philosophy of the Kyoto School made a substantial political contribution. It is well known that the Kyoto School philosophers, the most advanced philosophical school of the time in Japan, were intimately involved with the military government, with the navy in particular. The second generation of the school and four disciples of Nishida Kitaro, the founder of the school and the prominent scholar of Japanese existentialism, including Nishitani Keiji, Kosaka Masaaki, Koyama Iwao and Suzuki Shigetaka, had frequent meetings with the navy. They also participated the roundtable discussion 'the Philosophy of World History' and provided rationale for the government's imperialist expansion of its territory overseas and for the outbreak of the war against the United States (Kosaka et al. 1943).

Some argue that their involvement with the government was an inevitable consequence of the oppression over civil society, and their intention was to 'steal' the meaning of the uncritically accepted war-promoting words such as national polity and Hakko Ichiu (Eight Corner under One Roof) in order to change the course of Japanese diplomacy (Ohashi 2001). Others interpret the involvement in a more critical manner and argue that the reason was their acceptance of 'Japan' as an essentialised pre-given political entity (Hiromatsu 1989; Shimizu 2015).

Another path was through religious practices of everyday lives. The Nishihongwanji temple was the biggest temple organization of the time, and had a substantial number of adherents. It is a common understanding that the atmosphere of total war and oppressive control over every aspect of civil society, after the sudden change from the extreme prevalence of liberalism and democracy (Harootunian 2000), were overwhelming at that period, and by no means ignorable. It is certainly not surprising that the Nishihongwanji temple of the time also made the case in relation to the imperialist regime. It was of course under the control of the oppressive government, and consequently forced to adjust itself to fit in the current atmosphere. This is particularly important in a sense that the imperial government's control over individual citizens was conducted through everyday lives and religious practices, and here the pragmatic orientation of Shin-Buddhism, particularly concentrated on everyday lives, worked to prompt the organization in incorporating with the prevailing imperialist structure.

In order to understand the religious state of the time in Japan, we need to focus upon Shintoism too, the native religion of the nation. Shintoism was regarded as the core of Japaneseness, and officially supported by the government of the time. It is sometimes regarded as a transformed form of Daoism fitting in Japanese society, although the transformation was substantial and barely leaves the original form in it (Sakade 2014). While it was not religion, rather morality, in the mainstream conservative's interpretation, the convergence of Shintoism and the emperor system naturally granted the religious mysticism to the national polity (Akamatsu 1989: 384). According to Kuriyama Toshiyuki, a contemporary critical Buddhist philosopher, the convergence of Shintoism and the emperor system was natural and inevitable simply because the emperor was defined as the descendent of God, the Creator of Japan in Japanese ancient legacy (Kuriyama 1989: 539). Shintoism represented the only source of political and social values of Japan; thus it inevitably possessed the anti-universalist orientation (Akamatsu 1989: 385). Other religions of the nation, particularly in the case of the Shin-Buddhism, had, on the other hand, a universal quality of socio-political construction such as equality among peoples, rationality of individuals, and plurality in society; they had to face the overwhelming demand of the imperialist government to support the ideology of the emperor system (Akamatsu 1989: 385–386).

One of the most enthusiastic Buddhist monks who promoted the synthesis of Buddhism and Shintoism was Akegarasu Haya. He argued that Buddhism and Shintoism were not separated, but unified. Buddha is not limited to Shaka Buddha, but also includes Amaterasu (Sun Goddess, who is supposed to have created Japan as a nation). He also contended that the emperor Jinmu, who institutionalised Japan as a nation, is equivalent to Amida Buddha. For Akegarasu, the present emperor was a living Buddha, and therefore a living god. The emperor is the holy representation of the transcending and universal truth (Omi 2016: 257–258).

Reacting to the outbreak of the Sino-Japanese War in 1937, the Nishihongwanji organization issued an announcement, *Kokka Sodoin to Shukyo no Kakugo* (The Total Mobilization and the Determination of Religion), claiming that the 10 million adherents of Nishihongwanji must accurately comprehend the current state of the nation, and that they must abolish personal desire in order to enhance the public unity (Tatsuzawa 1984). This apparently meant that the Nishihongwanji organization accepted the national mobilisation policy and built itself in the structure of the prevailing discourse of unifying national polity.

In order to become a part of national polity, the organization had to accept the government's interpretation of the Sino-Japanese War that the conflict was caused due mainly to Chinese military cliques, and the Japanese army was brought under attack by them. Therefore, according to the Nishihongwanji's announcement, the counter attack by the Japanese military was inevitable and by no means illegal (Akamatsu 1989: 387). As one might expect, the announcement was only the beginning. The organization successively issued the announcement in order to promote and encourage the followers to be obedient to the national polity before and during World War II (Kuriyama 1991: 536).

Buddhist involvement with the imperial government was not limited to the domestic context. Buddhist temples and organisations enthusiastically promoted Buddhism in the colonised areas such as Korea and Taiwan. The promotion was partly to increase the number of adherents of Buddhism for organisational reasons, partly to respond to the command of the imperial government to control the locals by using religions. The religions that tried to expand their influence over Korea and Taiwan were not limited to Shin-Buddhism. Other Buddhist sects such as Soto-shu and Rinzai-shu were not reluctant to get involved in the expansion and governance towards the colonised areas either. The religious plight of the locals was constantly surveyed by the colonial government, and all those religious sects involved in the colonial governance were under tight control of the government (Nakanishi 2016).

What made possible the organization's involvement with the oppressive government? Kuriyama argues that it had already lost its reason for existence far before World War II. As is well known, Japan of the time was quickly transforming itself towards Westernization. Capitalism, liberalism and democracy were widely accepted by the nation, and religion as the source of morality lost its place for reason. In the Sino-Japan War of 1894–1895 and the Russo-Japan War of 1904–1905, Nishihongwanji already established the way of 'service under war'. It was to convince the followers to transcend the life and death, and contribute to the nation with their lives. In this way, the organization gave away the reason of its existence to the national polity (Kuriyama 1991: 536–537).

A similar story was also reported by Akamatsu Tesshin of Ryukoku University, that the reliance of the Nishihongwanji on the concept of national polity became intensified throughout the 1930s. Akamatsu states that the intensification of the organization's reliance on the nation required the reconstruction of a substantial reformation of the organisational structure in order to promote the followers' physical and spiritual contribution to the national polity (Akamatsu 1989: 388).

Because of the overwhelming atmosphere of nationalist movement and the sense of crisis of Nishihongwanji for its reason of existence, the organisation was prompted to pursue the nationalist goal. In other words, the nationalist orientation of Nishihongwanji was partly promoted by the organisational reason in order to maintain its ascendance in the Japanese Buddhist community. It is often said that this makes a sharp contrast with the second generation of the Kyoto School philosophers, who sincerely struggled to achieve an ideal world order through the concept of Japaneseness and its history, which supposedly made clear distinctions from Western civilization, although they simply ended up with justifying the violent invasion of Japan over other Asian nations. Nishihongwanji's involvement was rather strategic, rational and more importantly pragmatic in a sense that they tried to survive through the dark age of Japanese history according to the interpretation of this sort. However, even if the involvement was strategic, we can antedate that they needed to postulate a religious justification of some sort in order to convince their followers.

What was significant in justifying the organisation's support for the nationalist government? In what way could they come to terms with the violent move of the Japanese imperialism while they remained as purely religious and following the teachings of Buddha? While Buddhist organizations had to immediately answer these questions at the time of the war, they had to face these questions from the beginning of the modern Japan. Modernisation and Westernisation on the basis of rationalism and the scientific truth mainly imported to Japan after the Meiji Restoration naturally resulted in widely questioning the meaning of religion.

What helped the organization in this context was Shinran's saying of *Shinzoku-nitai* (Absolute and Conventional Truths). The original meaning of *Shinzoku-nitai* was substantially different from the way it was interpreted by the Nishihongwanji temple in the twenty years' crisis of Japan. The original purpose of *shinzoku-nitai* was to illuminate the contradiction in describing the transcending primary truth which was often described as 'emptiness' in ordinary everyday language. As the concept of 'emptiness' is defined as indescribable and can be obtained only through Buddhist practice, it is far beyond the ordinary everyday language. However, if Buddhism is to be understood by ordinary people and to promote Buddhism among them, it is indispensably required to illustrate the absolute Buddhist truth in conventional languages (Minami 2018: loc.1464/3103).

Shinran similarly introduced *Shinzoku-nitai* in order to clarify that the Buddhist statutes were just about forms and nothing imperative in terms of Buddhist beliefs. In other words, it was to announce to be cautious about the idolatry, and promote the belief in the truth. Usually *Shintai* is called *paramārtha-satya* or the 'primary truth', and means the absolute truth, which is transcendental and influenced by no social or political elements. *Zokutai*, on the other hand, has been regarded as secondary, and it is the truth socially and politically recognized and of course under the profound influence of the worldly context.

However, *Shinzoku-nitai* became a decisive means in relation to the justification of the Nishihongwanji's involvement with the dominant regime according to Kuriyama. He argues that while it guaranteed the commitment of Buddhists' adherence to the religious truth at least at the superficial level, the Nishihongwanji was able to maintain the number of followers under the extreme nationalist atmosphere for the purpose of the organizational existence by aligning itself to the imperial government. In order to preserve the number of followers as well as the good relationship with the government of the time, the organisation was destined to take a pragmatic stance and continuously provide religious interpretations of the aggressive foreign policies of the dominant regime in line with the *Shinzoku-nitai* (Kuriyama 1991: 556). For example, while a Buddhist principle tells that killing living creatures is a serious sin, Buddhist organisations contended that the reason why Japan should go to war against China was because of the China's rejection of Buddhist benevolence. Because Chinese people do not accept Buddhism, it was inevitable to regard them as 'enemies' (Omi 2016: 254).

While the Kyoto School's discourses reached readers through printed forms such as book and magazines, the new interpretations of *Shinzoku-nitai* were distributed through the channels of Nishihongwanji's announcements and orders to each Shin-Buddhist temple spread out all over the nation. It is also worth noting that the highest monk of Nishihongwanji, equivalent to the the pope in the Vatican, frequently visited the battlefields during the war against China for consolation, and himself was conscripted in 1939 (Omi 2016: 255). In order to make sure the institutionalisation of the organization's comprehension of Buddhism, which was repeatedly reorganised time to time, the Nishihongwanji even re-structured its organisational bodies in accordance with the new interpretation of the *Shinzoku-nitai* (Akamatsu 1989).

Analysis

The Nishihongwanji's story of pragmatic and strategic involvement with the imperial government parallels to the story of Kitaro Nishida, the leading philosopher of the Kyoto School. The central concept of Nishida's philosophy, the place of nothingness, was said to be developed by referring to Buddhist teachings (Nishida n.d.). It is particularly interesting that his philosophy is said to have been under profound influence of Zen-Buddhism and Shin-Buddhism. It is said that the experiences of the second generation of the Kyoto School philosophers, many of whom were Nishida's disciples, were somehow different from that of Nishihongwanji. Usually it is interpreted that while Nishihongwanji's involvement was out of its pragmatic organizational reasons, the Kyoto School's incorporation was more philosophical and theoretical. However, Nishida's Buddhism-based philosophy was interpreted and reinterpreted by Nishida's disciples in order to make sense of the militarist regime's territorial expansion towards the Asian continent before and during World War II, and this tells the pragmatic and contextual stance of the Kyoto School. While the concept of place of nothingness was supposed to reify the all-inclusive space in which multiculturalism is materialized as the Buddhist teachings repeatedly claimed, the concept of nothingness was reinterpreted by the second generation of the Kyoto School to mean a transcendent state of mind, which could supposedly be realized only by Japan. In this way, Japanese military government gained the strong support of the Kyoto School intellectuals to send their troops abroad (Shimizu 2011).

While Nishida's disciples were enthusiastic in promoting this interpretation to ordinary citizens that Japan was materialising the transcendental and superior truth to the West, Nishida was not all that keen. He was aware of the contradiction his disciples' aggressive move towards pragmatism might involve. This is one of the reasons why he successively published political writings in his later years, striving to change the meanings granted in the prevailing political phrases and propaganda of the dominant regime. For example, Nishida used a word *Kokka Minzoku* (state-nation) in referring to world politics by putting nation and state the other way around to the ordinary expression of *Minzoku Kokka* (nation-state). By using 'nation' as a noun and 'state' as an adjective, he expressed his cosmology in which 'nation', thus 'culture', would be the main focus of world politics. Here, Nishida repeatedly mentioned that culture is an open-ended system of thought, thus opposite to such a closed system as 'state' (Shimizu 2011).

There were two exceptional Kyoto School philosophers who were against the pragmatism of the conservative Kyoto School scholars: Tosaka Jun and Miki Kiyoshi, both of whom died in prison around the end of the World War II. They left a number of writings before their tragic deaths, and now many scholars are working on what they saying during the dark age (Harootunian 2000; Shimizu 2014). These two philosophers, Tosaka in particular, were self-proclaimed Marxists and often referred to as the left-wing Kyoto School philosophers. Their arguments will be introduced shortly.

In the case of Buddhism, there seem to be not many Buddhist monks who were against Nishihongwanji's pragmatic move. One of the exceptions was in the Mie prefecture, Ueki Tetsujo. He was not associated with Nishihongwanji but with another nationwide Buddhist organization called Otani-ha, based in the Higashihongwanji temple. Although Ueki's anti-war actions were known simply because of his son, Ueki Hitoshi, who became a nationwide comedian in the post-war period, not much has been written about him (Ueki 1987). Ueki was from an outcast community in Mie prefecture, and later involved in the socialist movements. He became a monk in 1929 by inheriting a temple of his wife's family. During the war, he continuously taught the adherents and supporting members of his temple that the war was not justifiable, and shoot somewhere else when you are ordered to shoot the enemy (Ueki 1987).

Another rare example was Takenaka Shogen, who was also a monk of Otani-ha. In 1937, Takenaka publicly announced that the prayer for the war was against the principle of Shin-Buddhism. For him, war was sin, and he showed strong objection to the Shin-Buddhism's involvement with the imperial government. However, he was accused by the government as well as by his colleagues, and eventually forced to retraction. It was an extremely brave and demanding action at that time to fight against the imperial government's bellicose attitude, and maintain the struggle against the war (Omi 2016: 253).

Then, what went wrong in the case of Nishihongwanji and the Kyoto School? One possible explanation is the denial of multiple discourses within the Kyoto School or Nishihongwanji. Miki and Tosaka were never accepted by the Kyoto Imperial University, but could get positions in Tokyo; both worked for Hosei University. They were self-regarded Marxists, and their critical analyses of contemporary capitalism were never accepted by the mainstream Kyoto School philosophy. Similarly, while Buddhist teachings are oriented to promote a multicultural and diverse society, Nishihongwanji never allowed different interpretations of *Shinzoku-nitai* for maintaining the organizational power. On the other hand, Ueki Tetsujo repeatedly preached for human equality and an open society, but he remained outside the mainstream organizational groups of Buddhist temples (Ueki 1987).

The denial of diversity directly means the disappearance of the public in the Arendtean sense. Hannah Arendt argues that diversity and plurality among citizens are the prerequisites for democracy and sound political community. When they disappear, totalitarianism will straitjacket society (Arendt 1958). The cases of the Kyoto School philosophy and Nishihongwanji are typical examples. The

Kyoto School philosophers' denial of different discourses on the basis of historical truth and Nishihongwanji's totalized control over adherents grounded in pragmatism worked in denying diversity and wiping out a space for dialogue. As a result, those who have been expelled from the space of intellectual engagement, Tosaka and Miki, died in prison before World War II ended, and Ueki was repeatedly arrested by the police until the war ended.

Another possible explanation is that the pragmatic principles of both the Kyoto School philosophy and Nishihongwanji fail to provide ethical argument for a just world. The school and Buddhist organisations both concentrate on the 'present' rather than progressive linear development of time. The former is frequently witnessed in the discourses of 'Eastern' ancient thoughts such as Confucianism, Daoism and Buddhism, while the latter is typical in the 'Western' philosophy. It recently became popular among Asian scholars to focus on the 'present' and its open-ended system of thought (Shih and Ikeda 2016). In fact, the pragmatic attitude of East Asian IR is indeed applicable to the territorial disputes of Diaoyu/Sekaku and Dokdo/Takeshima between China, Taiwan and Japan, and South Korea and Japan respectively. In these cases, the nations are more concerned with the immediate consequences of the disputes and tend to avoid definite answers. As a result, the negotiations often become the repetition of the postponement. In this sense, time appears to be cyclical.

However, the pragmatism in East Asian politics holds an extreme weakness when it comes to the issue of ethics. This is because the idea of morality and ethics often requires the linear progressive path of time. William Connolly states 'the dominant image of morality is bound to a progressive image of time'. This is because 'it must be possible to realize them' if there are such thing as 'laws to be obligatory' (Connolly 2005: 113–114). Thus, he maintains;

> we must project the possibility of continual progress toward their attainment. To act morally it is . . . *necessary* to project the subjective potential of long-term moral progress. For 'ought' implies 'can', and the obligation to be moral presupposes that it is possible to be so.
> (Connolly 2005 – emphasis original)

Morality in this context requires progress, a linear historical projection of the future. What lacks in the pragmatic time concept of the present is precisely this projection. The cyclical time does not have this progress, and finds itself with the difficulty of setting and defining what is right and what is wrong. In Confucianism, this is anticipated in the figure of the benign king, which is characterised by the established virtue and selflessness (Yan 2013). In other words, the possible ethical principle in the context of the cyclicality of time is virtue ethics only, and this is one of the reasons why it is often difficult to grasp ethics in the non-Western context in the form of Kantian deontology or Benthamite utilitarianism. However, the virtue ethics sometimes fails to provide a power of resistance as it lacks concrete programmes of ethical conduct. Indeed, under the military rule of Japan where there was no such king, but only the aggressive imperial government, virtue ethics provided no referencing point for those engaging with religions or non-Western philosophy.

Then what is the ideal ethics if the cyclical time framing is the norm like the Asian context? Although I have no definite answer to this question, probably Tosaka Jun's articulation of morality would be suggestive in this context. Tosaka argues that morality only becomes possible when we reflect upon people's lives. Morality must reflect the experiences of individuals. However, the term *individuals* here must not be confused with the individuals in relation to the universal. The individuals in relation to the universal are the standardised people who only exist as an oppositional existence to the universal. Therefore, they totally lack peculiar experiences or characteristics. They are like numbers which completely hide the differences among them. On the other hand, what Tosaka calls the self is a socio-political existence which holds peculiarities and memories of difference. The peculiarities and differences make a one and only self.

In order to draw political meanings out of a self, we must focus on the representation of the differences such as self-portrait and autobiographical novels. They will convey to the readers the authors' own experiences and perceptions towards society, which inevitably lead us to a society based upon plural experiences. Tosaka contends that these different experiences and diversified identities will question the prevailing socio-political orders and relativise the given norms. In sum, Tosaka's morality only lies in the pluralist society and political engagements with critical investigation of the prevalent socio-political structure (Tosaka 1966). Of course, this critical engagement is not confined to autobiographical novels. It must include arts, music, performances, films, acting and so forth. All sorts of expressions of subjectivity must be taken seriously as representations of the selves. By including these representations and establishing a pluralist society, we may become aware of the morality in cyclical time.

Conclusion

In this chapter I tried to introduce the hidden history of Buddhism in Japan. As explained, the Nishihongwanji temple was deeply involved with the mobilisation regime of imperial Japan. What was lying behind this involvement was the Nishihongwanji's pragmatic attitude and rational calculations towards the prevailing order. This pragmatism was intimately related to the *Shinzo-nitai* concept, which allowed the temple to interpret their pragmatic and secular attitude as acceptable. However, the totally pragmatic stance towards politics inherently lacked the ethical consideration and the temple failed to question and reflect upon its political position. It had to wait until the 1980s to revisit the issue and critically assess its politics during the war.

There seem to be some further key questions to ask in the case taken up in this chapter. One of them is the question of whether Nishihongwanji's and the Kyoto School's pragmatism should be defined as religious. This is because while religion and Buddhist philosophy were frequently used mainly to distinguish the Japanese self from the West which had been repeatedly exemplified by such concepts as state sovereignty and secularism, their pragmatism actually prompted them to legitimize the sovereignty of the state. In the contemporary nationalisms, religion is often used to represent the non-Western quality, but this seems to be problematic as basing their contention on the binary opposition of West/non-West is itself rational and secular as the previous examples evidently proved. In this sense, it is extremely imperative to carefully investigate religion in the context of nationalism, particularly when it comes to Asia, where the dichotomy of secular/religious is not as clear as in the Western traditions.

Second, it would be useful to question the relationship between religion and nation-state in the Asian context. As mentioned already, the boundary between secular/religious is not as clear in Asia as in the West. This is because the binary opposition itself is a product of a particular cultural tradition. However, rejecting the nation-state model is also dangerous in a sense that it gives the power in the region a free hand in the name of different cosmology such as *hakkoichiu* or Great East Asian Co-prosperity Area. While these ideas surely provided an alternative to the nation-state model of Westphalia, their argument was within the model justifying the state monopoly of violence, imperialist expansion and exploitation of natural resources for economic growth. What is needed in this sense is not the nation-state model in disguise. The new alternative should start with a critical question of what nation-state means in the contemporary world affairs, and this inevitably requires profound knowledge of religion, particularly in the context of Asia. Otherwise researchers may end up with putting everything into the black box of religion and simply labeling it with 'others'. Unless the question of nation-state and religion is properly addressed, any attempt at alternatives would end up returning to the nation-state model.

References

Akamatsu, T. 1989. *Hongwanjikyodan ni okeru "Senji Hokoku Taisei" no Kakuritsu: Iwayuru 'Chugogoku Kyoryoku Kaigi, Chuoshingikai, Kenkyukai nado oyobi Gakushikisha' no Yakuwari*. In Senjikyogaku to Shinshu. Kyoto.
Arendt, H. 1958. *Human Condition*. Chicago: Chicago University Press.
Aydin, C. 2007. *The Politics of Anti-Westernism in Asia*. New York: Columbia University Press.
Carr, E.H. 1946. *The Twenty Years' Crisis: 1919–1939*. London: Macmillan.
Chan, S., and Mandaville, P. 2001. *The Zen of International Relations*. Eds. S. Chan, P. Mandaville, and R. Bleiker. New York: Springer. http://doi.org/10.1057/9780230286429
Connolly, W. 2005. *Pluralism*. Durham: Duke University Press.
Harootunian, H. 2000. *Overcome by Modernity*. Princeton, NJ: Princeton University Press, available at: http://doi.org/10.1093/acprof:oso/9780190664008.001.0001/acprof-9780190664008
Hiromatsu, W. 1989. *Kindai no Chokoku: Showa Shisoshi no Ichi Shikaku*. Tokyo: Iwanami.
Huang, X. 2001. 'The Zen Master's Story and an Anatomy of International Relations Theory,' in *The Zen of International Relations IR Theory from East to West*. Basingstoke: Palgrave Macmillan.
Inoue, T. 2011. Sennen Nihon no Gurobarizumu: 1930 nendai no kyokun. Tokyo: Shinchosha.

Kosaka, M., Nishitani, K., Koyama, I., and Suzuki, S. 1943. *Sekaishiteki Tachiba to Nihon.* Tokyo: Chuokoron.
Kuriyama, T. 1991. *Senji Kyogaku: Shinzoku Nitai no Kiketsu. In Senji Kyogaku to Shinshu.* Kyoto: Nagata Bunshodo, pp. 535–568.
Ling, L. H. M. 2013. *The Dao of World Politics: Towards a Post-Westphalian, Worldist International Relations.* Abrington: Routledge.
Minami, Jikisai. 2018. *Choetsu to Mujo [The Transcendence and Evanescent].* Tokyo: Schinchosha.
Nakanishi, N. 2016. *Shokuminchi Taiwan to Nippon Bukkyo.* Kyoto: Sanninsha.
Nishida, K. n.d. 'Mu no Jikakuteki Gentei,' (The Self-Conscious Determination of Nothingness) Nishida Kitarō Zenshū [The Collected Works of Kitarō No.9.
Oguma, E. 1995. *Tanitsuminzoku no Kigen: Nihonjin no Jigazo no Keifu.* Tokyo: Shinyosha.
Ohashi, Y. 2001. *Nihonkaigun to Kyoto Gakuha: Oshima memo wo megutte.* Tokyo: PHP.
Omi, T. 2016. *Nyumon Kindai Bukkyo Shiso.* Tokyo: Chikuma.
Sakade, Y. 2014. *Nihon to Dokyo Bunka.* Tokyo: Kadokawa.
Schmitt, C. [1919] 2011. *Political Romanticism.* Abrington: Routledge.
Shih, C-Y., and Ikeda, J. 2016. 'International Relations of Post-Hybridity: Dangers and Potentials in Non-Synthetic Cycles,' *Globalizations*, 13(4): 454–468. http://doi.org/10.1080/14747731.2016.1143729.
Shimizu, K. 2011. 'Nishida Kitaro and Japan's Interwar Foreign Policy: War Involvement and Culturalist Political Discourse,' *International Relations of the Asia-Pacific*, 11(1): 157–183. http://doi.org/10.1093/irap/lcq021.
———. 2015. 'Materializing the "Non-Western": Two Stories of Japanese Philosophers on Culture and Politics in the Inter-war Period,' *Cambridge Review of International Affairs*, 28(1): 3–20. http://doi.org/10.1080/09557571.2014.889083.
Shinran, and Kaneko, D. 1957. *Kyogyo Shinsho.* Tokyo: Iwanami.
Sueki, F. 2006. *Shiso to Shiteno Bukkyo Nyumon.* Tokyo: Transview.
Tansman, A. Ed. *The Culture of Japanese Fascism,* Durham: Duke University Press.
Tosaka, J. 1966. 'Dotoku no Kannen,' in *The Collected Works of Tosaka Jun No.4.* Tokyo: Keiso Shobó.
Tatsuzawa, A. 1984. 'Senjika no Shinsyukyogaku'. *Indogaku/Bukyogaku Kenkyu*, 65: 266–269.
Ueki, H. 1987. *Yume wo Kui Tsuzuketa Otoko.* Tokyo: Asahishimbum.
Yan, X. 2013. *Ancient Chinese Thought, Modern Chinese Power.* Princeton, NJ: Princeton University Press.

7 Political modernity in East Asia
Religion, nationalism and subversion of imperialism

Atsuko Ichijo

The current chapter examines the development of political modernity in East Asia in the early twentieth century through an exploration of the ways in which ideas about political community were produced, used and appropriated by both the imperialists and the colonised. Inspired by the theory of multiple modernities (Eisenstadt 2000) which rejects the teleological assumption of conventional modernisation theories – an eventual convergence of various societies to the European experiences of modernity – the chapter focuses on the ways in which Asianism,[1] a discourse of resistance to European/western hegemony, was developed and acted upon by Eastern Asian intellectuals to define modernity in their own terms. In particular, the chapter reviews the ways in which various ideas associated with Asianism, articulated within the context of the philosophy of world history by the Kyoto School, were engaged by colonial intellectuals in Taiwan, Korea and China, which, the chapter argues, represented an exercise of agency in a broad, sociological sense and subjectivity on the part of the colonised.[2] These ideas include schemes such as the East Asian Community and the East Asia League. These initiatives clearly constituted oppressive Japanese imperial rule; but in some instances, attempts were made by intellectuals in various parts of the Japanese Empire to make use of these ideas in order to resist, challenge and even subvert Japanese imperialism. Their attempts were limited, cerebral and short-lived and did not lead to tangible outcomes. The fact that these attempts existed does not compensate for the brutality of Japanese imperialism, either. However, by examining the ways in which the oppressed and subjugated tried to mobilise the ideas of the oppressor in order to resist and subvert the oppression, the chapter calls for a more agency-centred investigation of the ideas used by the colonised and the oppressed in the unfolding of modernity.

The question in what ways an examination of various manifestations of Asianism and how they were mobilised relates to the issues of religion and nationalism needs to be addressed first. Asianism can be understood as a form of supranationalism, an ideology and movement to overcome division created by nationalism (see Szpilman 2007); it is also often understood as one of the guises Japanese imperialism adopted, thus, as an expression of expansionist nationalism (see Doak 2007). In this context, the relationship between Asianism and nationalism is evident but not that between Asianism and religion. The chapter addresses the problem by treating Asianism as a civilisational discourse as suggested by Prasenjit Duara (Duara 2002). Since civilisation is a totalising concept which draws from both material and spiritual dimensions of life, treating Asianism as civilisational discourse allows us to approach the underlying spiritual or, even, religious components that support Asianism as touched upon in the introduction to the volume (Shani and Kibe 2019).

At this juncture, some more definitions of key concepts that underpin this chapter should be given. In this chapter, nationalism, a nebulous concept, is seen as a totalising view of a political community. Nationalism could be a driving force for people to win liberation from various forms of oppression as the examples of the American and French Revolutions as well as a number of independence movements in Asia and Africa in the post–World War II era attest. Another aspect of nationalism as a force to impose conformity also needs to be recognised. In discussing the idea of culturalism as conceptual equivalent to nationalism in late nineteenth/early twentieth century China and India, Duara presents an understanding of nationalism as a totalising force in a somewhat roundabout manner. In challenging the claim that emphasises the novelty of nationalism as a form of consciousness which proves radical discontinuity between pre-modernity and modernity suggested by leading theorists of nationalism such as Benedict Anderson (1991) and Ernest Gellner (1983), Duara puts forward an argument that the novelty of nationalism as a form of consciousness lies in its insistence on the co-extensiveness of political and cultural communities, a totalised vision of a community. Furthermore, he argues that a totalising view of a community is not new in China, where culturalism traditionally provided 'totalizing representations and narratives of community', hence nationalism as a totalising force was not new in the East of the nineteenth century (Duara 1995, 1996, 1999). This is the basis to reject the conventional idea of the spread of nationalism from Europe but suggests that attempts by the colonial intellectuals in East Asia should be understood as endogenous movements rather than acts of adaptation and acculturalisation.

Religion in this chapter, following the argument in the introduction, does not refer to a particular denomination but a discursive formation or 'a fragmentary narrative' (van der Veer 2013: 661) which offers a set of worldviews to various actors, and as such, as briefly discussed previously, a constitutive part of Asianism. As a historically formed and maintained discursive formation offering explanations to ontological and existential questions, religion underpins a variety of ideational structure including Asianism and the philosophy of world history, often in reference to ethics and spirituality, the two key sets of ideas about modernity and subjectivity in this chapter.

Since the chapter is inspired by the theory of multiple modernities, the key to our investigation to political modernity in East Asia is subjectivity. The chapter first examines Asianism and the philosophy of world history which exercised heavy influence on the shape of Asianism produced in Japan in the first half of the twentieth century. Both represent non-western or 'post-western' subjectivity.[3] It can be seen as post-western in a sense that the intellectuals engaged with the production and articulation of ideas about Asianism often claimed the aim of their endeavour was to overcome the West (Isomae 2010). Both constituted the background against which intellectuals of various parts of the Japanese Empire articulated their thoughts and presented strategies for resisting and subverting Japanese imperial rule.

Background: Asianism and the philosophy of world history

Asianism

Asianism as a collection of thoughts and ideas is notoriously difficult to define mainly because the category of Asia is not indigenous. The idea of 'Asia' was probably coined by the ancient Greeks as a way to distinguish themselves from the Persians and other barbarians. The category was brought to East Asia by Jesuit missionaries in the sixteenth century but was not incorporated in popular consciousness till the nineteenth century within the context of the expansion of the West (Saaler and Szpilman 2011; Frey and Soakowsiki 2016). Another reason why Asianism is difficult to pin down is that as in the case of nationalism (Freeden 1998), transcendental ideas such as Asianism are ideationally weak (Esenbel 2010). Consequently, Asianism is an ever evolving concept reflecting the acceptance, absorption, innovation, revision and maintenance of the idea of Asia and echoing various intellectual movements developed from Japan to China, to India, to Islamic Central Asia or even to some parts of Europe. While it is nebulous, Asianism has driven a number of political and social movements across the geographical area often associated with Asia since the nineteenth century.

That Asianism, in its broadest conception, was articulated using the language of civilisation is clearly seen in Sun Yat-sen's well-known lecture, 'Greater Asianism'[4] delivered at a girls' high school in Kobe, Japan, in 1924. In the Japanese translation, Sun uses both 'culture' and 'civilisation' but since he is developing his view with reference to the oppositional framework of the East vs. the West, it is quite clear the main reference point of his lecture was the contemporary debates on civilisation. Sun opens his lecture by asserting superiority of Asia by declaring 'our Asia is the birthplace of the oldest culture' which is *the* source of all cultures and civilisations of the world. He acknowledges that Asia, the most ancient and highly developed civilisation, has been eclipsed by the West for the last few centuries and now the West dominates and oppresses Asia. Sun sees the signs of Asia's fight back in the Japanese victory over Russia at the beginning of the century because of the fact itself (an Asian country defeated a European country and by so doing liberated itself from the yoke of unequal treaties) and because of how it was seen by Asians across the world. He then argues that the revival of Asia is not merely something to be hoped for but is inevitable, and in justifying this, Sun mobilises the spiritual East vs. the material West framework.

According to Sun, the western civilisation is essentially material and more importantly, 'a culture that threatens people with military power (might)'; the western civilisation therefore rules through fear, which Sun characterises as *badao* (覇道: the rule of might) in reference to Chinese classical thinking. In contrast,

Political modernity in East Asia 111

in the East, *badao* has been looked down upon as a principle of rule in favour of *wangdao* (王道: the Kingly Way) which is based on benevolence, justice and morality. In the East, the rulers do not threaten people with violence in order to secure their compliance; rather, *wangdao*, the Kingly Way, the fundamental principle in the East, puts onus on the ruler to demonstrate his exceptional morality and sense of justice in order to solicit voluntary compliance from the population. In Sun's eye, it is clear which is superior as the principle of organising society: *wangdao*. Because Greater Asianism, as Sun sees it, draws from this tradition of the Kingly Way, which prioritises morality, spirituality and justice over might and material comfort, Sun believes Greater Asianism is ultimately superior to western civilisation. Greater Asianism is not about dominating weaker groups but about justice and respect to all, a fundamentally egalitarian and moral principle. He then calls upon Japan not to forget its civilisational heritage of *wangdao*, although it has caught up with the West in terms of material culture, in thinking about its future. According to Sun, it is up to the Japanese to decide whether to become a poodle of western *badao* or a champion of the Eastern Kingly Way.

As seen in Sun Yat-sen's lecture, Asianism was sometimes seen as a form of solidarity to resist the advancement of western imperialism or as an identity which justified such action. Early forms of Asianism had a strong cosmopolitan orientation, emphasising the freedom and autonomy of Asian peoples against western imperialism. What Rabindranath Tagore (see Chapter 1 by Kaviraj, this volume) envisaged and what Ueki Emori (1857–1892), Tōyama Mitsuru (1855–1944) and his Gen'yosha were working for was this type of Asianism in order to realise the 'rise of Asia' in which Asian peoples would be liberated from imperial domination and prosper as equals in a global community. However, the development of Asianism overlapped with the rise of Japan as a major international power, and increasingly Asianism was intertwined with Japanese nationalism and imperialism. This type of Asianism was present in thoughts and activities of Ōkawa Shūmei (1886–1957) and Kita Ikki (1883–1926), and articulations by some members of Kyoto School of philosophy.

The philosophy of world history

The phrase 'the world-historical standpoint' appears in the title of a symposium ('The World-Historical Standpoint and Japan') organised and published in *Chūōkōron* which took place in November 1941. The symposium was one of the three *Chūōkōron* symposia in which Kōsaka Masaaki, Kōyama Iwao, Nishitani Keiji and Suzuki Shigetaka, all of them members of Kyoto School, took part. The three symposia, after being published individually in different *Chūōkōron* issues, were published in a book form under the title of *The World-Historical Standpoint and Japan* in 1943. These symposia are generally seen as 'the most important public debates of significance for Japan of the transformation of a European war into a global conflict in 1941' (Williams 2004: 55). The world-historical standpoint can be understood as a way of understanding history which emerged out of the deliberation as to how to deal with world history in philosophy, a deliberation mainly pursued by the members of Kyoto School in the early twentieth century.

The philosophy of world history is difficult to grasp partly because it is not systematically developed in one volume but rather referred to in various works, most prominently in the *Chūōkōron* symposia and its proceedings, *The World-Historical Point and Japan*. In the volume, the philosophy of world history is described as 'the unfolding of the very ideal of the world, a clarification of its genealogy' (Kōsaka et al. 1943: 178–179), which is rather cryptic. In the philosophy of world history, the 'world' is understood to be 'an objective, universal horizon that transcends the standpoint of particular nations' (Horio 1994: 296). As such the world is the basis of true history; it follows the aim in the philosophy of world history is to achieve a true awareness as a subject through becoming conscious of the global characteristic of the world (Horio 1994). According to the Kyoto School, 'history is moved not only by the forces of economics and learning. There is a more subjective, more concrete life-energy in a people' (Kōsaka et al. 1943: 101–102). This life-energy is called '*moralische Energie*' and it 'does not refer to an individual or personal morality, nor is it a matter of a purity of blood.' It is a power 'concentrated in the people of a country culturally and politically', in a people subjectively self-determined (Kōsaka et al. 1943: 107). Japan is, according to those philosophers, 'being called upon by the world to discover such a principle (i.e. *moralishe Energie*)' which is 'the historical necessity that has been put on its shoulders' (Kōsaka et al. 1943: 126).

The idea of the world-historical standpoint was built on an understanding of the contemporary situation as a world-historical era in which the western-centric world would disintegrate and the world would finally be truly unified. It is more of an expression of conviction that Japan was to play a significant role in the world where the existing order was collapsing than a clear proposition of methodology to study history (Koyasu 2007). According to the members of the Kyoto School, the world-historical era was deemed to be a period in which various states and nations would influence world culture through their unique characteristics. They further argued that Japan was to take the lead in this new era of history as a fully self-aware subject because of its history of developing by absorbing and digesting influences from both the West and the East, a clear echo of the civilisational discourse which was dominant at that time. In their own words:

> The basis of Japan's leadership in East Asia lies in its consciousness of this world-historical vocation. . . . [T]he Japanese are a world historical people of the present. . . . World historical peoples of the past were simply expanding oneself through the whole wide world and did not have the awareness to renew the order of the world while recognizing the subjectivity of the other.
> (Kōsaka et al. 1943: 157–159)

The war, at the time of the symposium, yet to develop into the Pacific War, had a particular 'world-historical significance' because it was to reveal 'a new idea of world history by realising unification of the East, thus, enabling the true unification of the world' (Suzuki 2010).

The influence of the rising civilizational discourse is evident in the articulation of the world-historical standpoint by the members of the Kyoto School (see Shimizu, Chapter 6, this volume). It is widely acknowledged that the western powers justified their imperial conquest as a civilising mission drawing from Enlightenment ideals. The western civilisation in this regard was conceptualised as singular and universal, but some alternative views of civilisation started to emerge in the mid-nineteenth century welcomed by intellectuals such as Herder and Alexander von Humboldt. The old, Chinese conception of *wenming* (文明), valorised by the Christian missionary, attracted particular attention. The Orientalist scholars were busy describing ancient civilisations to educate the West because some of these were understood to be the source of the contemporary western civilisation. There was also a Buddhist revival in the world. These new discourse of eastern civilisation with an emphasis on the spiritual aspect was affirmed in the West before it was in the East (Duara 2002, 2003: 92–93). By the conclusion of World War I, there was generalised anxiety about the state of western civilisation, and, as it is well known, another infamous symposium, 'Overcoming Modernity', was organised in reference to efforts made by Paul Valerie to examine the state of civilisation in Europe (Isomae 2010: 62–63). The focus on *moralische Energie* in the 'World-Historical Standpoint and Japan' symposium was therefore, at least partly, a reflection of the general intellectual climate of the time.

That Asianism as expressed in the deliberation of the world-historical standpoint was heavily influenced by civilisational discourse can also be seen in the inherent contradiction of Asianism as outlined previously; it was an exercise to justify Japanese imperial expansion in the universalist language with moral commitment to lead the resistance to the western powers' hegemony. This inherent contradiction did not go unnoticed by the oppressors and the oppressed alike; in the *Chūōkōron* symposia, one of the participants, Suzuki, expressed his uneasiness with the apparent contradiction, and Sun Yat-sen noted it in his lecture, as we discussed earlier. When Asianism was used by colonial intellectuals to subvert and overcome Japanese imperialism, it was often this contradiction in the philosophy of world history that was focused upon and mobilised.

Various guises of Asianism in circulation in the Japanese empire

Taiwan: East Asia as way of transcending division

The first example of the use of Asianism in order to resist and overcome Japanese imperialism can be found in the writings by Tsai Pei-huo (蔡培火, 1889–1983), a multi-faceted politician and teacher of Taiwan, the first colony of Japan. He started his career as a teacher. He campaigned to introduce the Latin script in order to improve literacy among Taiwanese. He became involved in the Taiwan Assimilation Society formally in order to encourage assimilation of the Taiwanese into Japanese society but in reality to demand equal treatment of the Taiwanese with the Japanese. As soon as it was founded, the Society was banned by the governor-general in Taiwan in 1915, suspicious of its demand for the improved treatment of the Taiwanese, and Tsai lost his job as a teacher and was exiled in Japan. While in Japan, Tsai played the key role in founding a bilingual (Japanese and Chinese) magazine, 『台湾青年 (*Taiwanese Youth*)』 in 1920. *Taiwanese Youth* was supported by both Japanese intellectuals and Taiwanese students and intellectuals residing in Japan and it counted eminent figures such as Uemura Masahisa and Yoshino Sakuzō as contributors. The magazine continued till 1922 and then was renamed as 『台湾 (*Taiwan*)』, which was further morphed into a newspaper, 『台湾民報 (*Taiwan People's News*)』 in 1923 (Yokoji 2004). Tsai went back to Taiwan during this period and petitioned the Japanese colonial office to install a local council for Taiwan.

Tsai was a nationalist as seen in his article, 'Our Island and Ourselves' in *Taiwanese Youth* in 1920. The article reviewed the relationship between Taiwan Island and the Taiwanese – what kind of place Taiwan was and what the Taiwanese who were born and lived on the island should aspire to. After examining Taiwan in reference to its climate, geology and natural resources, Tsai claimed that because of the accommodating natural environment, the Taiwanese were indifferent to their subjective being, which had resulted in Taiwan's subjugated position in the world. He then argued that the Taiwanese could no longer afford to remain seen as incapable. 'Taiwan is Taiwan in the Empire at the same time Taiwan of ours, of the Taiwanese' (Tsai 1920: 19), and he called for the equal treatment of the Taiwanese. In making his argument, Tsai made reference to the kind of Asianism propagated by the imperial centre that the Japanese Empire was working for oppressed peoples of Asia and demanded that Japan should keep its word by treating the Taiwanese as equals so as to progress towards the realisation of universal equality.

Tsai's use of Asianism as shaped by the Kyoto School of Philosophy in order to challenge Japanese imperialism is more clearly seen in his book, 『東亞の子はかく思ふ (*Thus Thinks the Child of East Asia*)』, written in Japanese and published in 1937. Tsai mobilises the *bagdao* (the rule of might) vs *wangdao* (the Kingly Way) framework right from the beginning to argue for peace between Japan and China (pp. 2–3). Driven by deep concern that the whole of East Asia was on the brink of catastrophic disaster due to war between Japan and China and more generally as a consequence of Japanese imperialism, Tsai declares that his nationalist concern for Taiwan was no longer relevant (p. 10). He then challenges the Japanese imperial centre to prove their world-historical credential by honouring its commitment to equality among five peoples in Manchuria (p. 5). He urges Japan to follow *wangdao* in its dealing with China by respecting it as a senior rather than by following *baodao*, the western way, with a threat of force because 'Japan has already qualified as the eldest brother in Asia' (p. 222). Being an elder according to Asianism as elaborated by Sun Yat-sen in his lecture and as shaped by the Kyoto School with an emphasis on the inherent ethical nature of the East means being obligated to act benevolently and morally in accordance to the true essence of eastern ethics. Tsai legitimately demands equal treatment of all peoples in the Japanese Empire by making use of its most dominant discourse. Demand for respect and autonomy, which was one of the reasons why the Taiwan Assimilation Society was banned by the governor-general some twenty years before, was now presented in the imperialists' language using their version of Asianism that Asia is inherently superior to the West because of its superior spirituality and Japan was uniquely placed to lead all peoples in the world to 'true history'. While his plea was largely ignored, Tsai was clearly acting as someone with full subjectivity seeking the ways through which to advance his and the Taiwanese cause by using a type of Asianism – that of empire. Because of the civilisational discursive framework of Asianism, the appeal to Asianism often assumed similarity to any appeal to religious ideals. The exercise of political agency by Tsai was therefore conditioned both by nationalism and religion in a roundabout manner.

The East Asian community

As the war with China became entrenched, then–Prime Minister Konoe Fumimaro issued a statement on 'the construction of a new East Asian order' on 3 November 1938 which was followed by another statement on the normalisation of Japanese-Sino relationship on 22 December 1938. These statements publicly proclaimed that the Japanese government no longer saw China as the enemy and that it would like to regard and treat China as a partner of their efforts to build a new order in East Asia, the redefined aim of its war efforts. These statements signalled the birth of the East Asian Community (東亜協同体) initiative.

The East Asian Community initiative was formulated by Showa Kenkyukai, a group of intellectuals which advised Konoe Fumimaro. One of its members, Miki Kiyoshi, seen as an unorthodox member of the Kyoto School, played a key role in providing theoretical foundation of the East Asian Community initiative. Drawing from the philosophy of world history, Miki argued that the unity of East Asia realised in the form of 'a new East Asian order' as a consequence of the second Sino-Japanese War would serve as the moment of overcoming the pre-modern and semi-feudal nature of Asia, which in turn would lead to the overcoming of adverse effects of capitalism, that is, imperialism, which had prevented Asian unity from emerging (Oota 2014). In other words, Miki justified the initiative from a world-historical point of view. He saw a universalist ideal in the initiative that would overcome the opposition of Japanese invasion and Chinese resistance. For Miki, the initiative was a mode of thinking that could overcome nationalism and contained an orientation for a new kind of cosmopolitanism. In his thinking, the universality and cosmopolitanism of the initiative would facilitate the solution of problems of capitalism and western hegemony. It would lead to a renewal of Japan, which would in turn become fully qualified to lead Asia to the world of new order (Yonetani 2005).

History shows this Japan-centric but in a way idealistic vision of the world was short-lived. It was met by a complete rejection from the Nationalist government of China, the main target audience. When the Japanese government was taken over by the Imperial Rule Assistance Association in 1940 for the purpose of total mobilisation for the war, the East Asian Community initiative was superseded by a more clearly imperialist plan of building the Greater East Asian Co-prosperity Sphere, from which a sincere engagement with the problems posed by Chinese nationalism was absent.

There is evidence that the short-lived East Asian Community initiative provided opportunities for the oppressed and subjugated in the Japanese Empire to resist, challenge and even subvert Japanese imperial rule. For instance, some left-leaning Korean intellectuals saw opportunities for social reform in Korea as well as in Japan in the initiative which was originally proposed as a response to the rise of Chinese nationalism (Tobe 2004; Yonetani 2005). They saw in the initiative an invitation to nurture and articulate agency among the subjugated in the new world order albeit a Japanese-led one; a means to overcome Japanese imperialism by making the most of their own idea. These intellectuals also saw the opportunity in the initiative to overcome some problems which they saw as particular to the Korean nation. The emphasis on the rejection of western hegemony and the acceptance of Japanese leadership in the act of challenging and overcoming western hegemony would ultimately suggest the means for preserving the integrity of the Korean nation. They also reasoned that the initiative, because of its anti-capitalist undertone as articulated by Miki, could also be used to address the entrenched class issue in Korea (Tobe 2004).

So In-Sik, for example, examined the East Asian Community initiative from the perspective of the philosophy of world history. In his 1939 article 'The Whole and the Individual in Culture', set in a framework of the understanding that the world was facing a fundamental shift from one world structure to another, So argued that the East Asian Community initiative could not be other than a new form of regionally based community based on the principle that when the political sovereignty and cultural independence of East Asian peoples were respected, all of them would organically and continuously collaborate for the sake of co-existence of the whole of East Asia (So 2004). In other words, the logical conclusion of this principle would be opposition to assimilationist policies directed to the Koreans (Yonetani 2005; Cho 2004; Workman 2013). He then challenged imperial Japan to fulfil its stated world-historical mission of realising the 'world of globality' which would transcend both the feudal East and modern West by making good of the principles behind the East Asian Community initiative (So 2004). Furthermore, So came to see in East Asian subjectivity as embodied in the Japanese nation-state a potential to overcome class society by solving problems associated with capitalism. So saw in the East Asian Community initiative a potential to develop a new, multi-centred domestic order, a regime which guaranteed subjectivity of multi-national and ethnic citizens.

Tobe (2004) collects and comments on three pieces on the East Asian Community initiative which appeared in a special section on 'The East Asian Community and Korea' published in the January 1939 issue of *Sanzenri*. These three pieces by Kim Myeong-Sik, In Chong-sik and Ch'a Chae-jŏng shed light on the ways in which left-leaning Korean intellectuals under Japanese imperial rule attempted to use the East Asian Community initiative to resist further subjugation and to establish Korean subjectivity by referencing their arguments to the philosophy of world history. Tobe (2004: 344–347) points out three common themes in these pieces which were independently written: (1) they all ostensibly supported the 'construction of new China' as the basis for the realisation of 'a new East Asian order'; (2) they all anticipated a strong momentum for revolution in Japan and (3) they evaluated rapid social change in Korea positively and expected the Korean people's support of the Second Sino-Japanese War. These themes are then interwoven with the version of Asianism heavily informed by the philosophy of world history and propagated by the imperial centre as strategies for recovering Korean sovereignty and subjectivity. Below each piece is briefly examined to outline the ways in which these intellectuals sought to use the dominant discourse of Asianism to their advantage.

In his piece entitled 'The Awareness of Construction and Advancement to the Continent', Kim Myeong-Sik (2004) sketched out his understanding how the proposed new order in East Asia could lead to an ultimate liberation of the Korean people. The role of the Korean people, against the background of the outbreak of the Second Sino-Japan War, was defined as a mediator between the Japanese and Chinese. He then identified the significance of the construction of a new East Asia as preparing the condition to realise Sun Yat-sen's three principles of the people. Because of this, Kim argued, the Korean people had to commit to the construction of new East Asia subjectively. The new East Asia to be built was a combination of democracy as the political principle, collectivism in terms of organising economy and humanism as a social ethic, in which all peoples in East Asia would be respected and treated as equals. Furthermore, in Kim's view, building this new East Asia was the same as the effort to develop historical consciousness that would transcend the division of the world into the East and West. Here reference to the idea of world-historical standpoint is evident. In this piece, the realisation of the proposed new East Asian order was supported as a way of achieving the liberation of the Koreans, which is presented as an inevitable consequence of what the philosophy of world history predicts.

In Chong-sik framed his piece with a clear reference to the philosophy of world history: 'unifying all of East Asia into a single economic and political unit can only mean that all of East Asia as a community actively participates in and contributes to the progress of world history as a unit' and 'it is a kind of historic holy war on the part of the Empire' (2004: 359, 360). He then placed the Korean people in the East Asian Community initiative: 'we the Koreans have to think about our future as a nation on the premises of a new order in East Asia to be built' (2004: 360). Having situated his treaties on the future of the Korean people firmly within the official, imperial discursive framework, he then argued for a full realisation of the unity of the Japanese and Koreans in the form of complete equality as an essential condition for the building of an East Asian community because it was an inevitable consequence of pursuing the ideal of a new East Asian order as presented by the imperial centre.

Ch'a Chae-jŏng also acknowledged the overall framework provided by philosophy of world history in his piece 'A New East Asian Order and Renovation': 'it is legitimate to acknowledge the . . . world-historical significance of the new

118 *Atsuko Ichijo*

East Asian order as a way of dealing with the outbreak of war with China' (Ch'a 2004: 370). He then proceeded with the analysis with clear reference to Marxism. According to Ch'a the East Asian Community initiative constituted part of renovation of Japan: 'the capitalist Japan must be overcome as the war concludes. Establishing a new East Asian order as an imperialist development of capitalist Japan not only loses its world-historical significance but also denies happy development of Japan' (ibid.). Ch'a concluded that the East Asian Community initiative represented a new direction of cosmopolitanism, a major correction to cosmopolitanism based in Marxism because it was embedded in ethnic and cultural foundations.

These left-leaning Korean intellectuals, who had maintained their nationalist stance despite being jailed at various points of their lives, 'converted' to faith in the Japanese Empire at the outbreak of the Second Sino-Japanese War. Their writings, briefly reviewed previously, show that while they ostensibly expressed their support for the East Asian Community initiative, it was clearly as a means of achieving their own goals: the recovery of full sovereignty and autonomy of the Korean people, the realisation of Korean political subjectivity. Their strategies did not work and the unity of the Japanese and Koreans were never realised in the manner they hoped for. However, it is important to acknowledge in thinking about political modernity in East Asia that these intellectuals subjectively engaged with the dominant, imperial discourse and sought ways to utilise it to advance their causes. For this is clearly an exercise of subjectivity, the hallmark of being modern. Moreover, it was pursued in a particular mixture of nationalism and religion.

The East Asia League in China

While the East Asian Community initiative, which met an immediate rejection in China, achieved limited and brief traction in Korea under Japanese rule, the East Asia League movement led by Ishiwara Kanji, a general in the Imperial Japanese Army and one of the main plotters of Mukden Incident of 1931, which effectively led to war with China, gathered some support. The movement was officially launched by the establishment of the Association for the East Asia League in Tokyo in 1939 but it is reported that Ishiwara started to develop the initial ideas for the East Asia League soon after the Mukden Incident, when he became involved with an organisation to promote co-operation between Japan and Manchuria established in 1932 (Saga 2015). As it is widely known, Ishiwara, an arch-supporter of the occupation of Manchuria at the time of the Mukden Incident, turned out to be a supporter of Muchuria's independence emphasising the slogans such as 'five races under one union' and 'ideal state through ethical and just rule' soon after the establishment of Manchukuo. The East Asia League, as envisioned by Ishiwara in response to Konoe's statements on a new East Asian order, had three principles in order to achieve peace: joint defence of Japan, Manchuria and China, economic integration of three countries and political independence of all. The League is framed in the discourse of ethical and just rule, the Kingly Way, (*wangdao*), a tradition in Confucian teaching and what Sun Yat-sen advocated. This was evident in the speech by Wang Jingwei, who headed the East

Asia League in China established in 1941 in Nanjing. Wang linked the East Asia League vision with Sun Yat-sen's Greater Asianism by evoking Sun's emphasis on the Kingly Way in order to strengthen the idea of China's equality to Japan (Cho 2007; Saga 2015).

However, Saga (2015) points out a twist added by the supporters of the Association: in the framework of the East Asia League movement, the discourse of ethical and just rule was not treated as an element of Confucian tradition but a superimposition of the righteousness of the Japanese emperors' rule on to the old idea of ethical and just rule. While this clearly represented a manipulation of the Confucian tradition by the Japanese intellectuals, it also made the supporters of the movement reject imperialist invasion of Asia; since the emperor's rule was moral and just and based on the ideal of multi-national harmony, disrespecting other people's independence necessarily meant disrespect for the emperor. The East Asia League movement therefore presented a slightly more acceptable face of nationalism/imperialism to people in East Asia.

In place for a conclusion

The all too brief and incomplete review of various ways in which ideas associated with Asianism and the philosophy of world history circulated and interacted with the colonised and oppressed suggests several things about ideas and their unintended consequences. Asianism, or in the guise of Sun Yat-sen's Greater Asianism (which should mean 'to treasure the East Asian world following the ideal of ethical and just rule' but often misunderstood (Wang 2015), was mobilised by both Japanese and colonial intellectuals to present their vision of a more just world. The idea of the world-historical standpoint, a shorthand for a range of ideas developed mainly by the Kyoto School in response to Japanese militaristic and imperialist expansion, for instance, is very complex and it contains contradictory orientations. The philosophy of world history is at one level a conscientious engagement with the idea of history from a philosophical angle and it also contains serious questioning of the existing order in which taken-for-granted western hegemony including capitalism, imperialism, communism and totalitarianism is challenged. At the same time, the way the world-historical standpoint was developed was clearly to justify why Japan had to lead the reformation of the world order contradicting the universalistic and cosmopolitan orientation embedded in the philosophy of world history. This inherent contradiction contained in the philosophy of world history or the world-historical standpoint was the key to opening a possibility for the colonised in Korea, Taiwan, China and Southeast Asia to become 'true subjects of history' by developing their own articulation of subjectivity. The philosophy of world history invited the colonised in the Empire to identify with Japan as a way of overcoming modernity, a modernity of the West, so as to gain full subjectivity. Because of this appeal to universalism, it legitimated the colonial intellectuals' call for equality and respect for their autonomy in the development of subjectivity (Isomae 2010). The colonial intellectuals briefly examined in this chapter exercised agency as self-determining beings by combining what was imagined by Japanese imperialists with their understanding of civilisational past and of western-originated discourses such as Marxism and liberalism.

This theoretical risk for the oppressor and an opportunity for the oppressed was in part realised as seen in the ways in which Taiwanese, Korean and Chinese intellectuals try to turn the table round by adopting the ideas, be it the world-historical standpoint, the East Asian Community initiative or the East Asia League movement. These ideas may not have been produced to support primarily Japanese hegemony, but they were produced in a specific socio-historical condition, and inevitably had elements of supporting or justifying Japanese imperial expansion and ultimately the Pacific War. However, efforts by Sun Yat-sen, Tsai Pei-huo, So In-Sik, Kim Myeong-Sik, Chong-sik and Cha'a Chae-jŏng show that the colonised still maintained the capacity to exercise their agency to be a true subject of history rather than passively accepting what had been imagined for them by the westerners. They saw an opportunity to make use of the Japanese imperial ideas to their advantage. Whether this is interpreted as an authentic use of weapons of the weak or traitorous collaborating action is not relevant here; the fact that these efforts did not result in clear outcomes that worked in the favour of Chinese or Korean people is beside the point. The point is that ideas, because of their open nature, prepare a space in which even the oppressed can engage with subjectively. Granted, those who were engaged in this type of activity were limited to a small number of intellectuals, whose experience was not probably fully representative of that of the oppressed. Still they had potential to inspire and guide certain responses to hegemonic domination. Paying attention to this potential in investigating the workings of nationalism, imperialism and/or domination is at the same time an act of reminding ourselves that the oppressed retain at least a degree of agency, and fully accounting for it probably means paying due respect to the subject of investigation.

Finally, returning to the questions the volume raises, the following can be suggested. Asianism as conceptualised in the chapter represents a combination of religion and nationalism; as it is framed by civilisational discourse, it is evidently developed in opposition to nationalism as a western materialism/secularised nation-state model while drawing from spiritual/ethical elements deemed to define the essence of the East. Still it presents 'Asia' as a totalised community, a nation writ large. As such, Asianism is used by various intellectuals to advance nationalist causes embedded in a quasi-cosmopolitan context. Asianism, therefore, serves as another example how religion as fragmented narratives feeds into nationalism as a totalising concept. This further suggests that not only the secularised nation-state model benefits from religion but also religion would counter-intuitively find more space in the former. This is because, as the introduction to the volume has clearly pointed out, it is impossible to apply a definition of religion as developed in the West to the non-western part of the world.

Notes

1 In this chapter, the term 'Asianism' is used as an umbrella term to refer to what is variably called 'Asianism', 'pan-Asianism' and 'Greater Asianism' in order to secure a level of clarity to the discussion.

2 The chapter is concerned that the colonised are not often seen as true subjects of history as protested by Partha Chatterjee (1993: 5): 'If nationalisms in the rest of the world have to choose their imagined community from certain "modular" forms already made available to them by Europe and the Americas, what do they have left to imagine?'
3 For a discussion of the 'post-western' and how it differs from the 'non-western' within the context of International Relations see Shani (2008).
4 The discussion here is based on the Japanese version translated by the Ministry of Foreign Affairs of Japan and collected in *The Collected Works of Sun Wen* published in 1967. Translation from Japanese to English is mine.

References

Anderson, Benedict. 1991. *Imagined Communities: Reflections on the Origin and Spread of Nationalism*. Revised ed. London: Verso.
Ch'a Chae-jŏng. 2004. '"A New East Asian Order and Renovation" in Tobe, Hideaki "Historical Documents and Witness Accounts I: Debates on the East Asian Community by Korean Intellectuals During the Second Sino-Japan War: Commentary",' *Quadrante* (6): 368–372.
Chatterjee, Partha. 1993. *The Nation and Its Fragments: Colonial and Postcolonial Histories*. Princeton, NJ: Princeton University Press.
Cho, Kwanja. 2004. 'The Philosophy of History of So, In-Sik: The Impossibility of World History and *My Fate*' (in Japanese), *Shisō* (957): 29–54.
Cho, Kyŏng-dal. 2007. 'The Expansion of the Japanese Empire and Korean Intellectuals: On the East Asian Community and the Unity of the Japanese and Koreans' (in Japanese), in Ken Ishida (ed.), *Bōchō suru teikoku/kakusan suru teikoku: Dainiji sekaitaisen ni mukau nichiei to ajia (The Expanding Empire/Diffusing Empire: Japan, Britain and Asia on Their Way to World War II)*. Tokyo: University of Tokyo Press, pp. 163–201.
Doak, Kevin. 2007. 'The Concept of Ethnic Nationality and Is Role in Pan-Asianism in Imperial Japan,' in Sven Saaler and Victor Koschmann (eds.), *Pan-Asianism in Modern Japanese History: Colonialism, Regionalism and Borders*. Abingdon: Routledge, pp. 168–181.
Duara, Prasenjit. 1995. *Rescuing History from the Nation: Questioning Narratives of Modern China*. Chicago: Chicago University Press.
———. 1996. 'Historicizing National Identity or Who Imagines What and When,' in Geoff Elley and Ronald Suny (eds.), *Becoming National: A Reader*. Oxford: Oxford University Press, pp. 151–177.
———. 1999. 'The Theories of Nationalism for India and China,' in Tan Chung (ed.), *In the Footsteps of Xuanzang: Tan Yun-Shan and India*. New Delhi: Gyan Publishing House.
———. 2002. 'The Discourse of Civilisation and Pan-Asianism,' in Roy Starrs (ed.), *Nations Under Siege: Globalization and Nationalism in Asia*. New York: Palgrave Macmillan, pp. 63–101.
———. 2003. *Sovereignty and Authenticity: Manchukuo and the East Asia Modern*. Lanham, ML: Rowman and Littlefield.
Esenbel, Selçuk. 2010. 'Pan-Asianism and Its Discontents,' *International Journal of Asian Studies*, 7(1): 81–90.
Eisenstadt, S. E. 2000. 'Multiple Modernities,' *Deadalus*, 129: 1–29.
Freeden, Michael. 1998. 'Is Nationalism a Distinct Ideology?' *Political Studies*, 46(4): 748–765.
Frey, Marc, and Soakowsiki, Nicola. 2016. 'Introduction,' in Marc Frey and Nicola Soakowsiki (eds.), *Asianisms: Regionalist Interactions and Asian Integration*. Singapore: National University of Singapore Press, pp. 1–18.

Gellner, Ernest. 1983. *Nations and Nationalism*. Oxford: Blackwell.
Horio, Tsutomu. 1994. 'The *Chūōkōron* Discussions, Their Background and Meaning,' in James Heisig and John Marald (eds.), *Rude Awakenings: Zen, the Kyoto School and the Question of Nationalism*. Honolulu: University of Hawai'i Press, pp. 289–315.
In, Chong-sik. 2004. ' "The Reorganisation of East Asia and the Koreans" in Tobe, Hideaki "Historical Documents and Witness Accounts I: Debates on the East Asian Community by Korean Intellectuals During the Second Sino-Japan War: Commentary",' *Quadrante* (6): 356–368.
Isomae, Jun'ichi. 2010. '*Overcoming Modernity* and the Kyoto School: Modernity, Empire and Universality,' (in Japanese) in Naoki Sakai and Jun'ichi Isomae (eds.), '*Kindai no chōkoku' to kyōto gakuha: kindaisei/teikoku/huhensei ('Overcoming Modernity' and the Kyoto School: Modernity, Empire and Universality)*. Tokyo: Ibun-sha, pp. 31–73.
Kim, Myeong-Sik. 2004. ' "The Awareness of Construction and Advancement to the Continent", in Tobe, Hideaki "Historical Documents and Witness Accounts I: Debates on the East Asian Community by Korean Intellectuals During the Second Sino-Japan War: Commentary",' *Quadrante* (6): 353–356.
Kōsaka, Masaaki, Nishitani, Keiji, Kōyama, Iwao, and Suzuki, Shigetaka. 1943. *Seiakshiteki Tachiba to Nihon (The World-Historical Standpoint and Japan)*. Tokyo: Chūōkōron-sha.
Koyasu, Nobukuni. 2007. 'The Time of The Philosophy of World History: The "World-Historical Standpoint and Japan" symposium' (in Japanese), *Gendaishisō*, 35(8): 8–17.
Ministry of Foreign Affairs (trans. and ed.) 1967. *Sonbun Zenshū (The Collected Works by Sun Wen)*. Tokyo: Hara-shobo.
Oota, Ryōgo. 2014. 'Miki Kisyoshi and Ozaki Hidemi: Isolated Intellectuals and the Discussions of the "East Asian Community",' (in Japanese) in Kyŏng-dal Cho, Keiichi Harada, Yūjirō Murata, and Tsuneo Yasuda (eds.), *Kōza: Higashi ajia no chishikijin (Series: Intellectuals of East Asia)*, vol. 4. Tokyo: Yūshisha, pp. 252–268.
Saaler, Sven, and Christopher, Szpilman. 2011. 'Introduction: The Emergence of Pan-Asianism as an Ideal of Asian Identity and Solidarity, 1850–2008,' in Sven Saaler and Christopher Szpilman (eds.), *Pan-Asianism: A Documentary History, Vol. 1: 1850–1920*. London: Rowan and Littlefield, pp. 1–41.
Saga, Takashi. 2015. 'The East Asian League Movement and China' (in Japanese), *Hōgakukenkyū*, 88(8): 51–86.
Shani, Giorgio. 2008. 'Toward a Post-Western IR: The Umma, Khalsa Panth, and Critical International Relations Theory,' *International Studies Review*, 10(4): 722–734.
Shani, Giorgio and Kibe, Takashi. 2019. 'Introduction,' in Giorgio Shani and Takeshi Kibe (eds.), *Religion and Nationalism in Asia*. London: Routledge.
So, In-Sik. 2004. ' "The Whole and the Individual in Culture" in Tobe, Hideaki "Historical Documents and Witness Accounts I: Debates on the East Asian Community by Korean Intellectuals During the Second Sino-Japan War: Commentary",' *Quadrante* (6): 372–382.
Suzuki, Sadami. 2010. 'The Overcoming Modernity Thesis in Inter-war and Postwar Years,' (in Japanese) in Sadami Suzuki and Kenki Ryū (eds.), *Higashiajia ni okeru kindai shogainen no seiritsu (The Genealogy of Various Concepts of Modernity in East Asia)*. Kyoto: International Research Centre for Japanese Studies, pp. 9–65.
Szpilman, Christopher. 2007. 'Between Pan-Asianism and Nationalism: Mitsukawa Kametarō and His Campaign to Reform Japan and Liberate Asia,' in Sven Saaler and Victor Koschmann (eds.), *Pan-Asianism in Modern Japanese History: Colonialism, Regionalism and Borders*. Abingdon: Routledge, pp. 85–100.
Tobe, Hideaki. 2004. 'Historical Documents and Witness Accounts I: Debates on the East Asian Community by Korean Intellectuals During the Second Sino-Japan War: Commentary,' *Quadrante* (6): 339–352.

Tsai Pei-huo. 1920. 'Our Island and Ourselves' (in Japanese), *Taiwanese Youth*, 1(4): 13–24.
———. 1937. *Tōa no ko kaku omou (Thus Thinks the Child of East Asia)*. Tokyo: Iwanami-shoten.
van der Veer, Peter. 2013. 'Nationalism and Religion,' in John Breuilly (ed.), *The Oxford Handbook of the History of Nationalism*. Oxford: Oxford University Press, pp. 655–671.
Wang, Ke. 2015. 'The "Kingly Way" as a Shared Knowledge of East Asia: The Contract Between Humanity and the Nature' (in Japanese), *Asteion* (82): 173–187.
Williams, David. 2004. *Defending Japan's Pacific War: The Kyoto School of Philosophers and Post-White Power*. London: RoutledgeCurzon.
Workman, Travis. 2013. 'So In-sik's Communism and East Asian Community (1937–40),' *Positions*, 21(1): 133–160.
Yokoji, Keiko. 2004. 'The Magazine, *Taiwanese Youth*: Its Overlapping Networks at Its Base' (in Japanese), *Border Crossings: The Journal of Japanese-Language Literature Studies*, 1: 155–170.
Yonetani, Masafumi. 2005. '*The Philosophy of World History* of the Colony/Empire' (in Japanese), *Nihonshisōshigau* (37): 11–19.

8 Religious nationalism with non-domination
Ahn Changho's cosmopolitan patriotism

Jun-Hyeok Kwak

Within the confines of Western political philosophy, religion has been frequently regarded as the very means of providing peoples with a strong commonality. This way of understanding about the role of religion in society is not limited to those groups who consider themselves chosen peoples (*goy qadoshi*), that is, nations chosen by God. In many different periods of ancient and modern Western political philosophy, religion was thought to foster a sense of duty to one's fellows. For instance, Aristotle believes that impiety diminishes the unity of a political community (Aristotle 1932: 1262a25–1262a32). The assumed role of religion in reinforcing civic affection was persistently syncretized with the notion of the Christian love (*caritas*), as we can see from Augustine's letter to Marcellinus (Augustine 1994: 205). And one of the most sophisticated cases can be found in Tocqueville's *Democracy in America*, where he argues that religion can moderate individualism by cultivating civic solidarity between peoples in a political community (Tocqueville 2000: 417–424).

Current theories of nationalism have a similar view of religion and its role in a political community. On the one hand, religion has been understood as a social institution whose political function in a society is analogous with nationalism. At this juncture, religion and nationalism are essentially identical, since both are perceived to form a distinctive collective identity and a specific communal obligation. For instance, Anthony Smith emphasizes the religious quality of nationalism in his theory of the ethnic origins of nations, calling nationalism a 'new religion of the people' (Smith 2003: 9–43). Many scholars have developed further arguments in which nationalism supplants religion with the myth of ethnic election (Gorski 2003; Riesebrodt 2006; Derrida 1998). Actually, nationalist narratives and national movements that displayed messianic tendencies and myths of divine selection have emerged everywhere, not only in Savonarola's 'New Jerusalem' but also in the modern analogies of medieval Christian millennialism (Anderson 2012: 150–247; Goodblatt 2006: 167–203; Weinstein 1970; Kedourie 1960: 32–61).

On the other hand, it has been argued that religion supplements secular politics. The recent theories of religious nationalism can be included in this category, since they present religion as an alternative to secular nationalism if the latter failed to offer a legitimate foundation of political power and a set of moral orders (Barker 2009; Rieffer 2003; Friedland 2001; Juergensmeyer 1993). Actually, scholars of religious nationalism believe that religion can shape a form of collective commonality by which nation-state, territory, and culture are thoroughly renewed. For instance, Rieffer argues that people desire to acquire not merely national sovereignty but religious recognition through national commonality (2003: 225). In a similar vein, Friedland maintains that "religious nationalism is a form of politicized religion, one in which religion is the basis of political judgment and identity, indeed in which politics take on the quality of a religious obligation" (2002: 139).

Religion undoubtedly functions to create a collective commonality which can be either analogous with or substitutable for secular nationalism. In particular, the recent turn of religious nationalism enables us to make a distinction between those groups who are fundamentally religious and those who are politically religious. Nevertheless, the compatibility of religious nationalism with universal values, such as human rights, still needs to be satisfactorily answered. Though conceptualized with a unique Western experience, the very idea of love of humanity is nonetheless global in reach. Respect for human rights has bolstered the idea of peaceful coexistence, although the different understandings of human rights have frequently embraced cultural tensions. The self-confirmation of militant nationalism is no less intriguing to many people who see the construction of the nation-state in the guises of human rights. Therefore, what we need at this juncture is to find a regulative principle with which religion can shape a collective commonality without degenerating into a bellicose chauvinism.

Based on these observations, this chapter examines Ahn Changho's writings, which reflect not only the longing for national independence but the aspiration of peaceful coexistence in Northeast Asia. Although it has been frequently noted that the connection between Ahn's advocacy of national independence and his suggestion of humanitarian cosmopolitanism may have been much closer than is usually assumed, there were only a few scholarly attempts to examine his conception of non-domination in terms of a coherent logic creating a synthesis of elements widely regarded to be mutually exclusive. By juxtaposing Ahn's political thoughts with the ideal of non-domination, I make the following two claims. First, I will argue that Ahn adheres to the politics of non-domination that gives epistemological coherence to his ideas, ranging from the advocacy of national independence to the assertion of peaceful coexistence in Northeast Asia. As we shall see subsequently, different from the general trend of Korean nationalists thoroughly overwhelmed by the Social Darwinian quest for power after the March First Movement, Ahn holds fast in the spirit of the movement which countered the politics of domination at the time. Second, I will maintain that Ahn's conception of non-domination, embodied in his religious aspiration for innocent humanity, demonstrates the need for overcoming the simple antimonies between patriotism and cosmopolitanism. Ahn's cosmopolitan patriotism sheds light on the ideal of non-domination as a regulative principle that can help better prevent nationalistic agitation for liberation from degenerating into a pursuit of domination.

Christianity and the March first movement

The March First Movement in 1919 was a turning point in the history of Korean nationalism, since it instilled the moral cause of self-determination in the struggle for national independence (Park 2000: 35–95). Different from the previous resistances after the 1905 Protectorate Treaty, more than a million people participated in the movement.

This movement, accompanied with the common people, continued until the summer of 1919 even under the violent crackdowns of the Japanese colonial government. And, stimulated by the popular aspirations for national liberation and self-government during the movement, the Shanghai Provisional Government, which was the most supreme and imperative among provisional governments, was organized in 1919. It can be said that the movement was successful, in the sense that it fostered full-blown constitutional debates among independent activists of all ideological stances, by giving them the inspiration for the need for creating a new state (Ko 1997; Lee 1997). However, the movement as a political bid for national independence was unsuccessful, since it could neither repudiate the foreign domination nor gain the support from the Great Powers at the Paris Peace Conference.

The political failure of the March First Movement apparently spurred the predominance of the Social Darwinian quest for power under which most of Korean nationalists at the time sought to debunk cosmopolitan humanism and humanitarian pacifism (Kwak 2008; Park 1992). This trend was no exception for the Christian nationalists, who had led the strategy of 'gradualism' which put forward the need for self-strengthening cultural and economic power rather than an armed struggle for national independence. As is widely known, Christian groups took a crucial role in organizing the movement. 16 out of 33 national representatives who signed the March First Declaration were Christians, and 24% of those imprisoned were Christians (Park 2000: 517).[1] But the fierce suppression of the movement, followed by the severe crackdown of the Japanese colonial government over Christian churches, twisted the Christian impetus for national independence by reconfirming the validity of gradualism among Christian nationalists. In a greater or lesser degree, the central figures of the Christian gradualists – which have been named by historians as 'cultural nationalists' – swung like a pendulum between the two extremes of reinforcing the project of self-strengthening and voicing publicly the impossibility of national independence. Ultimately, the Social Darwinian quest for power, which was entrenched in the psyche of Korean nationalists at the time, directed these extreme dispositions of the Christian gradualists to the pessimistic view of national independence.

Yi Kwangsu, a Protestant Christian nationalist who relentlessly insisted a gradualist project of cultural self-reconstruction before the March First Movement, is an exemplary figure in this respect. His *Kobaek* (Confession), in particular, clearly shows the idiosyncratic switch of the Christian gradualists after the movement.

> Self-determination was nothing but words, and it ultimately ended up dividing the land of the loser. Neither the promised freedom nor self-governing

authority was given to the people of India, who shed blood fighting for Great Britain. Rather, they were suppressed by military force, and their leader, Gandhi, was imprisoned. Come to think of that, there was no one who could deliver independence, in the name of self-determination, by taking Korea from Japan, one of the Allied Powers.

(Yi 1962a [1948]: 262, my translation)

In this memoir written after the national liberation of Korea in 1945 to justify his pro-Japanese collaboration, Yi tries to elaborate his conversion to the Japanese imperialism as a tactical decision by devaluing the movement as a futile endeavor. Although he admits the moral legitimacy of the movement, Yi chiefly portrays the movement as a reckless confrontation with the stronger. Especially, as indicated by the expression of "blood fighting," he pejoratively defines the doctrine of non-violence postulated by the national leaders of the movement as nothing but a politically naïve strategy whereby he alludes to his conversion as an inevitable strategic choice driven by the realistic recognition that the actualization of self-government for a weaker nation is nothing but an illusion.

Such a pessimistic view of national independence was shared widely with the Christian gradualists, especially those who refused to take part in the March First Movement. They reinstated the idea of cultural self-reconstruction through Christianity, and along the same line they urged a sincere belief in Christianity for its own sake (Wells 1990: 82–137; Kim 1989: 83–89). There was a tactical goal set by them which corresponded to something realistic in their situation (Robinson 1988: 137–166). However, their ideal of self-reconstruction as a tactical goal was impracticable from the very outset, since its realization thoroughly depended on the arbitrary will of the stronger. At this juncture, Yun Chiho's *Diary* is revealing.

I gave my three reasons for disapproving the movement. (1) The Korean question will have no chance for appearing in the Peace Conference. (2) No nation in Europe or America will run the risk of fighting Japan for Korean independence. (3) When a weak race has to live with a strong one, the best policy for the weak is to win the good will of the strong.

(March 6, 1919: Yun, *Diary* 7:264)

Yun Chiho, one of the most influential leaders of Christian gradualism during the Japanese colonization, overtly laments that the diplomatic goals of the movement were unattainable. In addition, he steps further to contend that the destiny of the weaker nation should be entrusted to the stronger. It can be said that his interview with the *Keijo Daily News* – the official bureau of the Japanese governor-general of Korea – was prudently intrigued for avoiding an unnecessary trouble under the strict censorship. But (1) and (2) were mentioned again and again in his *Diary* (7:257–293), and (3) was also brought up frequently in various contexts especially after the Japanese invasion of Manchuria in 1931. For instance, criticizing Rev. Frank Buchman and his 'Moral Re-Armament' movement, he reveals his strong conviction of Social Darwinism: "Moral Re-Armament will bring no real world peace until great nations make first Economic Redistribution just and fair to all" (March 14, 1940: Yun, *Diary* 11:276). The upshot is that the pessimistic view of national independence interwoven with the Social Darwinian quest for power paved a way toward the fatal political fault that the Christian gradualists did not hold to the future goal of national independence.

After the outbreak of the second Sino-Japanese War in 1937, Yi Kwangsu voluntarily adopted Japanese imperialism. In a similar vein, Yun Chiho plumply spoke out the impossibility of national independence as well as the inevitability of the subjection of Korea to the Japanese Empire. Interestingly enough, they perceived Japan as a new empire through which their aspiration for survival as well as domination could be realized.

> Through taking part in the establishment of the Greater East Asia Co-prosperity Sphere, Koreans as subjects of the Japanese Empire become the masters and the leaders. They become the gubernators of all nations in East Asia. Have Korean ever been endowed with such a great mission before? Their glorious status can only be acquired when Koreans are subordinated to the Japanese emperor. Now, we have the tie of all times.
> (Yi 1962b [1941]: 152, my translation)

As we can see, Yi argues that the future of the Korean people does not depend on national independence but on its incorporation into the Japanese empire. The motivation for such statement does not appear to be simply driven by the fear of Japanese colonial control but by his longing for being a member of the powerful empire. We can find a similar statement from Yun's *Diary*.

> Fifty-six years ago when I first went to Shanghai I was deeply grieved to see a long shingle with these words in Chinese and English "No dogs and Chinese are admitted," hung at the entrance to the part just across bridge over the Soochow Creek as you went into the proud English settlement. . . . Now Japan has risen almost unconsciously to tear their shingle down and say to the white race: "Live and let live." Oh, I pray that Japan may succeed.
> (December 11, 1941: Yun *Diary* 11:408)

The Japanese empire was the manifestation of an Asian empire Yun Chiho yearned for. Thus, for him, the assimilation of Koreans into the Japanese empire was rather an opportunity not only to become the leader of civilization but also to create a new civilization. At this juncture, voluntary subjection could be justified under his aspiration for domination, a civilization-leading power.

Certainly, the cases of Yi and Yun cannot rule out the diverse groups of Korean Christianity and their evolutions during the Japanese colonization. However, they throw light on the degeneration of the Christian gradualists whose patriotic agitation for self-reconstruction was steadfastly empowered by Social Darwinism. With respect to religious nationalism, their distinctive peculiarities can be summarized in the two aspects. First, their pathos of distance from a direct confrontation with Japan after the March First Movement was not driven by Christian faith in divine justice but by the pessimistic view of national independence. Although their relentless urge of self-reconstruction echoed a similar voice by the Churchless (*mukyokai*) Christianity in early Showa Japan, they did neither wish to prioritize love of God over love of the world nor to withdraw themselves from politics.[2] Their real motivation for self-reconstruction was chiefly shaped through the desire to find Christian sources that they considered necessary for modernizing Korea. Second, their Christian faith was not enough to tame their longing for domination. Although Christian identities were clear in their sociopolitical statements, their Christian faith was not so much salient as their conviction of Social Darwinism. Ironically, their Christian faith functioned later as a leitmotif for their deference of Japanese imperialism. For them, Japan was the most successful example of industrial modernization in East Asia and by the same token, Japan was a chosen nation to cope with the conquering Western nations. At this juncture, a religious faith could not regulate their desire for domination which was expected to be realized through the subordination to the stronger.

Non-domination in Ahn Changho's patriotism

Ahn Changho (1878–1938) has been controversial chiefly due to his close relationship with the Christian gradualists, particularly Yi Kwangsu (1892–1950).[3] Certainly, Ahn and Yi had a lot in common between them in addition to their Christian identity. Both of them were born in the northwestern province of Korea, whose sociopolitical voices were marginalized before the Kanghwa Treaty in 1876. And they shared with one another an immense sensitivity to the problems of the traditional Korean society, which was a typical mindset of intellectuals in the region virtually affected by its locality in the border between China and Korea. Their recognition of Korea as a periphery of the world facilitated their receptiveness to foreign cultures and ideas, and their Christian faith mediated individuality and collectivity in their considerations of subjectivity on the one hand and particularity and universality in their pursuits of modernity on the other hand (Jung 2014: 9–16, 154–204). As a matter of fact, the sociopolitical inclinations which were in common between them include their thoughts over personal liberty, self-reformation, self-strengthening, and modernity. But Ahn did not share the pessimistic view of national independence which was predominant among the Christian gradualists after the suppression of the March First Movement:

> The day of March 1st is the most sacred day. It is the birthday of liberty, equality, and justice, which has been approved by Heaven. This day was not determined by one or two persons but by the twenty million Koreans, and it was not done by voices but actualized by the blood of impeccable men and women.
> (Ahn 1990[1920]: 143, my translation)

At the anniversary of the March First Movement in 1920, Ahn recalls the spiritual gist of the movement which compounded the principles for self-government along with the need for national independence. Especially, as we can see from the previous passage, he emphasizes the fact that the movement was carried out by the common people. Different from the Cultural gradualists who looked down on the capability of the common people, he elucidates the fact that the movement was accompanied with the awakened masses. Furthermore, contrary to the Christian gradualists whose cultural projects for self-reconstruction were gradually dissociated from the vision of national independence through direct struggle for liberation, Ahn believes that a direct confrontation with the foreign domination was not inimical to the realization of national independence. For him, "blood fighting" during the movement was neither a "futile endeavor" nor a "politically naïve strategy" but a historical achievement for uplifting the national consciousness of the Korean people.

Ahn's distinctively optimistic view of national independence was firmly anchored in his idea of non-domination. Although he was also preoccupied with Social Darwinism in forming his circumstantial judgments over Korea, his vision of national independence never gave way to the idea of the impossibility of national independence. His persistent appeal to self-reconstruction was clearly based on his abhorrence for any sort of enslavement. By the same token, any idea inviting foreign powers for national independence was unquestionably reprimanded.

> We are facing with an urgent situation in which all of us will become slaves and thereby our nation will be annihilated. . . . Should the independence of Korea give rise to any benefit for their national interests, the superpowers would help us out. If otherwise, there wouldn't be any reason for them to help us. Rather they would use violence against us. . . . Let's gear up for war against foreign powers in the future.
> (Ahn 1907: 24, 27, my translation)

Lamenting the military incapability of Korea to wage war against foreign powers, Ahn claims that strengthening ourselves rather than seeking assistance from superpowers is the only way to secure self-government against the coercive interference of foreign powers. Different from Yun, who envisaged the benevolence of foreign powers for modernizing Korea (Yun *Diary* 2:58), he clearly delivers a sharp reproach against the idea that "our nation will be happy through collaborating with Japan" (Ahn 1907, 27). For him, the intervention of any superpower including Japan in Korea is nothing but the dire enslavement of the Korean people by foreign domination.

> We are the people who are free, thus we shouldn't act like slaves. Because what can command us should be solely each individual's consciousness and reason, we must not let ourselves follow any individual or any association slavishly. We are the owners of Korea, thereby we don't have to boast about personal contribution as an employee does. If all goes well with Korea, it will be enough [for our rewards].
> (Ahn 1990[1924]: 10, my translation)

As seen previously, the incapability of self-government is portrayed through the image of enslavement, and the reproach against any type of enslavement repeats again and again, and it ultimately culminates in the spirit of national independence. For Ahn, as his contribution to the establishment of the Shanghai Provisional Government shows (Lee 2017; Ko 2000), the most imperative condition with which the moral and material foundations for national independence could be actualized should be the establishment of a "democratic republic" that was defined with the ideal of non-domination (Ahn 1990 [1919]: 100). Shortly put, his vision of national independence was articulated with the ideal of non-domination which was postulated by him to play an important role in securing individual as well as collective freedom.

The upshot is that not only did Ahn insist on self-strengthening a credible background for national independence but his vision of national independence was firmly anchored in his ideal of non-domination. The ideal of non-domination shaped through his awareness of the enslavement of Korea by foreign domination led him to incorporate as sources for national independence that the cultural gradualists would ordinarily exclude: the direct confrontation with foreign domination and the positive view of national independence. He thought of the pessimistic view of national independence as the "fatal disease" caused by spiritless despair that should be overcome by strenuous preparation for war against foreign domination (Ahn 1907: 27). Although he was also preoccupied with Social Darwinism, his project of self-reconstruction did not degenerate into the envisagement of foreign assistance or the theory of the impossibility of national independence. Furthermore, the ideal of non-domination also led him to suggest a democratic republic in which all including the common people should be placed in an equal and free footing. All in all, his longing for national independence and his desire for self-government were mediated through the ideal of non-domination. In this context, it is not surprising to see that his vision of national independence was gradually evolved into the hope for the establishment of an "exemplary democratic republic" (Ahn 1990 [1919]: 10).

Cosmopolitan patriotism with love of humanity

According to Maurizio Viroli, the republican aspiration for self-rule – as opposed to the nationalistic agitation for liberation – situates the idea of the republic conceptualized with liberty as non-domination within the patriotic love of a self-governing political community (Viroli 1995: 9–10). What is clear in all cases, however, especially with respect to national liberation, is that whatever the difference of national independence from republican self-rule, the longing for "freedom from foreign domination" is of necessity shared in common. And when a shared national culture is emphasized as something indispensable for democratic solidarity and self-government, the distinction between patriotism and nationalism becomes so blurred that the conflation of the former into a mere emotive underpinning for the latter or vice versa appears to be inevitable (Miller 1995: 17–80, 2000: 81–96). Furthermore, the conflation of patriotism into nationalism can be intentionally devised by political actors who seek to realize the republican ideal of self-government in the process of nation-state building (Kwak 2014: 29–33).

Ahn's cosmopolitan patriotism in this regard is peculiar. His vision of national independence was always associated with his desire for self-government, and his longing for self-rule was firmly anchored in his ideal of liberty as non-domination.

> What we can trust and want is nothing but "our strength." Independence genuinely means to live with and rely on my own strength. In contrast, it is slavery to trust and rely on others' power.
> (Ahn 1990 [1920]: 413, my translation)

As mentioned before, Ahn was also captivated by Social Darwinism. The aforementioned phrase "rely on my own strength" is certainly grounded in the Social Darwinian quest for power, and the notion of trusting "my own strength" suggests that his conception of self-rule is directly or indirectly interwoven with the theory of capacity omnipotence. However, portraying dependency as a form of slavery to the arbitrary will of others, he differentiates his vision of national independence from other nationalists who championed the quest for power beyond self-preservation or self-government.

> We should be ready for military struggle. If our task cannot be accomplished peacefully, we should carry it out militarily. Some might laugh at us, but the blood of humanity and justice can defeat Japan's strong military power.
> (Ahn 1990 [1919], 101, my translation)

For Ahn, self-government does refer to the very condition of non-domination in which "we do not live at the mercy of the powerful and thereby we live in accordance with laws we give ourselves." In the similar vein, he considers military preparations for national independence to be solidly fixed in the principles of humanity and justice. In this reasoning, the restoration of national independence must exhort not only loyalty to a particular nation but also a universal duty to promote justice in the world. In other words, one's special affection for a particular country should be concurred with the principle of humanity and justice.

More importantly, empowered and enforced by Ahn's Christian faith, all converged into a genuine request for love for humanity. As widely known with his commitment to Heungsadan (Yong Korean Academy), he consistently suggested "the cultivation of mutual love" (*Jungui-donsu*) as a necessary remedy for the incompetence of Korean nationality. His conception of "mutual love" was vested primarily with the Christian charity (*caritas*) of humanity, but being combined not only with Confucian "filial piety" but with the Buddhist concept of "mercy" (Ahn 1990 [1926]: 1–20). At this juncture, his conception of "mutual love" retained the ideal of non-domination in an unaltered form.

> When we were deeply moved for the sake of the love of our nation, we heard [this idea] like a voice in the desert saying "water." But the desperate longing

for love in our society became too common to keep its genuine sincerity and authenticity; now it sounds like looking for "water" in the Yangtze River. So I am asking you what kind of love we are longing for. No one looks for true love in its genuine meaning. This is because we are fallen into selfishness that betrays the central tenet of Christianity, which is love for all people.

(Ahn 1990 [1919]: 120, my translation)

Faced with the reluctance of Korean Christians abroad to take part in the struggle for national liberation, he urges them to prioritize national independence over personal prosperity. For winning over them, he puts forward the Christian "love" defined later by him as "the essence of Christianity from Genesis to Revelation" (Ahn 1990 [1919]: 120). At the same time, as we can see from the previous quote, he employs the Christian neighborly love, whose object is ultimately eternity, to transform selfish craving for material gain to altruistic love for the fatherland. For him, the Christian neighborly love reaches at its highest good in the secular world when it contributes to liberating Koreans from their enslavement by Japan. Along the same line, he repeats that the divinely imposed goal of love cannot be attained by the pursuit of national liberation without a love for humanity.

I don't want to see Japan perish. Rather I want to see Japan become a good nation. Infringing upon Korea, your neighbor will never profit to you. Japan will profit by having 30 million Koreans as her friendly neighbors and not by annexing 30 million spiteful people into her nation. Therefore, to assert Korean independence is tantamount to desiring peace in East Asia and the well-being of Japan.

(Quoted from An 1971 [1932]: 34)

He highlights previously that the exhortation of national independence rooted in love of the fatherland can be supported by the Christian neighborly love, only when it is not disentangled with the ultimate devotion to love for humanity. Needless to say, his account of peaceful coexistence in East Asia contains love for humanity that simultaneously evokes the vivid hope for reciprocal non-domination between countries in the region. In brief, the divine sources of humanitarian pacifism enabled him to build a bridge between love of the fatherland and love for humanity, thereby backing cosmopolitan patriotism as the divine reciprocal duties of nations and presenting his vision of national independence as a means of realizing the ideal of non-domination.

Ahn's advocacy of "mutual love" as a prerequisite for national independence is similar to Mazzini's exhortation of love for humanity. As is widely known, Mazzini rejected both groundless cosmopolitanism and ethnocentric nationalism: "On the one hand, there are those who have sought to rouse the people in the name of humanity without teaching them about their fatherland. On the other hand, there are those who have been speaking of nationality without any reference to the law of humanity (umanità). In the first case, the movement lacked both starting point and a means of support; in the second, it lacked an ultimate purpose"

(Mazzini 2009 [1860]: 53). In a similar vein, Ahn considers love for humanity, granted by God, as the regulative principle designed to steer nationalism into universalistic criteria. In this proposition, there is no discrepancy between patriotic duty to establish a just state and humanitarian duty to pursue peaceful coexistence. In his ideal of non-domination, no legitimate patriotic pursuit can be directed to national independence and human prosperity without a love for humanity, which is incorporated into the Christian neighborly love and thereby is equally shared by all human beings.

As mentioned earlier, the Christian gradualists whose guiding principles lacked an immanent logic that could regulate their insatiable quest for power ended up with the idiosyncratic pursuit of domination through subordination. Their initial pessimistic view of national independence after the March First Movement was incorporated into their unilateral deference to Western imperial powers firstly and their banal idea of imperial intervention for modernizing Korea later. Such a desire for domination can be found in other Korean nationalists who were exhaustively preoccupied with Social Darwinism. Their desperate resistance against the Japanese imperialism during the wartime period inevitably counteracted cosmopolitan pacifism. Their skepticism about the feasibility of peaceful coexistence was incorporated into their reformation of Korean nationality by denying the backward elements of traditional culture while appealing to genuine national traits formed throughout history (Shin 2006: 41–56; Schmidt 2002: 139–198). In this degeneration of Korean nationalism into ethnic nationalism, the gradual eclipse of non-domination from nationalist discourses contributed to the incorporation of the quest for power into the moral causes of the struggle for national independence.

In contrast, Ahn's vision of national independence which was also grounded in the Social Darwinian quest for power was effectively attuned by his Christian love for humanity to the pursuit of non-domination. As we have seen so far, his patriotism was framed in terms of the permissibility of accepting other nations as neighbors, and it was ultimately aimed at ensuring peaceful coexistence, rather than domination or conquest. In his cosmopolitan patriotism, the ideal of non-domination that evolved through his awareness of the enslavement of the Korean people by foreign domination successfully steered his Social Darwinian quest for power within the boundary of national self-determination. He derived his thoughts about love for humanity from exhaustive reading of the Christian Bible. As clearly demonstrated by his emphasis of "mutual love" in his speeches, he was particularly impressed by the Christian neighborly love in the New Testament. In this context, the idea of imperial intervention for modernizing Korea was reproached straightforwardly, and the struggle for national independence without considering any substantial sense of moral or ethical loyalty to humanity was rejected decisively.

Conclusion

This chapter has sought to present Ahn Changho's cosmopolitan patriotism as an alternative to the realistic pessimism of the Christian gradualists empowered by the Social Darwinian quest for power and its degeneration to the politics of domination through the subordination to Japanese imperialism. As the Christian gradualists, especially Yun Chiho, wished to reform the Korean society with Christianity, Ahn also appealed to the cultural and political sources of the Western Christianity in a way to replace the traditional representations of Korean neo-Confucianism with the modern reflections of individual freedom. In a paradoxical way, drawing on the Christian sources of modernization which were taken by him as the viable means for national independence, Ahn sought to overcome the Western incursions with the Western modernity, which simultaneously was envisioned as the trajectory of Korean modernity from enslavement to non-domination. In essence the Christian gradualists failed to keep the vision of national independence, for they looked to power to provide a confirmation of Korean modernity. On the contrary, regulated by the Christian neighborly love for humanity, which was enforced by his ideal of non-domination, Ahn's preoccupation of Social Darwinism was directed to the cosmopolitan patriotism with which he pursued not only the national independence of Korea but the peaceful coexistence with other neighboring countries in East Asia including Japan. At this juncture, Ahn's religiosity shaped through the Christian neighborly love for humanity functioned as a regulative principle that constrained his militant pursuit of national independence within the ideal of non-domination.

There has been a good deal of discussion of religious nationalism in which religion may be justified as the moral and political foundation for collective commonality. Ahn Changho's cosmopolitan patriotism offers us a set of insights for the current debate on religious nationalism. First, a religious claim for national commonality should be driven as a regulative principle that prevents secular politics from leading to regressive consequences rather than a prophetic vision for establishing a chosen nation. A religious form of collective commonality, in which group identity is culturally embedded in the practice of the political community, is not sufficient to regulate its possible degeneration to the tyranny of collective selfishness whose justification by virtue of belonging to the religious group is chiefly conceptualized in a prophetic disguise of special particularity. Second, the compatibility of religious nationalism with universal values such as human rights and democratic deliberation needs to be considered more seriously as an imperative measure for its political soundness. Ahn's Christianity in his cosmopolitan patriotism was concretized and articulated with a set of sociopolitical principles successfully underpinning the ideal of non-domination. In the ideal of non-domination, exemplified by his awareness of the enslavement of Korea by Japan as well as his pursuit of peaceful coexistence with Japan, the Christian neighborly love functioned to regulate his revolutionary militarism in significant ways. Certainly, there have been various endeavors to see about the role of religion in moderating the chauvinistic propensity of collective commonality. However, these attempts need to be accomplished together with a scholarly endeavor to find a regulative principle with which religion can help better shape a collective commonality without degenerating it into a bellicose exclusion. In this context, I suggest that the combination of religiosity with non-domination might be a viable approach to religious nationalism.

Notes

1 The number of Christians arrested during the movement outnumbered the total number of the other religious groups arrested including Chondogyo (the Way of Heaven Religion), and defined by the Japanese colonial government as bases for the movement, 47 churches and 2 church-affiliated schools were burned (Lee 2017; Kentaro 1955).
2 During the Japanese colonization period, there was a group of Christians who followed the founder of the Churchless Christianity in Japan, Uchimura Kanzo. Identifying Korea with ancient Israel in Egypt, this group advanced a prophetic vision for national liberation. Different from the Christian gradualists analyzed in this chapter, this group kept hold to the goal of national independence (Wells 1990: 94–98, 133–137). Some scholars have tried to take account of this group as an example of the religious indifference to politics in Korean Christianity at the time. But their sources are not so much reliable, since they are biased in favor of the missionary reports which were couched exceptionally in religious passion. According to Shogimen (2010), the Churchless Christianity in Japan was bifurcated after the death of Uchimura in 1930. One accommodated with the Japanese imperialism by symbolizing religious indifference to politics as an ingenuity of Christianity, while the other advocated a "true" patriotism as opposed to the Japanese government during the wartime period. Both the Cultural gradualists and the Churchless Christian group in Korea can hardly be identical with either Churchless group in Japan.
3 Ahn's lifetime cooperation with the cultural gradualists has been taken by some historians as an indication of his "possible" collaboration with Japan or an evidence of his admiration for Japan for its modernization. For instance, taking the same speech in 1907 quoted later in this section, Seo Joong Seok maintains that Ahn stood by Japan for its imposition of the new protectorate treaty with Korea in 1907 (Seo 2007: 28–29, 15). However, his interpretation is textually groundless at least in the speech taken by him as an example for Ahn's pro-Japanese deviation. As we can see later, by saying "they wish to rely on someone who cannot be trusted," Ahn sharply criticizes the idea of collaboration with Japan for its imprudence (Ahn 1907, 27). Although Ahn kept hold to his cosmopolitan patriotism grounded in love for humanity, he never gave up the vision of national independence (Kim 1996: 135–169, 249–268). In this context, Ahn's militarism needs to be examined closely together with his moral pacifism. Regarding Ahn's revolutionary militarism, see Pak (2012).

Bibliography

Ahn, Changho. 1907. 'Yeongsul [Speech],' *Seo-U.*, 7: 24–27.
———. 1990. *Ahn Changho Junjip 2* [Works of Ahn Changho 2]. Ed. Ahn Changho Memorial Foundation. Seoul: Bumyangsa.
Anderson, Baden P. 2012. *Chosen Nation*. Eugene, OR: Cascade Books.
An, Pyong-Uk. 1971. 'Tosan: The Man and His Thought,' *Korea Journal*, 11(6 June): 33–42.
Aristotle. 1932. *Politics*. Trans. H. Rackham. Cambridge, MA: Harvard University Press.
Augustine. 1994. *Political Writings*. Trans. Michael Tkacz and Douglas Kries. Indianapolis, IN: Hackett.
Barker, Philip W. 2009. *Religious Nationalism in Modern Europe: If God Be for Us*. London: Routledge.
Derrida, Jacques. 1998. 'Faith and Knowledge: The Two Sources of "Religion" at the Limits of Reason Alone,' in Jacques Derrida and Gianni Vattimo (eds.), *Religion*. Stanford, CA: Stanford University Press, pp. 1–78.
Friedland, Roger. 2001. 'Religious Nationalism and the Problem of Collective Representation,' *Annual Review of Sociology*, 27: 125–152.

Goodblatt, David. 2006. *Elements of Ancient Jewish Nationalism*. New York: Cambridge University Press.
Gorski, Philip. 2003. *The Disciplinary Revolution: Calvinism and the Rise of the State in Early Modern Europe*. Chicago: University of Chicago Press.
Juergensmeyer, Mark. 1993. *The New Cold War? Religious Nationalism Confronts the Secular State*. Berkeley, CA: The University of California Press.
Jung, Joo-a. 2014. *Seobookmunhak-kwa Locality* [The Literature of Korea's Northwestern Province and Its Locality]. Seoul: Somyung.
Kedourie, Elie. 1960. *Nationalism*. London: Hutchinson University Library.
Kentaro, Yamabe. 1955. 'San-ichi undo ni tsuite [On the March First Movement],' *Rekishigaku Kenkyu*, 185, July: 13–28.
Kim, Hyung-chan. 1989. 'Portrait of a Trouble Korean Patriot: Yun Ch'i-ho's Views of the March First Independent Movement and World War II,' *Korean Studies*, 13: 76–91.
———. 1996. *Tosan Ahn Ch'ang-ho: A Profile of a Prophetic Patriot*. Seoul: Tosan Memorial Foundation.
Ko, Jung-hyoo. 1997. 'Seching Hansungjungbu Jojikjuchewa Sunpokyeongwuie deahan Gumto' [Investigation on the Organizing Subject of Hansung Provisional Government and Its Establishment Process], *Hankooksa Yeongu*, 97: 167–201.
———. 2000. 'Danhanminkuk Imshijungbuui Tonghapjungbu Suripundonge Deahan Jaekumto' [Reconsideration on the United Movement of the Korean Provisional Government in Shanghai], *Hankookhyeondaesa Yeonku*, 13: 34–71.
Kwak, Jun-Hyeok. 2008. 'Domination Through Subordination: Yi Kwangsu's Collaboration in Colonial Korea,' *Korea Observer*, 39(3): 427–452.
———. 2014. 'Patriotism and Nationalism: "Republican Patriotism" in the Northeast Asian Context,' in Jun-Hyeok Kwak and Koichiro Matsuda (eds.), *Patriotism in East Asia*. London: Routledge, pp. 28–45.
Lee, Hyeon Joo. 1997. 'Samilundongjikhu Kookmindaehoewa Imsijungbu Suripundong' [On the National Convention Right After the March First Movement and Provisional Government Movement,' *Hankook Kunhyundaesa Yeongu*, 6: 111–159.
Lee, Ki-baik. 1984. *A New History of Korea*. Cambridge, MA: Harvard University Press.
Lee, Man-yol. 2017. 'Samilundongui Jongkyosajuk-jungchisajuk Uiyi [The Significances of the First March Movement in the History of Religion and Political History],' *Kidogkyo Sasang*, 699: 7–17.
Lee, Yun-gab. 2017. 'Dosan Ahn Changhoui Minjokundongkwa Konghwajuui Shiminkyoyuk' [Ahn Changho's National Movement and Republican Civic Education], *Hankukhak-nonjip*, 67: 37–92.
Mazzini, Giuseppe. 2009[1836]. 'Humanity and Country,' in Stefano Recchia and Nadia Urbinati (eds. and intro.), *A Cosmopolitanism of Nations*. Princeton, NJ: Princeton University Press, pp. 53–65.
Miller, David. 1995. *On Nationality*. New York: Oxford University Press.
———. 2000. *Citizen and National Identity*. Cambridge: Polity Press.
Pak, Jacqueline. 2012. 'The Ahn Changho Controversy: Rescuing a Patriot from Colonial and Postcolonial Myths,' *The Journal of Northeast Asian History*, 9(2): 181–227.
Park, Chan Seung. 1992. *Hankuk Geundae Jeongchisasang Yeonku* [Study on Modern Political Philosophy Korea]. Seoul: Yeoksa Bipyeong.
———. 2000. 'Iljae jibaeha hankuk minjokjuuiui hyungsungkwa bunhwa' [Development and Diversification of Korean Nationalism under Japanese Domination], *Hankukdoklipundongsa yeonku*, 15: 35–95.

Park, Yong-Shin. 2000. 'Protestant Christianity and Its Place in a Changing Korea,' *Social Compass*, 47(4): 507–524.
Rieffer, Barbara Ann. 2003. 'Religion and Nationalism: Understanding the Consequences of a Complex Relationship,' *Ethnicities*, 3(2): 215–242.
Riesebrodt, Martin. 2006. 'Religion in Global Perspective,' in Mark Juergensmeyer (ed.), *The Oxford Handbook of Global Religions*. New York: Oxford University Press, pp. 597–610.
Robinson, Michael. 1988. *Cultural Nationalism in Colonial Korea, 1920–1925*. Seattle, WA: University of Washington Press.
Schmid, Andre. 2002. *Korea Between Empires 1895–1919*. New York: Columbia University Press.
Seo, Joong-Seok. 2007. *Korean Nationalism Betrayed*. Trans. Do-Hyun and Pankaj Mohan. Kent, CT: Global Oriental LTD.
Shin, Gi-Wook. 2006. *Ethnic Nationalism in Korea: Genealogy, Politics, and Legacy*. Stanford, CA: Stanford University Press.
Shogimen, Takashi. 2010. '"Another" Patriotism in Early Showa Japan (1930–1945),' *Journal of the History of Ideas*, 71(1): 139–160.
Smith, Anthony. 2003. *Chosen Peoples: Sacred Sources of National Identity*. New York: Oxford University Press.
Tocqueville, Alexis de. 2000. *Democracy in America*. Trans. Harvey Mansfield and Delba Winthrop. Chicago: University of Chicago Press.
Viroli, Maurizio. 1995. *For Love of Country: An Essay on Patriotism and Nationalism*. New York: Oxford University Press.
Wells, Kenneth M. 1990. *New God, New Nation: Protestants and Self-Reconstruction Nationalism in Korea 1896–1937*. Honolulu, HI: University of Hawaii Press.
Weinstein, Donald. 1970. *Savonarola and Florence: Prophecy and Patriotism in the Renaissance*. Princeton, NJ: Princeton University Press.
Yi, Kwangsu. 1962a. *Yi Kwangsu Jeonjip* [Works of Yi Kwangsu] *7*. Seoul: Samjungdang.
———. 1962b. *Yi Kwangsu Jeonjip* [Works of Yi Kwangsu] *10*. Seoul: Samjungdang.
Yun, Chiho. 1986. *Yun Chiho's Diary Vol. 2, 7 & 11*. Ed. Kuksapyunchan Yuiwonhoe [National Compilation Committee], available at: http://db.history.go.kr (accessed 12 February 2019).

9 The structural problem of religious freedom in China
Toward a Confucian-Christian synthesis

Zhibin Xie

The problem defined

According to Rogers Brubaker's summary, the model of "religion as a cause or explanation of nationalism" is one of four approaches to the problem of religion and nationalism. This model is meant that "religious traditions have shaped particular forms of nationalism." "Religion contributed to the origin and development of nationalism not only through the political appropriation of religious symbols and narrative but also in more indirect ways" (Brubaker 2012: 6). For example, the Protestant Reformation contributed to nationalism "by generating new models of imagining and constructing social and political relationship" (Brubaker 2012: 6) Religious beliefs and religious community have an affinity with political community; it is in this sense I will in this chapter explore the structural problem of religious freedom in China – namely, the relationship of the state and social institutions (including religious ones) – from religious and ethical perspectives.

In his "A Research Agenda on Religious Freedom in China," Fenggang Yang lays out three aspects of religious freedom to be understood in China: conception, regulation, and civil society (Yang 2013). This general understanding may suggest scholarly study in these areas from philosophical, political, legal, sociological perspectives, among others. One major concern of these studies is how the Chinese government regulates religious activities and affects the development of religious groups. As I see it, the state plays a critical role in determining the space of religious practice and social impact in China. Still, someone may suggest that "religious freedom is not merely a nice thing tolerated by the state," as "religious communities are historically and ontologically prior to the modern state, and their autonomy deserves protection from overreaching political authorities" (Hertzke 2013: 6, 7). When reviewing the church-state issues in China and comparing them with the principle of church-state separation, Christopher Marsh and Zhifeng Zhong mention, "Under a system of church-state separation, the success and failure of religious organizations is in the hands of the people, not the state," and "The state's role is simply that of providing a system of religious liberty while also ensuring the public welfare" (Marsh and Zhong 2010: 42). An undeniable fact in China is that the survival and influence of religious believers and communities have always wrestled with the state. "In such a highly centralized political country as China, religion has had little chance to become independent of the state" (Yao and Zhao 2010: 128).

The current Chinese government's treatment of religion tends to be pragmatic. It neither encourages religion nor attempts to eliminate it, but requires religion to cooperate with the government under the principle of "accommodation of religion to socialist society," particularly underlying religious contribution to the government's expectation of social harmony. The state's tolerance of religion extends to certain officially recognized religions and their normal activities within the structure of state-sanctioned religious organizations. In principle, the state makes constraints on political appeals by religious believers, while managing religious affairs to ensure religious contribution to national well-being rather than placing emphasis on how to guarantee the freedom of the individual to choose his or her own faith and concrete practice.

I have to place great emphasis on the role of the state when thinking about the scope of free religious practice, growing religious interaction with government, and religious dynamics in Chinese society today. The focus of this article is to give a structural analysis of the relationship between the state, religious communities and other social institutions in an authoritarian state like China with the state's strict restrictions (Grim and Finke 2011: 120–159), yet with religious revival, growing religious dynamics and the demand for more autonomy. For this purpose, I attempt to integrate Confucian ideas of the state and association (including religious) with a Christian social theory of the state and social institutions in order to work out a proper philosophical and theological interpretation on the structural problem of religious freedom (the role of the state in particular) in China, with respect to traditional Chinese cultural and religious resources, political order, and the current religious situation.

There have been some comparative studies between Confucianism and Christianity regarding the ideas of god, worldview, human nature and some practical issues such as ecological ethics. Yet there is not much work on the dialogue on social and political theory between the two. Here I attempt to work in this line to develop and integrate both sources addressing religious freedom in China. What brings in Confucian and Christian resources in this study derives from my following research concerning: (1) the Confucian tradition regarding the space between state and family, (2) the problem of justification for religious autonomy, and (3) state authority toward religious exercise. I will try to show some complementary points between two regarding the problem of religious freedom in China.

Confucian idea of the family, state and association

Even though it is hard to give an exact measure on how much Confucian ideas impact political structure (including political arrangement of religious affairs) in communist China, I agree with Daniel A. Bell's position regarding Confucianism's far-reaching influence in East Asian societies, which states that "Rather than condemn any deviations from liberal goals, anybody who wants to engage with East Asian societies in respectful ways must understand the Confucian ethical thinking that informs social and political practices in that region" (Bell 2008: xi).

In the first place, Confucianism "takes as its theoretical and practical basis the natural order of things in human society: the family, neighbor, kinship, clan, state and world" (Tu 1994: 181). This order focuses on moral cultivation at all levels of society. Personal moral cultivation beginning with family life extends to the community in order, and then to rulers of the state, which require certain institutions such as "community schools, community compacts, local temples, theater groups, clan associations, guilds, festivals, and a variety of ritual-centered activities" (Madsen 2008: 9).

Under this framework, "Confucianism in many ways modeled its understanding of the state on its understanding of the family. In Confucianism, the ruler is unambiguously represented as the parent of the people, which reinforces an organic view of society as an enormous quasi family with the ruler as its paterfamilias" (Nosco 2008: 25). The Confucian state is expected to exercise parental function and the government has the power in controlling all social affairs, including religious ones. Under a wider administrative network, "religious attachment to the state is part of an overall ruling strategy" (Yao and Zhao 2010: 128). Of course, state authority and its goal to rule have roots in the moral and spiritual cultivation of the human person and his or her conformity to social norms, which serve to maintain a certain social order. As Desheng Zhang says, "Confucianism employs the ideal of value consensus, which focuses on the subjection of individual to social norms. If each person obeys the norms, order will be developed accordingly" (Zhang 2008: 181).

The basic purpose of social order which is attained by individual's conformity to social norms is stability and harmony rather than general solidarity. The pursuit of steady social order in Confucianism "overrides the affirmation of the conflict between personal interests and the attention to social equality" (Zhang 2008: 111). However, the principle of solidarity is to include strangers equally based on overcoming individual differences.

The ideals of social norms, stable social order and personal conformity to society enforced by Confucianism are binding together by the principle of the priority of totality. As Zhang Desheng states, "Confucianism always sees things from the totalistic perspective, viewing individuals as inseparable parts of society. This view results in the structural flaw of considering society solely without taking individual interest into account" (Zhang 2008: 180). From a sociological perspective, immersed in Confucianism, traditional Chinese society is a "large-community-centered society and these communities restrain individual rights and personal development. This rules out the space of the development of individual rights and personality and even reduces the space of autonomy of smaller communities" (Qin 2011: 277).[1]

We may see that due to emphasis on the totality, it is hard to find sufficient resources in Confucianism which support the development of small communities or organizations. Two points should be noted here regarding the Confucian idea of state and society. One is its focus on a stable society with a common moral basis. The other is the absence of an independent status of voluntary associations; all voluntary associations benefit from the state and yet the state is not out of necessity to form any voluntary or communal associations, which remain always subject to the state's control.

According to C. K. Yang's interpretation, the state's dominance over social organizations constrains the development of religious and other groups: "When voluntary religion was developed, it faced a well-entrenched political institution that had long assumed a controlling position over religious matters" (Yang 1961: 211–212). Another factor contributes to the limited independent organized religious organization (with separate functions and structure) is the diffused character of classic religion in China: "the classic religion in its actual operation was largely diffused into the social institutions, and thus it was not independent institutional religion competing against other religions" (Yang 1961: 21).[2]

Two other Chinese thinkers account for the absence of organizations in Chinese tradition. A Chinese philosopher, Shuming Liang, gives his famous account on his understanding of Chinese social structure compared to the Western one: Chinese tradition concentrates on familial life surrounding certain ethical values; in the West, organizations based on professionals, locality and religious beliefs, etc., depart from familial structure (Liang 1990: 72). In his view, Christianity contributes much to the formation of associations with their scope beyond family chains and relations (in Chinese tradition, *guanxi*), in that the extending objects of religious beliefs bring about the expansion of social institutions.

Here is the sharp contrast between organizational life and familial life: "The difficulty of co-existence of organizational life and familial life demonstrates the absence of associational life in China. Developing from familial life, it is questionable not only to build up a country but also to construct a real large local autonomous institution" (Liang 1990: 78). It is observed that it does not leave much space for the formation of autonomous associations in Chinese tradition. Norman Stockman explains Shuming Liang's positions about Chinese perceiving of organization in the following:

> On the one hand, he claimed, China had only a weakly developed concept of the individual self, of individual rights, individual self-development and individual freedom from interference by others. On the other hand, he argued that China had only a weakly developed notion of group, the organization, and of society as a whole, that might enable mobilization for the pursuit of collective societal goals. What is central to Chinese society is the quality of human relationships.
>
> (Stockman 2000: 72–73)

A Chinese sociologist, Xiaotong Fei, shares the similar ideas with Shuming Liang on Chinese social structure regarding the association problem. He contrasts Chinese "differential mode of association" (*cha xu ge ju*) with "Western organizational mode of association": "In the pattern of Chinese organization, our social relationships spread out gradually, form individual to individual, resulting in an accumulation of personal connections. These social relationships form a network composed of each individual's personal connections" (Fei 1992: 79), while in Western society "personal relationships depend on a common structure. People attach themselves to a preexisting structure and then, through that structure, from personal relationship" (Fei 1992: 71) where organizational life has a central place in one's life: "individuals form organizations. Each organization has its own boundaries, which clearly define those people who are members and those who are not" (Fei 1992: 61–62). By contrast, "Chinese social patterns, unlike Western ones, lack organizations that transcend individual personal relationships" (Fei 1992: 76). In China, social relationships (starting from kinship) is concentric and self-centered: "it is like the circles that appear on the surface of a lake when a rock is thrown into it. Everyone stands at the center of the circles produced by his or her own social influence. Everyone's circles are interrelated. One touches different circles at different times and places" (Fei 1992: 62–63). In this sense, "Confucius's difficulty is that, with a loosely organized rural society such as China's, it was not easy to find an all-encompassing ethical concept" (Fei 1992: 75).

In their introduction to Xiaotong Fei's text in English, Gray G. Hamilton and Wang Zheng explain: "With this mode of association, the society is composed not of discrete organizations but of overlapping networks of people linked together through differentially categorized social relationships" (Hamilton and Wang 1992: 20). And, these networks have four key features: discontinuous (not in single systematic way), defined in terms of a dyadic social tie (gang), without explicit boundaries, and situation specific morality (Hamilton and Wang 1992: 20–24). These explain the Chinese differential mode of association as an egocentric system of social networks rather than group-orientated association. "This is a society in which considerations of order, not law, predominate; and in this context, order means – to paraphrase the *Xiaojing* (The Classic on Filial Piety) – that each person must uphold the moral obligations of his or her network ties" (Hamilton and Wang 1992: 24). Within this network structure, one's obligations to family and kinship have a priority to more distant network people. Besides the priority of obligations to family and kinship networks, thus the egocentric system of social networks, there exists control of these networks of relationships, "in the patriarchal control of the family, in the elder's control of villages, and in the notable's control of other kinds of associational networks" (Hamilton and Wang 1992: 29). Therefore, "As Fei describes them, Chinese political institutions work in the way his metaphor about the spreading ripples of water would suggest: from the inside out. Institutions of control in families and lineages are more important for establishing social order than are those in locales, which are in turn more important than those in more distant government locations. Ties of kinship and locale create core sets of ego-centric networks, which individuals can manipulate and expand to take advantage of economic and other kinds of opportunities" (Hamilton and Wang 1992: 30).

Both Liang and Fei attempt to develop the Confucian logic of social relationships, the relationships between person, family, social life and the state. In general, traditional China society was characterized by a stable and totalistic social order supported by certain social norms and moral cultivation at different levels of society and a concentration on familial life surrounding certain ethical values. This resulted in the weak development of organizational life beyond family and kinship relationship, concentric circles and an egocentric system of social networks rather than group-oriented association, control of networks of relationships, and even state control of religious and other organizations. All of these understanding of Chinese social structure are connected to the idea of Confucianism in different ways.

In communist China, as C. K. Yang describes, "while certain politically neutral religious beliefs can theoretically continue to have a measure of independent existence in the mind of the believer, the religious organization must structurally become a part of the Communist sociopolitical organizational system and accept strict control from the Communist authorities. For the Communists, the religious organizations, like any other social groups, constitute an integral part of society and its system of political authority, and there can be no organizational separation of religion and the state" (Yang 1961: 393). Religious organizations again serve as one chain in the state's holistic administrative work toward various social groups. "Through these government agencies, religious activities and organizations are controlled and directed so that they function as part of the Communist sociopolitical order" (Yang 1961: 394).[3] Due to the communist atheist ideology, there developed more suspicion of religious belief and practice, which led to further control over certain religious communities. As Zhang Qianfan and Zhu Yingping point out, "In recent years the religious associations in China have increasingly become quasi-state organizations, with their independence continually declining" (Zhang and Zhu 2011: 814). In this sense, all religious associations are subject to governmental management. C. K. Yang also highlights the persistent problem of religious autonomy in China: "organizational autonomy of religious bodies in the Western sense never existed under the traditional government, and certainly does not under the contemporary Communist rule" (Yang 1961: 393). The autonomy problem of religious organizations under state authority stands as a good example for the common problem of social organizations in contemporary China.

Today, the Chinese government and society have to face new religious realities which have developed since the 1980s: there emerge more dynamic religious communities in terms of their interactions with state and society, such as the ongoing unregistered church movement, religious negotiation with government and even resistance to state control for the rights, interests and organizational autonomy of religious communities, and increasing religious engagement in social and political life in China while social and collective expression of religion is subject to administrative management by the state. The consistent pattern of religion-state relationship is being challenged and the reality calls for a reconsideration of the role of the state and the identity of religious organizations as well in China.

Both Suming Liang and Xiaotong Fei specify the relevance of Christianity to Western social organizational structure, yet they do not go deep so far regarding its theological foundations. They are concerned with the relationships among personal, family, social life and the state, which need deeper elaboration. Questions remain about social organizations (seen from religious groups in particular) and their relationship with the state, in which we may see more clearly the characteristic and weakness of Confucianism. For this purpose, I attempt to develop the idea of the state and social institutions from Christian social theory in terms of the reformed principle of sphere sovereignty and the Catholic social doctrine of subsidiarity to see how they may work together in contributing to a remodeling of the state with particular attention to religious practice in China. The reasons for turning to Christian social theory are basically theoretical considerations due to its different approach to the state and social institutions from the Confucian one.[4] Meanwhile, I have something in mind that as a matter of fact, there are emerging some unregistered churches in China which are practicing in the Calvinist tradition and striving for new church-state interactions while some Christian lawyers are getting more actively involved in some human rights matters (see Chow 2014; Ma and Li 2014); there are also cases of Catholic churches (both open and underground ones) which seek "religious freedom and resist government control": "Pro-government groups that support the government are weak in the dioceses, whereas groups advocating stances of negotiation and opposition are strong" (Chan 2013: 134). To some degree, we may expect some theological practice among Chinese churches may exercise certain impact regarding their relationship to the state and society as well.

Christian perspectives on the state and social institutions

Christianity is distinctive in its perspectives on the state and its relationship to various social institutions including religious ones. Both the Reformed principle of sphere sovereignty and the Catholic social doctrine of "subsidiarity" propose the idea of social pluralism either at the horizontal or vertical level.

The doctrine of subsidiarity is primarily concerned with the relationship between the state and lesser communities in endorsing "a divinely ordered hierarchy of qualitatively different communities" (plurality of communities) and supporting the principle of non-absorption of lesser communities by greater ones (i.e., the maintenance of communities' separate identity and independent value). "The state has a duty to offer lesser communities such help as is needed in order for the latter to realize their distinctive ends" (Chaplin 1993: 182). In Jonathan Chaplin's summary, the state may perform enabling, intervening and substituting activities toward lesser communities to support their flourishing and the common good of society.

According to Patrick McKinley Brennan, there is both negative and positive sense in the principle of subsidiarity: negatively, "it is a principle of non-absorption of lower societies by higher societies, above all by the state," and positively, "subsidiarity is also the principle that when aid is given to a particular society, including the state, it be for the purpose of encouraging and strengthening that society; correlatively, flourishing societies contribute to the flourishing of the great societies of which they are so many irreducible parts" (Brennan 2014: 35). The principle of subsidiarity endorses certain functions of the state toward various communities while confirming their independent identity.

On the Protestant side, the principle of sphere sovereignty suggests that God alone possesses ultimate sovereignty and is the origin of all earthly sovereignties; our lives are divided into separate spheres, each with its own sovereignty. The principle has been significantly developed by John Calvin, Abraham Kuyper, Herman Dooyeweerd, and others. The development of this principle has attended to the relationship between all social institutions, each of which should work out its characteristic function without interfering in one another's functional exercise. For Kuyper, he affirms the independent character of social spheres: "In a Calvinistic sense we understand hereby, that the family, the business, science, art, and so forth all social spheres, which do not owe their existence to the state, and do not derive the law of their life from the superiority of the state, but obey a high authority within their own bosom; an authority which rules, by the grace of God, just as the sovereignty of the State does" (Kuyper 1931: 90). In other words, the sovereignty of the state must stand alongside with that of other social spheres, without being deducible from the family or other spheres, nor applied to other spheres.

In this vision, each sphere with its uniqueness is sovereign within itself while co-operating with each other. Particularly, the state as "the sphere of spheres" is not allowed to intrude in the laws of other spheres: "In this independent character a special higher authority is of necessity involved and this highest authority we intentionally call – *sovereignty in the individual social spheres*, in order that it may be sharply and decidedly expressed that these different developments of social life have *nothing above themselves but God*, and the State cannot intrude here, and has nothing to command in their domain" (Kuyper 1931: 91). Yet, standing alongside other spheres, the state as the unique public authority involves the task of balancing and protecting the diverse social spheres, while state intervention may take place in such circumstances as the conflict of spheres, the abuse of power on individuals by other members of the sphere, etc.

In affirming the diversity of social life, Dooyeweerd developed this principle in terms of the "creation's ontic structure" into differentiation of institutions and relationships particularly in a way of modal analysis. For him, that diversity has creationally normative meaning; that is, "Created reality displays a great variety of aspects or models of being in the temporal order" (Dooyeweerd 1991: 278). Each of God's diverse creations is bound by its own laws. Therefore, "sphere sovereignty points us to God as the author of all diversity and unity and meaning in life . . . Social diversity is always connected with creational unity from a Christian point of view . . . to see how the full diversity of social life should be developed properly, each according to its own created nature – science, art, education, economic enterprise, politics, and so forth. Sphere sovereignty is simply a shorthand phase to express the idea that a diversity of creational arenas call for human obedience to God as part of humanity's unified service to the Creator" (Skillen and McCarthy 1991: 403).

Deriving from this creational principle of unity and diversity, Dooyeweerd's peculiar contribution to the development of the idea of sphere sovereignty lies in his interpretation of modal structure of reality, the complex nature of the typical "identity structures" (or individuality structures) of social reality. "Each existing thing, including every social entity, reveals a distinct qualifying aspect while functioning in all the modal dimensions of the creation. For example, a family is 'qualified' differently than a state or a business enterprise. A family exists normatively as a community of kinship love. A state, on the other hand, is qualified by a guiding juridical norm" (Skillen and McCarthy 1991: 404). Again, family and state should be distinguished from each other, each law of which cannot be applied or extended to the other. "[E]ach is qualified by a different modal 'leading function' which is constitutive of its peculiar identity and purpose. Thus, when the 'whole' institution or organization is analyzed with regard to its sphere of responsibility (or sphere of sovereignty), it displays a typical character (a distinguishable 'identity structure')" (Skillen and McCarthy 1991: 404).

The institutions and relationship are to develop in terms of their being as creatures, and this kind of development recognizes the function of the existing reality (including social reality) and their determined features, on the one hand, and embodies as humans' obedience and service to God in created order, on the other. Dooyeweerd's interpretation of sphere sovereignty has implications for the distinction "between the 'whole/part' relationship and 'sphere sovereignty,'" with regard to the role of the state in particular: "This allows for a better understanding of how the state can, thorough public law, integrate into a community of public justice all other institutions and societal relationships without thereby reducing them to 'parts' of a single whole" (Skillen and McCarthy 1991: 407). This principle supports social diversity without being absorbed into political entity, while recognizing the "public-legal integrating functions of the state." For Chaplin,

> The state is not responsible for the *internal* legal domain of a social structure; it may not impose compulsory dieting on persons or families, or set prices for private industries. It lacks the competence to fulfill such internal responsibilities and is empowered only to establish legally the external, public conditions in which these can be adequately pursued. . . . The state is to create a network of just interrelationships between the various social structures and persons within its territory. Not only is the state to refrain from violating the sphere sovereignty for other spheres, but it is to prevent any other structure from violating such sphere sovereignty.
>
> (Chaplin 2011: 225)

From Kuyper and Dooyeweerd, the principle of sphere sovereignty informs the basic relationship among individuals, social institutions and organizations and the state, involving the issues such as individual capacity and responsibility, identity and structure of institutions, and the integrating function of the state under God's ordinances. It affirms the relatively independent character and diversity of social spheres of life while encouraging personal vocational responsibility in developing these spheres. The principle also serves as an idea against state sovereignty (or limiting the state's authority) and many forms of authoritarianism and totalitarianism. (Spykman 1976).

Both Christian principles of subsidiarity and sphere sovereignty on the state and social institutions support the plural structure of society and reject the absolutism of the state or the individual by seeking to strengthen intermediate associations and balancing diverse associations. It attempts to overcome the flaws and dangers from "individualistic" or "collectivist" deduction of social structure. While both principles have different angles on the state and social institutions, both support the plural structure of society and reject the absolutism of the state or the individual by seeking to strengthen intermediate associations and balancing diverse associations through "solidarity" (see Van Til 2008). Regarding the state function, recent studies show the commonality between these two principles and a point to a synthesis of them by suggesting a Christian social vision of empowerment and the state's occasional and exceptional intervention within the different spheres of society when the authority of that sphere is abused (see Weinberger 2014; Mcilroy 2003). Chaplin suggests that the acknowledged diverse communities must be enabled by the state to pursue their own particular purposes and state intervention happens when the common good is in deficiency or distortion (for the doctrine of subsidiarity) or the state must "coerce all citizens to bear personal and financial burdens for the maintenance of the natural unity of the state" (Chaplin 1993: 185, 191, 196–197).

These positions are implied to religious communities and their relationship with the state, especially in the case of church autonomy (see Van Der Vyver 2004). For Chaplin, the church-state relationship is the "central implication of sphere sovereignty, as we saw, that all social structures receive their authority directly from God. It is also true that the church possesses penal (though not physically coercive) sanctions (e.g., excommunication), though these must be governed by the faith of the church, not by political principles" (Chaplin 2011: 247). The state must respect and protect the sphere sovereignty of the church. Here church autonomy stands. "The unity of the church cannot be based upon any external political criterion but only upon the internal criterion deriving from its qualifying functions of faith" (Chaplin 2011: 248).

Reflection: a possible synthesis, and how much religious freedom is granted in China?

In this case study in the problem of religious freedom, I examine the nation-state issue in China in its interaction with society and religion and recognize the resources of Confucian understanding of family, state and social association. Meanwhile, I suggest that the shape of the modern nation-state in China should take into account the fact of arising social groups, including the dynamic of religious communities and religious perception of state and society. In my case, I introduce Christian social theory of the state and social institutions in dialogue with and further integration with Confucian resources in reshaping the role of the state encountering the demand of growing social life, religious life in particular. As Karrie J. Koesel claims, "In authoritarian regimes, religious communities tend to represent the most diverse and robust forms of associational life outside the state" (Koesel 2014: 3). I also suppose that no other groups have such a strong and deep concern and struggle with their own rights and autonomy as do religious groups, which demand for state's creating space for them. It is at this sense I propose any discourse on the national-state problem in China would be not inclusive without religious engagement.

To this end, this chapter is to search for some complementary points between Confucian resources and Christian social thought as a way to reconsider the structural problem of religious freedom in China, which recognizes their significant difference. It seems that both concepts of solidarity and state's interference serve as bridge concepts for this study. On the one hand, the Confucian paternalistic perspective concentrates on a common moral basis and state control as necessary for the good of the whole nation. The relationships between the person, family, other voluntary associations, and the state are regarded as concentric circles, thus these associations including religious groups have never gained their own independent status while being immersed into the whole sociopolitical order in traditional and present communist China. On the other hand, Christian social theory acknowledges one kind of specific "order" (laws-structure) within creation in different social entities and "solidarity" for common humanity in different social institutions at both horizontal and vertical levels. It distinguishes the authority of the state from that of other spheres including family. My concern here is how the Christian idea of the state and social institutions may contribute to China's remodeling the role of the state while the state's power and intervention will still be regulated, limited and effective, yet social institutions including religious groups will practice their relatively independent tasks.

The relationship of religion and state has developed in the forms of subordination, cooperation, negotiation and resistance among various religious groups in China. Yet, the state is far stronger in terms of power when compared to religion and by no means will the state lose its dominant position: "political control of the voluntary types of religion was a consistent pattern in Chinese history" (Yang 1961: 211). At this point, rather than exploring such ideals as freedom of conscience and individual choice, I hesitate and yet have to ask the more limited and modest question: how much freedom may religion receive from the state in China? It seems to me that real freedom is granted only with a certain cost, either through some kind of compromise or through a struggle for the sake of religious autonomy.

The question of autonomy of religious groups, alongside with other social organizations, raises the question of the identity structure of these social institutions: the origin of the diversity of social life, their independent character, their internal law-structure and finally their relationship to the state. At its root, it calls for ontological understanding of the plural social structure particularly so as not to dissolve this diversity into the political whole. If diverse social institutions exist as parts of a whole for the whole purpose, they will lose their independent status and their autonomous development together with individuals' different responsibility in these institutions. In confronting the distinctive and characteristic function of social institutions, it is not allowed to overstate the function of "the whole." At this point, as public authority, the state, through its public-integrating function, can protect and promote the plural social structure.

Today, many are concerned with limited freedom given to religious worship in China from the perspectives of the religion-state relationship, religious policy and even the rule of law. We have to acknowledge constraints on religious practice, the problem of autonomy of religious organizations in China in particular. However, besides the traditional religion-state framework still being effective in contemporary China, we have to take seriously the following aspects of reality: the constitutional protection of normal religious activities, religious revival and growth since the 1980s, the wide impact of religion to people's life, positive influence of religious moral teachings such as benevolence and tolerance and religious contribution to the cultivation of a good citizen in community. The Chinese government has officially affirmed the positive side of promoting economic, social, cultural development by religious groups, especially religious philanthropy concerning medical service, education support, environmental protection and poverty cure, etc. Here it is essential to affirm normatively the differentiation of social spheres (such as agriculture, industry, business, transportation, arts, media, education, etc.), which has taken place in contemporary Chinese society and tends to broaden in the future. In these emerging spheres, religion, through its various works, is expected to get more engagement, promote its influence, and develop more organically in a pluralistic-orientated Chinese society. Furthermore, religious groups, along with their social participation in different spheres, constitute an important component of China's emerging "civil society," which, in spite of the restrictions imposed by the state, manages to create a greater social space. The space of religious autonomy depends on its interaction with the state and society as well.

In contemporary China, both the state's regulation of religious affairs and recognition of positive religious resources (moral force in particular) in society, from my point of view, will lead to one kind of collaborative relationship between religion and state, within which I am more concerned with religious public engagement in Chinese society. Under general guidelines on religion's social participation from the state authority, there are certain social and public spaces for religious believers and groups to get actively involved rather than passively. They may creatively explore specific issues in various social spheres and develop strategies accordingly. It is also the responsibility for religious circles to work together with the authorities and other groups (religious and otherwise) to find out a consensus concerning the common good of the whole society deriving from their unique religious insights, while not compromising with the core interests defined by the state. Under these circumstances, Chinese government is expected to take into account new problems arising from religion's social engagement and open more public space for religious groups through dialogue with them.[5] This proposal emphasizes social and public space for religious engagement as well as religious contribution to social development, which is operated under the state's guiding framework of religious activities. It demands the state's constructive role in regulating social institutions while acknowledging their diverse existence and interaction among them, with its affirmation of religion as societal force and willingness to become more open and allow more space for religious engagement. It aims to expand the role of religion in the social and wider public realm. In this way, it is my hope to strengthen religious practice in their public dimension, and to transform traditional subordination of religion to political dominance through promoting religious vitality in public life and religious interactions with the state, so as to foster religious freedom in China so far.

Notes

1 Here large communities specify nation, while small organizations contains kinship associations (such as family, kinship) and non-communities, such as villages, diocese and professional associations, etc.
2 In Chinese society, the different forms of diffused religion are ancestor worship, the worship of community deities and the ethicopolitical cults (see Yang 1961: 295).
3 Governmental agencies mean the State Bureau of Religious Affairs, the Department of Religious Affairs in the provincial and municipal governments and various patriotic religious organizations at national and local levels.
4 I understand that some other ideological types such as Marxism give impact to the state-society structure in China. My study in this chapter is limited to the approach of two resources (Confucianism and Christianity) to this structure, their difference and possible synthesis, even though I take into account the existing communist ideology to some degree to develop my thinking.
5 As Karrie J. Koesel states, in China, "top-down policies were instrumental in lifting the lid on religion and creating greater space for religious actives" (Koesel 2014: 160). Through comparative studying religion-state relationship in China and Russia, Koesel proposes the space of one kind of cooperation relationship rather than one of domination or resistance between religion and the authoritarian state. While Koesel's study is a political approach, my concern with religion-state-society problem in China is philosophical and theological.

Bibliography

Bell, Daniel A. 2008. 'Preface,' in Daniel A. Bell (ed.), *Confucian Political Ethics*. Princeton, NJ and Oxford: Princeton University Press, pp. ix–xiv.
Brubaker, Rogers. 2012. 'Religion and Nationalism: Four Approaches,' *Nation and Nationalism*, 18(1): 2–20.
Brennan, Patrick McKinley. 2014. 'Subsidarity in the Tradition of Catholic Social Doctrine,' in Michelle Evans and Augusto Zimmermann (eds.), *Global Perspectives on Subsidiarity*. Dordrecht: Springer, pp. 29–47.
Chan, Shun-Hing. 2013. 'Civil Society and the Role of Catholic Church in Contemporary China,' In Francis K. G. Lim (ed.), *Christianity in Contemporary China: Socio-Cultural Perspectives*. New York: Routledge, pp. 123–137.
Chaplin, Jonathan. 2011. *Herman Dooyeweerd: Christian Philosopher of State and Civil Society*. Notre Dame, IN: University of Notre Dame Press.
Chaplin, Jonathan. 1993. 'Subsidiarity and Sphere Sovereignty: Catholic and Reformed Conceptions of the Role of the State,' in Francis P. McHugh et al. (eds.), *Things Old and New: Catholic Social Teaching Revisited*. Lanham, MD: University Press of America, pp. 175–202.
Chow, Alexander. 2014. 'Calvinist Public Theology in Urban China Today,' *International Journal of Public Theology*, 8: 158–175.

Dooyeweerd, Herman. 1991. 'Roots of Western Culture,' in James W. Skillen and Rockne M. McCarthy (eds.), *Political Order and the Plural Structure of Society*. Grand Rapids, MI: Eerdmans Publishing Company, pp. 265–297.

Fei, Xiaotong. 1992. *From the Soil: The Foundations of Chinese Society* (A Translation of Fei Xiaotong's *Xiangtu Zhongguo*, with an Introduction and Epilogue by Gary G. Hamilton and Wang Zheng). Berkeley and Los Angeles, CA: University of California Press.

Grim, Brian J., and Finke, Roger. 2011. *The Price of Freedom Denied: Religious Persecution and Conflict in the Twenty-First Century*. New York: Cambridge University Press.

Hamilton, Gary G., and Wang, Zheng. 1992. 'Introduction: Fei Xiaotong and the Beginnings of a Chinese Sociology,' in Fei Xiaotong (ed.), *From the Soil: The Foundations of Chinese Society*. Berkeley and Los Angeles, CA: University of California Press, pp. 1–36.

Hertzke, Allen D. (ed.) 2013. *The Future of Religious Freedom: Global Challenges*. New York: Oxford University Press.

Koesel, Karrie J. 2014. *Religion and Authoritarianism: Cooperation, Conflict, and the Consequences*. New York: Cambridge University Press.

Kuyper, Abraham. 1931. *Lectures on Calvinism*. Grand Rapids, MI: Eerdmans Publishing Company.

Liang, Shuming. 1990. *Collected Works of Liang Shuming*, vol. 3. Jinan, Shandong: Shandong People's Publishing House.

Ma, Li, and Li, Jin. 2014. 'Remaking the Civil Space: The Rise of Unregistered Protestantism and Civil Engagement in Urban China,' in Joel A. Carpenter and Kevin R. den Dulk (eds.), *Christianity in Chinese Public Life: Religion, Society, and the Rule of Law*. Basingstoke: Palgrave Macmillan, pp. 11–28.

Madsen, Richard. 2008. 'Confucian Conceptions of Civil Society,' in Daniel A. Bell (ed.), *Confucian Political Ethics*. Princeton, NJ and Oxford: Princeton University Press, pp. 3–19.

Marsh, Christopher, and Zhong, Zhifeng. 2010. 'Chinese Views on Church and State,' *Journal of Church and State*, 52(1): 34–49.

Mcilroy, David H. 2003. 'Subsidiarity and Sphere Sovereignty: Christian Reflections on the Size, Shape and Scope of Government,' *Journal of Church and State*, 45(4): 739–763.

Nosco, Peter. 2008. 'Confucian Perspectives on Civil Society and Government,' in Daniel A. Bell (ed.), *Confucian Political Ethics*. Princeton, NJ and Oxford: Princeton University Press, pp. 20–45.

Qin, Hui. 2011. 'From Large-communities-centered to Civil Society: A Reconsideration on Traditional China and Its Modernization,' in Zhenglai Deng (ed.), *State and Civil Society: Chinese Perspectives*. Shanghai: Gezhi Publisher and Shanghai People's Publishing House, pp. 266–278.

Stockman, Norman. 2000. *Understanding Chinese Society*. Cambridge, UK: Polity Press.

Tu, Wei-ming. 1994. 'Embodying the Universe: A Note on Confucian Self-Realization,' in Roger T. Ames, Wimal Dissanayake, and Thomas P. Kasulis (eds.), *Self as Person in Asian Theory and Practice*. Albany: State University of New York Press, pp. 177–186.

Skillen, James W., and McCarthy, Rockne M. 1991. 'Chapter XXI: Sphere Sovereignty, Creation Order, and Public Justice: An Evaluation,' in James W. Skillen and Rockne M. McCarthy (eds.), *Political Order and the Plural Structure of Society*. Grand Rapids, MI: Eerdmans Publishing Company, pp. 397–417.

Spykman, Gordon J. 1976. 'Sphere Sovereignty in Calvin and the Calvinist Tradition,' in David E. Holwerda (ed.), *Exploring the Heritage of John Calvin*. Grand Rapids, MI: Baker Book House, pp. 163–208.

Van Der Vyver, Johan D. 2004. *Leuven Lectures on Religious Institutions, Religious Communities and Rights.* Leuven: Uitgeverij Peeters.
Van Til, Kent A. 2008. 'Subsidiarity and Sphere-Sovereignty: A Match Made in ...,' *Theological Studies*, 69: 610–636.
Weinberger, Lael Daniel. 2014. 'The Relationship Between Sphere Sovereignty and Subsidiarity,' in Michelle Evans and Augusto Zimmermann (eds.), *Global Perspectives on Subsidiarity.* Dordrecht: Springer, 49–63.
Yang, C. K. 1961. *Religion in Chinese Society: A Study of Contemporary Social Functions of Religion and Some of Their Historical Facts.* Berkeley, CA: University of California Press.
Yang, Fenggang. 2013. 'A Research Agenda on Religious Freedom in China,' *The Review of Faith & International Affairs*, 11(2): 6–17.
Yao, Xinzhong Yao, and Zhao, Yanxia. 2010. *Chinese Religion: A Contextual Approach.* London: Continuum.
Zhang, Desheng. 2008. *Confucian Ethics and Social Order: A Sociological Interpretation.* Shanghai: Shanghai Peoples' Publishing House.
Zhang, Qianfan, and Zhu, Yingping, 2011. 'Religious Freedom and Its Legal Restrictions in China,' *Brigham Young University Law Review* (3): 783–818.

10 Augustine's critique of religious identity and its implications for the Chinese church

Wei Hua

Religious identity is conferred upon an individual or a group on the basis of their religious belief. In religious interactions or conflicts with other individuals or groups, a sense of identity will be manifested or strengthened (Sandwell 2007: 3–4). From the Roman Empire in the fourth and fifth centuries to China in the twentieth century, the propagation of Christianity has been marked by schismatic sects bearing different religious identities. Governments usually demanded religious identity to be subordinated to political identity and therefore favored compliant sects, while suppressing resistant ones, which inevitably led to serious political-religious problems.

The religious Roman North Africa in the fourth and fifth centuries was basically composed of traditional Roman religions, Catholic Christianity, the Donatists, and a relatively small number of Jews and Manichees. The Roman Empire made great efforts in the process of Christianization in order to replace traditional Roman religions with Catholic Christianity. Meanwhile, the Empire suppressed heresies and schismatics in order to reshape its subjects' national religious identity and maintain social harmony and local stability. The North African Catholic church actively participated in the religious affairs of the Empire, including giving their strongest support to the construction of such a unified identity and sharply criticizing the localized religious identity of the Donatists. While all claiming to be Christian, the Roman Empire, the Donatists and the North African Catholic church had different interests and different arguments for their religious identities. As a result, the religious interaction among them was beset with group conflicts and theoretical conundrums. It was in such a severe conflict that Augustine of Hippo criticized the arguments by which the Donatists and the Roman Empire constructed their own religious identities.

This chapter will examine the emergence of the Donatists and then discuss how Augustine, in supporting the unity of the Catholic church, criticized the Donatists' localized religious identity and argued for the priority of the Catholic faith with his theory of two cities. Reflecting on the fall of Rome in 410, Augustine eventually abandoned the early Christian political theology championed by Eusebius and Orosius, and argued that Christians' identity should be eternal and transcendental and could not be restrained by time or an earthly state. In light of Augustine's argument on the state-church relation, we will then seek a possible solution for the illegal status of Protestant house churches and underground Catholic churches in mainland China.

The Donatists: a schismatic sect in Roman North Africa

Donatism originated during Diocletian's ferocious persecution of Christianity in 303–305. Some bishops surrendered (*tradere*) holy Bibles and vessels to be destroyed by the government. Such an action was regarded as a mild form of apostasy. After the persecution, the North African Catholic church debated heatedly on the validity of sacraments, such as ordination and baptism, administered by these *traditores*. Some bishops and believers rejected the validity of these sacraments. Nor did they recognize the bishopric of Caecilianus, the new ordained bishop of Carthage. Although appealing to Constantine on this issue, they refused to accept the verdicts made by three synods organized by the emperor. This controversy led to the split of the North African Catholic church. In 313, Donatus the Great, a Berber by birth, succeeded as the bishop of the schismatic sect. Since then this sect was called the Donatists (*pars Donati*). In North Africa, the Catholic church received full support from the Christian emperors, but the Donatists disobeyed the edicts of unity and endured political repression for a long period (Frend 2003).

Despite numerous heresies and schisms, the Christian faith provided the subjects of the Empire with a unified religious identity. This unified identity carrying different localized characteristics gave local peoples a sense of "ontological security" (Kinnvall 2004: 741–767). As a regional church, the Donatists claimed that they were always loyal to the tradition of the North African church since Tertullian and Cyprian. They regarded the North African Catholic church as a puppet of the Italian church. By resisting the romanization of the North African church and the Catholic Christianization promoted by the Roman Empire, the Donatists shaped for themselves a new localized but more genuinely African religious identity. As the majority group in North Africa, they not only threatened the unity and the security of the Catholic church in North Africa, but seriously weakened the authority of the Christian emperors' edicts. Being proud of their localized religious identity, the Donatists were also potential supporters of political separatism and religious extremism which would erode the grass-roots governance, the regional peace, and the national unity of North Africa (Heyking 2001: 240).

The Roman Empire: state religion and political loyalty

Judaism was an ethnic religion of the Jews. With their ethnic religious identity, they hoped for the coming of the Messiah to usher in a Jewish, politically independent country. While abiding by the policy of religious tolerance and pluralism, the Roman Empire advocated a national religious identity for the Roman people. The emperor was the chief priest (*pontifex maximus*) of the traditional Roman religions. The subjects had to manifest their political loyalty through the practice of emperor worship (Ferguson 1993: 198; Klauck 2000: 325–327). Apart from that, they did have freedom to worship various local deities. Through these two kinds of worship, the Roman people shared the same political identity, while simultaneously bearing different religious identities.

In the Jesus movement, Jesus, a Nazarene, was proclaimed as Christ (Messiah) and the Lord of lords. He commanded his followers to "give therefore to the emperor the things that are the emperor's, and to God the things that are God's" (Matthew 22:21, NRSV) and to fulfill the Law of Moses by loving God and loving neighbors as themselves. Therefore, it was not appropriate for Christians to participate in emperor worship or to sacrifice to pagan gods. As Jews and non-Jews, through converting to Christian faith, became Jewish Christians and gentile Christians, the early church began to face social repressions and persecutions from both non-believing Jews and the Roman Empire. For non-believing Jews, Christian faith was destroying their ethnic religious identity with the Mosaic Law as its core, abolishing their special status as the people of God, and overthrowing the theoretical basis of the Zionist movement. For the Roman Empire, the Christian faith was threatening the national religious identity, which had emperor worship as its core. Undoubtedly, these worries triggered a series of accusations for Christians, including political disloyalty, ethical immorality and unlawfulness.

However, Christianity in the first three centuries not only survived the insults, slanders and attacks, but expanded rapidly to the whole Empire and even became a strong religious group which could not be eradicated by persecutions. In 313, the Edict of Milan unprecedentedly recognized Christianity as a religion and established its legal status. Constantine, the first Christian emperor, generously offered his political, economic and legal support to the Catholic Church. He actively promoted the unity of the whole church in his Empire. For example, he did his best to alleviate the schism of the North African church and chaired the first Nicene Council in response to the Arian Controversy. Since then, Christian emperors tried to rejuvenate the subjects' national religious identity with Christianity. Following this road map, they began to promote the Christianization of the Empire, while repressing traditional Roman religions and various local beliefs. As a consequence, they desired to build the Roman political loyalty upon this new faith (Eusebius, *Historia Ecclesiastica* 10.7). Emperors were used to being masters of the Roman people, but now they became friends of the Christian God (Eusebius, *Historia Ecclesiastica* 10.9). In 380, Theodosius established Christianity as the official state religion. In 382, Gratian abandoned the emperor's title of *pontifex maximus*. In the 380s and 390s, Theodosius suppressed heresies and schismatics within the church and believers of traditional Roman gods outside the church (Stevenson 1989: 150).

Therefore, the religious policy of the Roman Empire experienced an abrupt turn in the fourth century. Formerly, the Empire tolerated almost all religions except Christianity, but now it turned to support Catholic Christianity only and no longer tolerated any other religions. However, behind this dramatic change, the pattern of the state-church relation of the Empire remained consistent and stable. They were Christian emperors who tightly controlled the developmental path of church affairs. As Robert Dyson wrote, Constantine and his successors "declared

Augustine and the Chinese church 157

themselves spiritual submission to the church, but in the world were the rule of the church" (Dyson 2005: 158). Thus, by ordering the Roman people to convert to the Catholic faith, Christian emperors actually integrated a unified political identity with a unified religious identity for their subjects. This new policy apparently would be helpful not only to eliminate political separatism and religious extremism, but also to promote political loyalty, regional peace and national unity.

Rome had grown from a city to an empire. During this long period, there was not a separate and private domain that belonged to individuals only, and religious belief was never a personal affair but the core part of the Roman constitution. The Roman Empire demanded the subjects' religious belief to be subordinated to their political identity, which meant that they must recognize the political theology of the Empire. After the legalization of Christian faith, the Empire transformed its holy tradition as expressed by Virgil in *Aeneid* to a new holy tradition as expressed by Eusebius in *Church History*. In this transformation, Aeneas was replaced by Constantine and the Christian emperors now became bishops for everything outside of the church (Eusebius, *Vita Constantini*, 4.24). In order to reshape a unified national religious identity, the Christian emperors insisted on the priority of political loyalty and made the religious power of the church part of their political power. Thus, the church was only responsible for religious affairs of the Empire. While making efforts to promote Catholic Christianity, the Christian emperors encountered a resistance from the Donatists, who were a localized religious community. In response to this challenge, they repressed paganism, heresies and schismatics by fines, exiles and deprivation of citizenship.

The main reasons for religious schism are as follows:

1 From believing the traditional Roman gods to believing the Christian God, the core aim of religious affairs was still to enhance the Roman people's political loyalty to the Empire. Julian the apostate once supported the Donatists and the Arians in order to slow down the process of Christianization of the Empire, but in vain. Unlike barbarian invasions from the north or the Persian war from the east, the splitting of the North African church did not seriously threaten the political stability and the national unity of the whole Empire and thus was never a primary concern of the emperors. Besides repressing political riots, the emperors wished to maintain the status quo of North Africa, which was favorable to the Donatists' rapid expansion.
2 Following the former pattern of the state-church relation, the emperors usually dealt with religious affairs according to their variable political needs and religious beliefs. In political struggles and doctrinal debates, they often supported different positions besides the Catholic church. In the Western Empire, Valentine II and his mother, Justina, had tried to force Ambrose the bishop of Milan to surrender a basilica for the worship of the Arians (Augustine, *Confessiones* 9.7.15). In the Eastern Empire, Athanasius and John Chrysostom were even exiled several times. The political environment required that, in the conflict with the Donatists, the North African Catholic church had to seek support from the emperor in the name of political loyalty. However, even if

being supported by the Christian emperors, the Catholic church could only be an equal side of the debate in the Council of Carthage.

3 In the context of this doctrinal controversy and ecclesiastical split, the imperial favor of one side unavoidably led to the other side's extreme enmity, so that there was no chance for dialogue or even legal coercion to dispel these divergences and hostilities. The Donatists were under the harsh political pressure to join in the Catholic church after being defeated in the Council of Carthage. This coercive unity was not stable, and Donatism lasted at least until the middle fifth century.

As a powerful opponent of the Donatists, Augustine not only persistently refuted their doctrinal errors, but also appealed to local officials and the emperor to take decisive measures. Augustine participated as a leader in the Council of Carthage, and because of his efforts, he and his friends completely reversed the difficult situation of the North African Catholic church. On the one hand, Augustine criticized the localism and isolationism of the Donatists and argued that Christian faith must be Catholic and that the holy church of Christ must be unified throughout the world. On the other hand, after the fall of Rome in 410, Augustine criticized the nationalism and political loyalty of the Roman national religious identity supported by the emperors and argued that Christian faith must prioritize religious devotion over political unity, which, as the earthly city, had limited value in comparison to the city of God.

Augustine: replacing localism with Catholicism

Even if relying on the support of the Empire, the North African Catholic Church for quite some time lacked strong leaders who could compete with the two Donatist counterparts, namely, Donatus (313–355) and Parmenianus (355–391). In Hippo, the threat of Manichaeism, though prohibited by the Empire, was real. With the ordination of Augustine as priest of Hippo in 391 and Aurelius as bishop of Carthage in 393, the situation began to turn around. By founding a monastery beside the church, Augustine trained a number of clergy and appointed his friends or followers as bishops in various cities and towns. Thanks to these vigorous efforts, Augustine efficaciously waged a doctrinal and political battle against the Donatists and finally defeated them (Hua 2015: 332–348).

The Catholic church and the Donatists both recognized the North African church tradition and commemorated Cyprian the bishop of Carthage on the same day. They shared almost the same doctrines except the doctrines of baptism and church. The Donatists insisted that the baptism of the Catholic church was invalid because its bishops were ordained by the *traditores* and thus these Christians must be rebaptized. Augustine refuted them with the following argument: (1) The effectiveness of baptism did not depend on the holiness or purity of a bishop but on the authority of the Trinitarian God. As long as a person was baptized in the name of the Trinity, his baptism was valid. The Donatists retraced the idea of rebaptism to Cyprian's thought, though he made a doctrinal mistake in his effort to maintain the unity of the North African church during Decius's persecution. The Donatists not only inherited his erroneous theory, but also caused the splitting of the church (Eusebius, *Historia Ecclesiastica* 7.2–6; Augustine, *Contra Cresconium grammaticum* 2.32.40). (2) There would always be the righteous and the sinful in any church, who would be separated only at the last judgment. "Who are you to pass judgment on servants of another" (Romans 14:4, NRSV). (3) Since the Gospel will be spread "to the ends of the earth" (Acts 1:8, NRSV), and "Christ is the head of the church" (Ephesians 5:23, NRSV), churches on the earth must be Catholic and unified. The sign of which was that they believed in the same doctrine and performed the same liturgy. However, the Donatists were only restricted in North Africa (Augustine, *Epistulae* 43.9, 49.3, 66.2, 86.2; *Contra epistulam Parmeniani* 2.108; *De baptismo* 3.19). (4) Christians must accept the secular authority of the Roman Empire and love their neighbors as themselves and never resort to violence when dealing with disagreements among believers.

With regard to doctrinal disagreements and sectarian division, Augustine initially insisted on peaceful dialogue and theoretical persuasion, but did not receive positive responses from the Donatists. Instead he received violent attacks from the Circumcellions. In view of the Empire's effective repression of the Donatists who were involved in the rebellions, Augustine began to accept the necessity of the policy of religious coercion which was initially carried out by the Empire. He no longer simply emphasized that the unity of church must be based on the Donatists' free choice of will; instead, he began to argue that their fear of coercive edicts would be slowly healed by Christ's love (Augustine, *Epistulae* 93.16–20; *Retractationes* 2.5). Because of this transition, he then requested the emperor to issue new edicts and urged local officials to implement anti-heresy laws (Augustine, *Epistulae* 61.1; Six-Means 2011: 176). Regarding this historical transition, Peter Brown commented that "some profound and ominous changes had taken place in Augustine's attitude to the church and society in his first ten years as a bishop" (Brown 2000: 231).

According to Jesus's distinction between Caesar and God as well as Paul's teachings in Romans 13, Augustine not only accepted the emperor's political authority, supported the Christianization of the Empire, but painstakingly participated in the governance of North Africa at the grassroots level. While local officials implemented the emperor's coercive policies, he endeavored to propose that, for stubborn Donatists: (1) the most appropriate penalty was a fine but any physical punishment, including the death penalty, should be banned, because it would stimulate their passion for martyrdom; (2) while imposing fines, it was not proper to bring them into extreme poverty, for their daily bread must be guaranteed (Augustine, *Epistulae* 134.4, 139.2, 153.18). Augustine reasoned that religious coercion was a means to enforce Christian disciplines in order that the Donatists would be forced to return to Catholic basilicas first and then their souls would have a chance to accept Catholic teachings leading to a final unity of all churches.

By clarifying Christian doctrines, refuting schismatics, and introducing imperial power to protect the unity of church, Augustine essentially continued the political manipulation initiated by Constantine, namely replacing a localized religious identity with a national religious identity. However, he recognized religious devotion instead of political loyalty as the core of this identity (Lee 2016: 41–63). While rebutting the Donatists' viewpoint of church, he attempted to argue that it was necessary to move beyond the early Christian political theology as represented by Eusebius and Orosius. In this sense, he was both a sincere Roman and a true opponent of Rome.

Augustine: replacing political loyalty with religious devotion

After a political and military struggle with Honorius's court in Ravenna for more than ten years, Alaricus led the Visigoths into Rome on August 24, 410, and plundered the city for three days. A large number of people fled to North Africa and then traveled to the eastern provinces. Compared to the other disasters in the history of Rome, this fall of Rome neither caused serious damage to the city nor became a historical turning point in the late Roman Empire. However, in the eyes of the pagans and a vast majority of Christians, Rome as an "eternal city" was still the spiritual capital of the Empire and so its fall caused a great psychological shock in them. After hearing this news, Jerome in Bethlehem mourned for it repeatedly as was evident in his writings (Jerome, *Epistulae* 127.12,126.2; *The Commentary on Ezekiel*, Vol. 1 preface; Vol. 3 preface).

Besides the psychological shock, the fall of Rome triggered a heated debate over who should be responsible. The pagans blamed the Roman Empire for converting to Christianity, causing them to lose the protection of their traditional gods. Facing this blame, Augustine first responded in his five sermons (Augustine, *Sermones* 24, 81, 296, 105, and 397). From 412, he began to write *The City of God* as a complete refutation. After the first ten volumes, he ordered his student Orosius to compile a reference book containing past human catastrophes.

In *Church History* and *The Life of Constantine*, Eusebius, a representative of church historians in the fourth century, warmly welcomed the legalization of Christianity and the Christianization of the Roman Empire. He praised the emperor as a friend of God and the Empire as a kingdom of God. It was out of God's divine plan that the Empire gave up its former polytheism and converted to Christianity. According to this kind of historical narrative, Orosius wrote *Historiarum Adversum Paganos Libris VII*, which recounted the history of mankind from the creation of Adam to the present. By comparing Rome with other countries and the age before Jesus Christ with the age after him, Orosius argued the following points: (1) The Roman Empire, chosen by God, was superior to all other countries. (2) After Jesus Christ's coming, this age was superior to any time before. (3) With the blessing of God on the Empire, the pagans also received benefits though they falsely attacked this Christian era.

The historical development of Rome from a kingdom to a republic was illustrated by Virgil's *Aeneid*. As a descendant of Jupiter, Aeneas suffered many calamities and finally came to Latium, where his heirs established the city of Rome. With the protection of the traditional Roman gods, the city expanded its power to the entire Mediterranean world and became an empire. Emperors, from

Octavian to Diocletian, inherited Virgil's political theology. The development of Rome from a city to an empire seemingly had proven the effectiveness of this enduring political-religious system. Thus it was very natural that the emperors constructed a unified national religious identity for the Roman people. As we have seen, the process of Christianization of the Empire was also a process of Romanization of Christianity, but the political theology behind it had not changed. An emperor still claimed that he was appointed by God. He continued to manage religious affairs of the Empire but replaced the Roman gods with the Christian God and pagan temples with Christian basilicas. Being a Catholic Christian was defined by law as the national religious identity. In this sense, from Virgil to Eusebius, and then to Orosius, the argument for the Roman political-religious system was in the same vein. However, there was a serious crisis which they did not foresee or dare to face.

Like Orosius, Augustine admitted that Alaricus respected Christian faith by not harming Christians and pagans who fled to basilicas. This was contrary to the general custom of war after a victory. However, unlike his predecessors, Augustine criticized three interpretations of the Roman history mentioned previously. (1) Virgil's interpretation was self-contradictory from its beginning. Since the traditional Roman gods did not have the capacity to defend Troy so that Aeneas had to carry their statues to escape, how could they defend the growth and prosperity of Rome (Augustine, *De civitate Dei* 1.1–1.7)? (2) Eusebius's interpretation could not explain why the city of Rome fell in 410. Since the emperor had become "a friend of God," how could the spiritual capital of the Empire be plundered by barbarians in this Christian era? (3) Orosius's interpretation could not respond to the mortal fate of an earthly empire. If he would see the third fall of Rome in 455 and the ending of the Western Roman Empire in 476, how could he prove that God was blessing and protecting the Christian Empire? Thus, how to interpret the political changes of an earthly regime in light of Christian doctrines became an urgent and difficult question for Augustine. This was the very reason for his writing of *The City of God* (Augustine, *De civitate Dei* 1 prologue).

Since the origin of Rome could be traced back to the fall of Troy, it was difficult to argue that its subsequent expansion was due to the help of the traditional Roman gods. Moreover, Jupiter's promise to the Romans had been broken by the Roman emperors' conversion to the Christian God (Vergil, *Aeneid* 1. 223–296). Based on this historical narrative, Augustine gave his unprecedented argument. (1) There was not any causal relation between believing a religion and the prosperity of a country. (2) The rise of Rome was not due to the promise of Jupiter or virtues of the Romans, but two desires – lust for liberty and lust for domination. The former referred to the banishment of Tarquin the Proud and the foundation of the Republic; the latter referred to the military conquest of the Republic and the Empire. However, both were rooted in a desire for honor, which was the sin originating from the fall of Adam (Augustine, *De civitate Dei* 5.12).

Although the Empire had converted to Christianity since Constantine, Augustine still criticized the Christianized Empire, arguing firstly that the conversion of the Empire was simply a replacement of the traditional Roman religions with Christianity. The existing pattern of the political-religious relation had not changed, because it still required that religious identity be unified with their political identity and prioritized political loyalty in religious life. Secondly, he argued that the conversion did not guarantee God's blessing and protection to the Empire, which had been proven by the fall of Rome and would be proven by the ending of the Western Empire. Moreover, like ordinary Christians, a Christian emperor should differentiate his religious identity from his political identity and set religious devotion to God as the first priority in his pursuit of eternal life (Augustine, *De civitate Dei* 5.26).

Although Augustine did not witness the third fall of Rome and the demise of the Western Empire, the fall of Rome in 410 forced him to deeply reflect on the fate of any secular political entity. He proposed the idea of the separation of state and church and the separation of the earthly city and the city of God. Augustine argued that, given the limited space and time of a political state, we must view the Christianization of the Empire from a critical perspective, understanding that Christianization does not guarantee a promising future for the state. Secondly, he pointed out that the political power of the emperor was a gift from God. Given the respective functions of the Empire and the church, the Empire should deal with secular affairs and take care of the subjects' body, and the church should deal with sacred affairs and take care of their soul. Finally, Augustine suggested that, following the teachings of Romans 13, Christian subjects should fulfill their secular obligations to the Empire, including paying taxes or tributes, and fulfill their religious obligations to the church (Augustine, *Expositio quarundam propositionum ex epistula apostoli ad Romanos* 72; *Epistulae* 134.1–3).

While rebutting the localized religious identity of the Donatists, Augustine also criticized the national religious identity constructed by the Roman Empire with his theory of two cities. He separated religion from politics and faith in God from loyalty to the Empire. With entering the city of God as their ultimate goal, Christians should differentiate their religious identity from political identity and make their religious devotion the first priority in earthly life. They also should refuse religious violence; but love their neighbors as themselves and wait patiently for God's last judgment. Only then would it be possible for them to achieve universal peace in this world and eternal salvation in the next.

Based on an eschatological view, Augustine did not approve Eusebius's position to defend the Empire, but tried to transcend the earthly territory. He refused the idea that the Empire after Constantine was a Christian kingdom on earth. Unlike Orosius, Augustine wanted to move from secular time and space to eternity and the heavenly kingdom in order to validate the Christian faith in the coming of the city of God. The Catholic Church should respect, but not be subordinated to, the imperial political authority. Christians did not have to defend the Empire's past or pray for its future. Rather, they should break away from the uncertain destiny of any secular regime in order that by God's divine authority they can achieve their eternal salvation. In the city of God, the heavenly kingdom would transcend any geographical location and historical time.

"Political Augustinianism"?

Religious freedom and religious coercion were the two sides of the religious policy of the Roman Empire. The basic principles were to build a national religious identity for the subjects and promote their political loyalty to the emperors. Before the fourth century, the policy was embodied in the emperor worship. The subjects were ordered to sacrifice to the emperor. Caligula had attempted to put his portrait in the sanctuary of the Jerusalem Temple. After the fourth century, the policy presented itself in the emperor's control and interference of church affairs in accordance to his own belief, for example, promoting the Nicene Creed or Arianism. Julian the apostate even restored the altar of victory in the Roman senate and planned to revive the traditional Roman religions.

From the persecution of unlawful Christianity before 313 to the suppression of heresies and sectarians after 380, the construction of a national religious identity neither solved nor alleviated the theological-political problems of the Empire. In the late fourth century, like the "Circumcelliones" (supported by the Donatists), Christian mobs (supported by some of Catholic bishops) threatened the social harmony and local stability of the Empire (Gaddis 2005: 151–207). Facing this challenging situation, Augustine defended the necessity of religious coercion from the Empire, but advised that the subject's Christian belief should be independent of their political obligations, so that the Catholic church could maintain a safe distance from the aggressive political power of the Empire. Only upon this appropriate separation of church and state was it possible to maintain a healthy relation between the two.

However, in the earthly city, the relation between state and church is always one of the most delicate questions in politics. The solution provided by Augustine is dynamic and complex such that over-emphasizing any side will lead to horrible errors. On the one hand, with his insistence on the limited value of secular politics, Augustine's theory can easily be used to defend a dangerous position of anti-state or anti-political community so that the value of this life is totally replaced by the value of the afterlife. In such cases, the debate on politics is replaced by the debate on religion. And the political, economic or cultural conflicts on earth are reduced to religious conflicts between the pagan and the orthodox, between the fall and salvation, state power and church power, political obligation and religious duty. On the other hand, his affirmation of the independence of church can be used to argue that divine affairs are higher than secular affairs and that the sacred power of the pope is superior to the secular power of kings, as was evidenced in medieval society.

In the fourth century, some Catholic bishops believed that their bishopric power should be independent of the emperors' secular power and even challenged political authority with the authority of faith. For example, Ambrose criticized Theodosius's mishandling of the Thessalonian slaughter and persuaded Valentine II to disallow the restoration of the altar of victory (Ambrose, *Epistula* 17, 18, 40, 41, 51; Paulinus of Milan, *Vita Ambrosii* 26). However, these bishops were passively reacting to the emperors' political decision rather than positively seizing political power or economic interests. By equating the Catholic church with the realization of the city of God on earth, the medieval Catholic church reinterpreted Augustine's theory of two cities such that the pope was guaranteed the power to "appoint, teach and punish" all kings. This new interpretation is called "political Augustinianism" (Dyson 2005: 142–145). However, this is a serious distortion of Augustine, as he himself never thought that the Catholic church could represent the fulfillment of the city of God on earth, because in his view any church in this world was unavoidably a mixture of sinners and the righteous, even among bishops.

Implications for the Chinese church and government

Like the Roman Empire, from the Qin Dynasty to the Qing Dynasty, the Chinese Empire had always endorsed emperor worship. The Chinese emperor was seen as the son of the highest god acting as the high priest in the national spring sacrifice and autumn sacrifice. Based on this political theology, the Chinese subjects should be politically loyal to the emperor and all religious powers should subordinate to the political power; otherwise they would be destroyed. The adverse fortunes of Taoism and Buddhism in ancient China had clearly shown this principle.

In the late Ming and early Qing dynasties, Catholic Christianity came to China and soon triggered "the Chinese Ritual Controversy." The Holy See prohibited Chinese Catholics from participating in sacrifices to ancestors and Confucius because these rites were regarded as idol worship. Nevertheless, the Kangxi Emperor of the Qing Dynasty, along with the Jesuits in China and most of the Chinese Catholics, opposed the prohibition. The serious challenge of pontifical power led to Kangxi prohibiting the expansion of the Catholic faith in China. Since then, the Catholic mission in China suffered a major setback (Hua 2016: 78–98). In the nineteenth century, Protestantism was introduced into China. Because of the Western colonial aggression and the weakness of China, the Qing court could not effectively control and manage various Protestant missionary associations. During the Republic of China, the Christian mission was not subject to interference by the government, giving the Christian mission the opportunity to be flexible and active in the fields of education, medicine and publication. In the 1930s, the Holy See revoked the ban on Chinese rituals, for they were no longer seen as idolatry but a traditional custom of China. The ordination of Catholic bishops was also respected by the government of the Republic of China. Therefore, in the first half of the twentieth century, the bishopric power was independent of China's regime and departed from the original model of state-church relation.

After the founding of the People's Republic of China in 1949, the Chinese government strengthened its management of religious affairs, banished all foreign Catholic and Protestant missionaries and clergy, and established the three-self (self-supporting, self-governing and self-propagating) church. Three-self churches, being completely obedient to the political authority of the Chinese government, were managed by the State Administration for Religious Affairs and the Ministry of Civil Affairs at all levels. As an integral part of the state, they accepted the ideological guidance and other interventions from the Communist Party of China and the central government. Political loyalty of Christian leaders took the priority over their religious faith. The Chinese government only recognized the legitimacy of the churches that were under their control. Nevertheless, since some Protestant Christians and Catholics did not accept the ideological guidance or political intervention from the party or the government, their churches could not be registered in the Ministry of Civil Affairs as legitimate religious organizations. Subsequently they were called "house or family church" and "underground" Catholic church, resulting in serious church division and social isolation. With the partial implementation of religious freedom in mainland China in place since the 1980s, the house church and the underground Catholic church have grown rapidly. However, the Chinese government has been unable to effectively control them, and the division and misunderstanding between the government-approved church and the "underground" church are deep.

The Chinese scenario is similar to the Roman Empire in the fourth and fifth centuries: (1) In the view of the Chinese government, the religious rights of its citizens must be subordinate to their political obligation and their political identity also takes precedence over their religious identity. As such the government has absolute power to intervene in church affairs and to dominate the doctrinal interpretation and organizational development of Chinese Christianity. The core cause of the church division in China is that the house church and the underground Catholic church firmly oppose any doctrinal and organizational intervention from the government and refuse to express political allegiance in their religious life. (2) Like the Donatists, the suppressed churches develop a sense of pride in their illegal religious identity, and openly express their dissenting voice and even hatred to the official churches. Believers of each side almost never associate with the other, let alone hold an open dialogue to resolve their religious disagreement. As the Chinese government insists in the priority of political loyalty, its negotiation with the Holy See moves slowly.

Unlike during the age of Augustine, the freedom of religious belief and the separation of church and state have become a common practice in the modern world and Augustine's argument for religious coercion is no longer recognized. Today, religious faith is seen as a matter of the private sphere, while political power pertains to the public sphere. For this reason, the government need not intervene in the personal religious belief of its citizens. No modern state can impose penalties including "fines, exiles and executions" on citizens simply because of their religious belief. Nor can the church support Christian mobs or participate in political riots. In China, the house church and the underground Catholic Church recognize the political authority of the Chinese government in the public sphere and are required to be registered as a legal social organization. They do not encourage believers to participate in any political protest. But being prophets of the day and out of their religious convictions, they do speak against the social ills and personal sins of the Chinese society.

Although modern states no longer try to establish a national religious identity for their citizens, Augustine's argument on Catholicism, the priority of faith, and a healthy separation between church and state can still shed light on the problem of the Chinese church today. Without religious coercion, the Chinese church still needs to insist that "Christ is the head of the church" (Ephesians 5:23, NRSV), and "one Lord, one faith, one baptism, one God" (Ephesians 4:5–6, NRSV). This means the house church and the underground Catholic church should abandon their pride and hostility toward other members of the body of Christ (Romans 12:5; 1 Corinthians 12:12–27; Ephesians 3:6 and 5:23); instead, they should have a congenial and edifying dialogue with official churches as "joint heirs with Christ" (Romans 8:17, NRSV). With the love for God and neighbors, these two types of Chinese churches should strive for unity. While it may be challenging in actual practice, the clergy of the three-self church should neither pursue their personal political advancement nor let the government's ideology interfere with the teaching and liturgy of the church. Meanwhile, the Chinese government should also recognize the legal rights of the house church and the underground Catholic Church. After withdrawing the internal control of religious affairs, the government can provide external service and supervision to the Chinese church. Only in this way can the Chinese church achieve final unity and thus promote the social harmony and national prosperity of China.

Note

This paper is supported by National Social Science Foundation of China (Grant No. 14CZJ002).

Bibliography

Brown, Peter. 2000. *Augustine of Hippo: A Biography*, a new edition with and epilogue. Berkeley and Los Angeles: University of California Press.
Dyson, Robert. 2005. *St Augustine of Hippo: The Christian Transformation of Political Philosophy*. London: Continuum.
Ferguson, Everett. 1993. *Backgrounds of Early Christianity*. Grand Rapids: William B. Eerdmans Publishing Company.
Frend, W. H. C. 2003. *The Donatist Church: A Movement of Protest in Roman North Africa*. Oxford: Clarendon Press.
Gaddis, Michael. 2005. *There Is No Crime for Those Who Have Christ: Religious Violence in the Christian Roman Empire*. Berkeley: University of California Press.
Heyking, John von. 2001. *Augustine and Politics as Longing in the World*. Columbia: University of Missouri Press.
Hua, Wei. 2015. 'The Unification of Church and the Harmonious Society: On St. Augustine's Debate Against the Donatists,' in Xinping Zhuo and Kui Cai (ed.), *Christianity and Harmonious Society Construction*. Beijing: China Social Science Press, pp. 332–348.
———. 2016. 'Pauline Pneumatology and the Chinese Rites: Spirit and Culture in the Holy See's Missionary Strategy,' in Gene L. Green, Stephen T. Pardue and K. K. Yeo (eds.), *The Spirit Over the Earth: Pneumatology in the Majority World*. Grand Rapids, MI: William B. Eerdmans Publishing Company, pp. 78–98.
Kinnvall, Catarina. 2004. 'Globalization and Religious Nationalism: Self, Identity, and the Search for Ontological Security,' *Political Psychology*, 25(5): 741–767.

Klauck, Hans-Josef. 2000. *The Religious Context of Early Christianity: A Guide to Graeco-Roman Religions*. Trans. Brian McNeil. Edinburgh: T & T Clark.

Lee, Gregory W. 2016. 'Using the Earthly City: Ecclesiology, Political Activity, and Religious Coercion in Augustine,' *Augustinian Studies*, 47(1): 41–63.

Sandwell, Isabella. 2007. *Religious Identity in Late Antiquity: Greeks, Jews and Christians in Antioch*. Cambridge: Cambridge University Press.

Six-Means, Horace E. 2011. *Augustine and Catholic Christianization: The Catholicization of Roman Africa, 391–408*. New York: Peter Lang.

Stevenson, J. (ed.) 1989. *Creeds, Councils and Controversies: Documents Illustrating the History of the Church AD 337–461*. W. H. C. Frend revised. London: SPCK.

11 Post-Chinese reconnections through religion

Buddhism, Christianity, and Confucianism

Chih-yu Shih

Amid the rise of religious tension in the 21st century, nationalist leaders and fundamentalist activists rely on and employ religious resources willingly and without hesitation. However, this does not seem to reflect developments in China despite Chinese leaders likewise resorting to Chinese nationalism in their attempts to reinforce the legitimacy of Communist Party rule. By complicating the categories of "China," the "Chinese," and "Chineseness" this chapter aims at trivializing the role of religion in the reconstruction of cultural as well as political nationalism in China. It will enlist the anthropological notion of post-Chineseness in order to present the nuances that restrain the political use of religions from reproducing, in Giorgio Shani and Takashi Kibe's words, the "spiritual, moral and timeless essence" of the Chinese nation.

Despite Marxism, the Communist Party state of China has witnessed a revival of religion (Johnson 2017; Yang 2011; Marsh 2011). Even President Xi Jinping has resorted to Buddhist wisdom, along with Confucianism as a practical religion, in his public speech. Many Chinese leaders have been known for their faith since the beginning of the Republic (Katz 2014). For example, Chiang Kai-shek and former president of the Republic of China Lee Teng-hui in Taiwan were dedicated Christians and consistently nationalist leaders. Chiang and Xi are apparently Chinese nationalists and Lee is a determined Taiwanese nationalist. Nevertheless, religious beliefs have not intervened in the formation of their nationalist sensibilities given the largely secular inclination of the Chinese population compared with the ethnic Indians (van der Veer 2013). To that extent, the role of religion in the Chinese politics of nationalism is different (Faries 2010; Bovingdon 2010; Katz and Rubenstein 2003). To say the least, the nationalist leadership did not intend to relate to religion beyond the level of self-disciplining.

I regard religions mainly as faith. Abiding by certain sacred texts, religious nationalism is conceived as the belief in a presumably common faith in order to build, reproduce, or protect an imagined nation. Religious nationalism has not been a common practice in historical as well as contemporary China, though. Consider Chinese religions "supernatural beliefs and related practices." Their practical aspect tends to reinforce those secular purposes coming outside of religious values and practices instead of deriving from the gospel or the apocalypse (Yukong 2013). Thus, religion constitutes Chinese selfhood in two mundane ways. First, religion provides an imagined relationship between believers and their gods, as if gods are obliged to bless the believers who worship them (Sutton 2003). Religiosity distinguishes the believers from others mainly sociologically. Second, religion reminds and urges self-sacrifice and self-discipline at the individual level to sustain the virtue of perseverance, devotion, and benevolence in a relational habitus that encompasses the believers (Yu 2012; Rošker 2016; Tang 2016; Keenan 2011). Thus, Chinese religions are neither inevitably nationalist nor provide outright resistance to nationalism projects. They promote a peculiar kind of cultural nationalism shared by a population beyond any definitive territorial scope or, where territoriality prevails, motivate a kind of nonresistance, or at most soft resistance, to an encountered and presumably stronger rival via the sporadic construction of an unyielding volition. Cultural nationalism in China is not entirely compatible with statist nationalism embedded in territoriality.

This chapter tackles Shani and Kibe's question about "diverse configurations of nationalism and religion in Asian context" by interrogating how the emerging character of post-Chineseness informs the cultural function of Chinese religions and the ineffectiveness of statist nationalism in the religious sphere.

In short, post-Chineseness is about the process of relating between strategically self-acknowledged Chinese populations so that they can individually reconnect with an alleged Chinese trait. Reconnection refers primarily to reimagining, rediscovering, and reproducing one's own Chinese trait. Whether or not the target group of reconnection acknowledges its Chinese trait is a different matter. Therefore, post-Chineseness can be either reciprocal or unilateral. Cultural nationalism here refers to the process of reconnecting between populations by incurring, reciprocally and unilaterally, imagined sharing of the same cultural practice, which, in the religious realm, includes the worship of ancestors, Buddha, or earthly gods.

As populations at different sites improvise their connection or disconnection differently, post-Chineseness enacts differing epistemological perspectives that engender wide-ranging cultural nationalism for different constituencies, which resemble Wittgenstein's (1986: 31) notion of family resemblance that defies any definitive scope. Post-Chineseness is, in other words, about self-imagination of one's little self that results in cultural nationalism of a greater self that encompasses the same membership of other little selves. The self and the other are therefore not necessarily mutually exclusive or even paired. Post-Chinese identities of this sort reproduced through constant and differing reconnections necessarily embrace the normative implications of Chineseness being ontologically unquestionable and yet epistemologically undefinable, culturally unproductive, or socially unstable.

Cultural nationalism as the purpose of post-Chineseness

Post-Chineseness, as the process of reconnection between related self-recognized and other-designated Chinese groups, can rely on religious resources. I discuss three of these religious resources, namely, Buddhism, Christianity, and Confucianism. (Examples of folk religions will be briefly mentioned at times.) Targeting either a Chinese group or a non-Chinese group is possible when reconnecting with

170 *Chih-yu Shih*

an imagined Chinese trait of one's own. Therefore, one can choose either of the two purposes: (1) discovering a shared Chinese trait of another Chinese group, i.e. the quest for purity and (2) exploring the potential of a non-Chinese group to acquire a Chinese trait, i.e. the quest for hybridity. Depending on one's self-identity, either constituted by an imagined national being as in political nationalism to reproduce a definitive scope or by a process of constantly becoming as in cultural nationalism to transcend a definite scope, one can identify one's own relationality as constituted by (1) spatiality defined by a physical scope, such as a body, a kin network, a site, a security community, a tax regime, or a sovereign border, or (2) temporality embedded in an evolutionary trajectory, such as a common origin, an overlapped historiography, a joint civilization, or a shared cultural identification.[1] (Table 11.1)

Cultural Chineseness in a multi-religious state

Cultural Chineseness is the consequence of the incurrence of a symbol of non-territorial national identity and its practice that engenders imagined resemblance among the audience and worshipers (Kuehn, Louie, and Pomfret 2014). Intended incurrence does not necessarily contribute to the nationalist consciousness, whereas unintended cultural sharing may (Katzenstein 2012; Louie 2004). The following discussion on cultural nationalism refers to the process of producing and enhancing imagined resemblance of a population. Thus, cultural nationalism can either reinforce an extant non-territorial national identity or produce a relationship between those not already constituted by a collective identity. For a population of multiple religions, an agency to craft imagined resemblance on behalf of the imagined cultural nation can rely on religious beliefs and transcend borders and ethnicities.

The nuances of religious practices remind and distinguish between groups (Clayton 2010). Religious practices that have no recorded historical origins make a consensual origin easily imagined by appealing to a sacred text, a school or scholar, a god, or a site, which constitute and connect contemporary disciples (Truman 2011). The incurrence of religious belief or practice embedded in imagined historiography to reconnect with other Chinese overcomes the obsession with territorial Chineseness. Such reconnection reconstructs Chineseness

Table 11.1 The purpose and the relationality of post-Chinese reconnection

Purpose Relationality	Pure	Hybrid
Temporal	Cultural Chineseness Religion as culture	Cosmopolitan Chineseness Religion as cross-culture
Spatial	Political Chineseness Religion as statehood/ethnicity	Postmodern Chineseness Religion as sitedness

Source: Author

(Yao and Zhao 2010). Cultural nationalism can be a challenge to political leadership wherever its scope does not overlap with political Chineseness to include and exclude certain populations and can be embarrassing to the connected group that politically owns a separate citizenship.

Reconnections for the sake of inclusion or exclusion of targeted groups are all about one's agency of reimagining and reconstituting one's own relationality (Shih 2015). Therefore, reconnection is strategic in consequence, if not by nature. Goddess Mazu worship, for example, can be a cultural strategy for the Chinese authorities on China's southeast coast to engender resemblance to Taiwanese believers in order for their relationship to become conducive to a sense of shared Chineseness.

Political Chineseness in a multi-religious state

Within a multi-religious scope of territory, religious beliefs that support political nationalism are difficult to attain because disciples inevitably spread across borders, which undergirds a kind of contemporary political membership usually rendered irrelevant by religious connection. Instead, religious beliefs inspire in the peculiar manner of instilling devotion, concentration, and determination into individual leadership. Leaders that subscribe to political nationalism acquire strength from their conviction that they have the support of the supernatural spirit. Religious transcendence takes place at the agential level, rather than the communal or national level. Thus, the individual faith of leaders and organizations disregards mundane concerns in the pursuit of their own political nationalism that does not arise directly from religious beliefs. Rather, the perseverance revealed in their pursuit benefits from their faith in god (Formicola and Morken 2001).

Any faith leaders can derive strength from their religion. Leaders of different faiths can cooperate to pursue or resist the same political cause, such as Chinese nationalism. This is not because their religious beliefs are identical but because a shared political identity with Chineseness or counter-Chineseness connects them. Religious faiths are conducive to their post-Chinese connection only indirectly because they provide self-confidence in whichever political ideology they choose (e.g., Cagle 2016; Ahmad 2015). A demonstration effect is revealed as disciples subscribing to the same religious belief acquire a political mission to actualize the strength of their faith. A mobilization effect exists as politically neutral disciples elsewhere may come to help because of religious brotherhood/sisterhood. One example of this are the leaders of the Boxers in the late Qing period who inspired anti-foreign nationalism through the use of Daoist superstition. In this regard, faith leadership provided by religious organizations is an indirect and yet plausible source of nationalism (Cismas 2014).

Cosmopolitan Chineseness in a multi-religious state

Cosmopolitan Chineseness is about reconnection consented to by putative out-group individuals who seek reconstitution of their selves through owning

Chineseness. Relying on religious resources to connect with others can reconstitute the individual identity to the effect of engendering relations across fixed boundaries (Yeh 2000). This cosmopolitan Chineseness reflects the pursuit of self-fulfillment at the individual level. Religious resources are conducive to bridging politically and culturally distinctive groups. This has to be the choice of individual members of the out-group. Encountered groups imagine resemblance to each other through the media of religious agency, which introduce and translate cultural meanings that are incomprehensible or even unnoticeable without the religious media. Cultural exchanges through religious means can be either threatening due to their sometimes obscuring effect on orthodox positions or relaxing due to their lack of immediate or specific political intention.

For noticeable examples, post-Chineseness spread to Europe through the media of the Christian missionary, to South Asia through the media of Buddhism, and in the 21st century through the establishment of the Confucius Institute, to younger generations everywhere. Even where a believer in Daoist shamanism is attracted to a spiritual medium in another Chinese society, a peculiar kind of cosmopolitan Chineseness can ironically emerge to reflect connectedness. Thus, religious reconnection between Chinese and non-Chinese groups is more effective with an agency that is culturally familiar with both sides (Liu 2015) The other groups, who were more comfortable with Chineseness, tolerate the first few members who begin to appreciate, enjoy, and own Chineseness to make the scope of Chineseness truly open-ended.

Postmodern Chineseness in a multi-religious state

Postmodern Chineseness is about the reconnection of individuals at a conventional site, who use religious resources to craft resemblance among themselves. Reconnection through the mutual recognition of difference at each site, amid the appreciation of some dubious common Chineseness, informs certain self-other sensibilities. These self-other sensibilities can either embrace a variety of individualized claims of each being differently Chinese or facilitate a sited ethnicity that conveniently performs being different. The ethnic practice of religion that constitutes individual identities enables a claim of distinction from others. To resist religious synchronization across sites, actors of sited identities view those religious resources that encompass the encountered groups suspiciously as totalizing projects to be cautioned against. In contrast, to construct a sited distinction, religious resources are open-ended since all sites can share in their own ways, resulting in boundary spanning (Carlson 2009). A sited religious identity, such as Islam, exists as a condition of curiosity toward differences (Israeli 2007), as opposed to national unity. Ironically, the purpose of reconnection in the postmodern context is to expound on how and why reconnection cannot and should not be integrated or assimilated.

The practice of postmodern Chineseness sometimes risks overemphasizing differences embedded in territoriality. For example, Tudigong (Lord of the Soil) worship that cannot be shared outside its site always accepts outsiders passing through to mimic indigenous worship. Thus, postmodern Chinese reconnection fulfills the function of differentiating outside Chinese without resorting to causing estrangement. Such an exercise of othering aims at reciprocal recognition as opposed to the orientalist construction of an inferior other. The appropriation of post-Chinese nuances on a particular site can proceed through political, economic, or cultural vehicles, depending on what composes the agency for difference (Hirono 2008). An economic agency consumes religious resources to meet the desire for individuality and subjectivity to resist any totalizing, authenticating, or essentializing project; a political agency mobilizes religious resources to reproduce nationalism as a way to resist synchronizing globalization; and a cultural agency appropriates religious resources to resist statist nationalism.

Post-Chinese Buddhism (Table 11.2)

Historically, Buddhism has assisted its followers in various incompatible ways. In areas neighboring China, Buddhism has been the only religion that enabled its followers to powerfully resist the suppression of external and internal controls (Harris 2013; Benn 2007). Examples include the resistance by the Vietnamese, Cambodian, and Burmese to the Confucian court of Vietnam, the Chinese invasion, and the US puppet regime in Saigon during the Cold War. Buddhism has attained emperorship in history but was rarely devoted to nationalism. Buddhism assists in the Confucian adoption of modernity by providing the theme of transcendence so that, philosophically, modernity does not reduce Confucianism to sheer materialism in its resistance to Western imperialism. Similar to Confucianism, Buddhism is not conducive to nationalism despite its occasional rescue of Chinese nationality. No historical experiences in China have tied Buddhism to a particular nationalist position (Tan 2015; Sen 2003). Circumstantial passion and sympathy for the masses can nevertheless inspire Buddhist intervention.

Cultural Chineseness and Buddhism

Chinese Buddhism is not as territorially or ethnically bound as in Sri Lanka, Myanmar, or Thailand. Buddhism does not own or define Chineseness, and, today, PRC China does not own Buddhism. Chinese Buddhist priests are concerned with

Table 11.2 Buddhist mechanisms of post-Chineseness

Purpose / Relationality	Pure	Hybrid
Temporal	Cultural Buddhism Master Hsing Yun	Cosmopolitan Buddhism Suma Ching Hai
Spatial	Political Buddhism Master Taixu	Postmodern Buddhism Buddhist Tourism

Source: Author

Chinese followers and understand their conditions better; so are Tibetan priests with Tibetan followers. Nevertheless, Tibetan Buddhism that enhances ethnic consciousness is not territorially bound (Yu 2014). Rather, Tibetan Buddhism is culturally ethnic (Goldstein 1998). In addition, a string of secularized Humanist Buddhisms (*renjian fojiao*) has emerged from Taiwan and is now widespread all over the world, including Chinese communities everywhere. Disciples actively spread blessings and provide benevolence regardless of their identity. A major leader, Hsin-yun, has been keenly aware of the reality that, although his current base and strength arise from the devoted Chinese community in Taiwan, the continuous growth of Buddhism lies in the return of Buddhism to mainland China. Thus, the future of Chinese communities staying together harmoniously in politics becomes a religious mission. Buddhism across Chinese communities, for example the circulation of Buddha statues/images/representations to different sites, helps Chinese across different borders reconnect and engenders a pressure on politics to refrain from mutual estrangement (Yang 2008). Hsin-yun is particularly worried that the pro-independence leadership of Taiwanese nationalism hinders Buddhism's prospects by inhibiting its quest for a reconstituted Chineseness of a broader scope.

Political Chineseness and Buddhism

During national crises, history shows that followers of Buddhism can always join forces with other fellow patriots to defend the nation, even to the extent of committing "compassionate killing" (Yu 2011; Walton and Hayward 2014). Historically, Buddhist intervention in national defense took place in Korea, China, Japan, Vietnam, and in contemporary Tibet (Woeser 2016). Taiwanese Buddhism has been involved in Taiwanese and Chinese nationalism. A well-known modern example in China was Master Taixu (1890–1947), who supported the anti-Japanese war. He was able to inspire his followers into reform action. Dispensing benevolence to demonstrate transcendence over mundane politics is conducive to the formation of a reciprocal relationship between the givers and the receivers (Pittman 2001). Political Buddhism possesses a privileged position that allows it to take advantage of its apolitical image and selfless sacrifice if it chooses to support nationalism (Tikhonov and Brekke 2013). The purpose of Political Buddhism is to either overcome sub-nationalism as in the case of Sri Lanka and Myanmar or resist suppression as in the case of Tibet. Political Buddhism is presumably transient and yet hinders reconnection with non-Buddhist Chinese.

Cosmopolitan Chineseness and Buddhism

Buddhism can spread around the world to develop new worshipers because its transcendent views of the world inspire new subscribers who look for alternatives to the promise of modernity (Crook 2012; Guruge 2005). People outside of Asian Buddhist circles do not usually become Buddhist by being providers or receivers of benevolence. They become followers to contemplate or listen to Buddhist wisdom, which leads to an image of this world that is unreliable and transient and in which mundane interests cease to provide incentives. One well-received nun, Master Ching Hai (1950–), who comes originally from a Vietnamese community, uses different languages with different audiences in the West and explains the wisdom of simple *zen* in a straightforward manner so that the audience will be enlightened and released from the burden of mundane life (Ching Hai 2011). Ching Hai has a colorful career, thought, and outlook, which stand in sharp contrast with simplicity. Consistently, her preaching is intentionally cosmopolitan. Her disciples in the West seek her advice individually as opposed to worshipers in Chinese societies who seek for benevolence. Themes embedded in the imagined afterworld they share with Chinese followers informed their post-Chineseness.

Postmodern Chineseness and Buddhism

The representation of Chineseness through Buddhism is common in China wherever historical Buddhist temples exist. Given that praying and tourism in Buddhist temples have flourished, Western and Chinese worshipers frequently mingle with tourists (Chau 2008; Granoff and Shinohara 2005). Each temple usually has its own glorious history. Tourist trips to China would be incomplete without visiting at least one characteristic temple (Sheperd 2013). However, Taiwanese temples are usually not historical but postmodern, as they are the earliest to adopt electronic technology, such as laser beams during family funerals and to attract tourist curiosity. Tourism has become so powerful in Chinese Buddhism that worshipers complain that tourism has reduced Buddhism to no more than an economic instrument. In addition to the commodification of Buddhism is Xi Jingping's habit of citing Buddhist sayings. For example, Xi urges communist cadres to look beyond mundane interests in their service to the nation (Lim and Blanchard 2013). Communism and capitalism coexist in the sense that Buddhism is their common retreat. In other words, Buddhism can become an easily consumable representation that provides an otherwise dry position a characteristic identity so that one remains connected in one's secular Chineseness.

Post-Chinese Christianity (Table 11.3)

Judging from the fact that Anson Burlingame (1820–1870), the first Chinese ambassador to Europe, was a US priest, it can be argued that Christianity constituted at

Table 11.3 Christian mechanisms of post-Chineseness

Relationality	Purpose	Pure	Hybrid
Temporal		Cultural Christianity Chiang Kai-shek	Cosmopolitan Christianity The Jesuit Sinology
Spatial		Political Christianity The Taiwan Presbyterians	Postmodern Christianity Three-self Patriotic Church

Source: Author

least part of the Chinese image. Robert Hart, an Irish Christian who worked for the Qing Dynasty for half a century, single-handedly built the Chinese custom system and composed what John King Fairbank called the Manchu-Han-West synergy. The Church joined imperialism to rob Chinese land and wealth and bring down the Qing Empire but intervened in the subsequent nation building. China was the single most important nation to be saved in the practices of the US churches. For example, Chiang Kai-shek's renaissance movement evolved into a Christian campaign under the supervisory of Mme. Chiang, who came from a Christian family. Her baptized elder sister, Song Qingling, was the only woman who became a member of the national leadership of the People's Republic of China. Despite the devastating interlude during the Cultural Revolution, more Chinese have been converted in the 21st century to make China a plausible candidate for the largest Christian state in the world (Stark and Wang 2015). However, for the Chinese, Christianity as a religious identity is not a cultural identity. Rather, Christianity constitutes individuality more than collectivity (Madsen 1998). Exempt from the pressure of choosing a collective identity for China, Christianity is an uneasy, yet accessible resource for believers to transcend the political rivalry between Chinese communities plagued by the politics of identity and ease post-Chinese reconnection wherever a volition to reconnect exists (Fulton 2015).

Cultural Chineseness and Christianity

Although Christianity is not in itself a national identity for the Chinese, Chinese political rivals that subscribe to Christianity can shelf their struggle against each other in the context of a common faith in God, hence constituting a quasi-cultural group. It can support a collective identity broader than the nation-state. For example, Chiang Kai-shek was able to keep his faith in a greater Chinese nation that has never been unified since the Republican revolution. Chiang's conviction in the Chinese nation was not only sustained by historical experiences, but also by the soul he acquired through the Church that supported him throughout (Kyounghan 2009). His scope of the nation extended far beyond territorial China. From an imagined string of successions embedded in the spirit of the Confucian Dao, Chiang considered himself the latest carrier of a line that could be traced back to the Emperors Yao and Shun of primordial time. This half-racial, half-philosophical perspective has little to do with Christianity as a religion (Taylor 2011); however, Christianity supported Chiang to spiritually overcome the political failure and continue believing in his moral appeal to every Chinese in the world (Wang 2014). To that extent, Christianity is more a psychological than a cultural base to withstand his cultural nationalism.

Political Chineseness and Christianity

Making nationalist consciousness out of religion, as is the case in Catholic Poland, is unfamiliar to China (Zubrzycki 2006). Similar to the psychological strength required to make cultural Chineseness a convincing project for Chiang, political nationalism can acquire strength from the faith in God to drive a realistically questionable project of nationalism. Political nationalism is most clear in the case of the Presbyterian Church in Taiwan, which has been an ardent advocate for Taiwan's independence and Taiwanese nationalism (Coe 1980). Nevertheless, another separate Presbyterian Church division in Taiwan supports strong reconnection with the Chinese Mainland, which indicates that the Church is able to reduce political tension among its politically divided Taiwan followers (Hsu 2016). Moreover, the pro-independence Taiwanese Presbyterians continue to interact with Chinese Presbyterians in their common world organizational frame, which indicates that the Church can keep political discord from breaking out. Although political reality disallows the quest for statehood of Taiwan to succeed, Taiwanese Presbyterians could register their volition in the spirit of resistance embedded in the Presbyterian tradition (Coe 1993).

Cosmopolitan Chineseness and Christianity

Jesuit Sinologists who were able to interpret China and the West to each other best illustrate cosmopolitan Christianity. The churches retreated from China on the eve of the Communist Revolution. Many stayed in Hong Kong. They further withdrew in the face of the coming return of Hong Kong to China and moved to Taiwan (Morrissey 2008). The Jesuit fathers who were simultaneously trained Sinologists never stopped their learning of Chinese culture and politics. A notable example is their publication of *China News Analysis*, which used to rank as one of the most consulted intelligence works for Chinese experts globally (Heyndrickx 2005). Their interpretation of events in China was derived from their observations of local affairs and cultural perspectives engrossed in their Sinological training (Domes 1990). Their professional dedication was intellectually prepared under the Church system of pedagogy and financially sponsored by the Church. Thus, they could be cultural translators between China and the world. Their staunch anti-Communist beliefs, propagated by the Church, made them all determined researchers. Cosmopolitan Christianity aimed at integrating Chineseness and Christianity.[2] Pope Francis, the first Jesuit Pope, has worked steadily toward mutual recognition between the Vatican and the People's Republic of China.

Postmodern Chineseness and Christianity

The nationalization of Christianity has been an official line since the Communist Party came to power in 1949. The subsequent reorganization of the churches in China resulted in the establishment of the Three-self Patriotic Movement Church (i.e., self-govern, self-support, and self-preach) in China, which emphasizes the independence of Chinese Christians from the influence of the pope. The Communist Party tolerated only patriotic Christians. Thus, notwithstanding the Marxist aversion to religion, Church dogma and pedagogy still were permitted. Coexisting, alternative house/family churches were ostensibly illegal but still realistically practiced (Lian 2010). With the end of the Cultural Revolution and the revival of folk religions, family churches came back strongly, particularly following the spread of urbanization (Kang 2016). Patriotic and house churches can operate only within China because patriotism refers exclusively to Chinese patriotism (Entwistle 2016; Shan 2012). Nevertheless, the Vatican and international churches outside China actively seek reconnection with any Chinese Christians inside (Baugus 2014; Hirono 2008). Such reconnection compels the connection seekers to reassess how they would accommodate Chinese patriotism to constitute Christianity as they fulfill their duty as workers of God. By contrast, Chinese churches have to strategize on the newly acquired international relationality in the process of reconstituting Chinese Christianity.

Post-Chinese Confucianism[3] (Table 11.4)

Confucianism has inspired two particular modes of thought that can indirectly contribute to Chinese nationalism, namely, unification and self-strengthening. Unification specifically refers to those splinter regimes or lost lands that subscribe to Confucianism embedded in imagined kinship; thus, it is usually oriented toward a certain kind of poetic territoriality (Han 2011; Chan 2001; Hsu 1991). Moreover, kinship is dubious because the common practices of mixed blood and political marriage disallow any definitive scope. Imagined resemblance exists because of the myth of common ancestors enacted by the ritual of ancestor worship, which, together with the national worship of heaven and sagehood, allows Confucianism to be categorized as a religion (Taylor 1990). If successful, then the practice of mixed blood requires no resistance to alien regimes, whose leaders could adopt ancestor worship through cultural assimilation. A highly motivated leadership can engage in self-strengthening to restore an allegedly authentic Confucian regime (Roetz 1993: 160–165). In the 21st century, PRC neo-Confucianists even advocate a revival of a Confucian state. Although self-strengthening can make an ethical inspiration to the effect of fighting alien invaders, cultural mingling remains a viable strength of Confucianism. The string of Confucian nationalisms continued on both tracks of value – assimilation and self-strengthening.

Cultural Chineseness and Confucianism

Confucianism most vividly contributes to contemporary cultural nationalism in Sinological studies (Makeham 2008), particularly among the Southeast Asian

Table 11.4 Confucian mechanisms of post-Chineseness

Relationality \ Purpose	Pure	Hybrid
Temporal	Cultural Confucianism SE Asian Living Sinology	Cosmopolitan Confucianism Confucius Institute
Spatial	Political Confucianism Xi Jinping	Postmodern Confucianism East Asian Confucianism

Source: Author

Chinese intellectuals. Veteran Chinese Southeast Asian scholars describe the scholarship as "living Sinology" (Shih 2014). A typical Sinological agenda covers classic humanities during the millennia of dynastic China; thus, Southeast Asian Sinologists endeavor to record the evolving strings of classic humanities in the writings of the migrant scholars of the Chinese diaspora. Their Sinology continues to live and develop in sharp contrast to the lifeless classics, which Sinologists elsewhere work on. A genealogy that leads to the contemporary scholarship establishes a sense of longevity and infinity of Chineseness that enhances the self-respect of the Chinese population facing the indigenous Southeast Asian populations that continue to practice ethnic politics. Living Sinology reconnects the Southeast Asian Chinese population to a dubious China but distinguishes itself through its imagined living characteristics. Living Sinology can enable a nuanced claim on the distinction of indigenous Chineseness from China and can alternatively inspire the population to embrace various routes of re-Sinicization during the rise of China (Hau 2014).

Political Chineseness and Confucianism

Given that Confucianism is historically alienated from territoriality, its contribution to political nationalism is at best ambiguous. During the crisis of modernization, Confucianism has been a major target to blame. One could trace from the beginning of the Republic of China in 1912 a series of anti-Confucian campaigns, which include the May Fourth Movement and, at a much later time, the Cultural Revolution. Confucianism can contribute to nationalism to the extent that it offers a sense of difference because of the highlighted contrast with the Western civilization (Chang 2009). Nevertheless, Confucianism finally restored its recognition in 2012 as emerging Chinese president Xi Jinping intensively cites Confucian classics in almost all of his public speeches. Xi means to incorporate Confucian values in his effort to revive Chinese civilizations (Zhang 2015). However, Xi has been keen in uplifting the moral consciousness of his cadres. His quest for national greatness and the associated China dream are registered within the Chinese sovereign borders, rather than among Confucian disciples (Terrill 2016). Therefore, his use of Confucianism primarily focuses on individual ethics regarding how to be a good Communist. Making Chinese citizens a disciplined population for the sake of state building is a peculiar kind of post-Chineseness. However, in practice, no discursive or philosophical restraint exists on how a conscious use of Confucian wisdom will evolve, even to the extent of becoming alienated or critical of Communist leadership (Wang 2000).

Cosmopolitan Chineseness and Confucianism

In practice, the state-sponsored Confucianism spills over territorial borders in the 21st century to produce post-Chineseness beyond definitive borders. The establishment of the Confucius Institutes all over the world, which are staffed by language teachers sent and paid for by China, is a policy premised upon the Confucian indoctrination of these teachers who are expected to introduce the Chinese culture in their teaching (Kluver 2014; Li, Mirmirani, and Ilacqua 2009). Neither teachers nor their alien students can be immune from cross-cultural exchanges in their encounters. Students come upon their own initiative and are clearly interested in a career prospect that may be related to China (Wheeler 2015). Students fulfill their own localized or individualized decisions in the process of them becoming familiar and even comfortable with the Chinese civilization and language (Hartig 2012). Confucianism constitutes their new identity indirectly, each in their own way. The post-Chineseness of the Confucius Institute secularizes Confucianism where it connects the students and the teachers at the expense of a widely considered Confucian ritual trait. However, such a loss in the process of expansion guarantees a kind of cosmopolitan post-Chineseness embedded in individualized trajectories that are unrestricted by borders.

Postmodern Chineseness and Confucianism

Multiple Confucianisms become an imperative in the postmodern condition to preserve the local identities of those societies to protect their own Confucianism from any totalizing definition. This quest for a distinctive identity can easily find a shelter embedded in mutually exclusive sitedness that cannot be shared. The East Asian Confucianism that stresses the common origin but different trajectories of improvised hybridity due to sited genealogy represents the postmodern Confucianism that combines Chineseness, Western modernity, and indigeneity (Ivanhoe 2016; Huang 2015). All can appreciate the Chineseness of one another, whereas most remain sensible to their own differences (Barmé 2005).[4] How Confucianism continues at several sites is premised upon an imagined common origin that ensures the othering of one another to proceed in a mutually appreciated manner. A hybrid and special mode of Confucianism is possible because the relaxation on ancestor worship, together with pedagogy offered by international Confucian scholars, can create post-Chineseness that enables all sides to practice different Chineseness.

Conclusion

I have complicated essentialist understandings of Chineseness by enlisting religious cases and presenting nuances in their applications to the study of Chinese nationalism. I have also shown how, once complicated, Chineseness evolves into multiple strings of post-Chineseness, which constantly reconstruct Chineseness via all sorts of strategic reconnection enacted by those self-regarded cultural Chinese. In this sense, cultural nationalism is the practice of reconnection. Chinese cultural nationalism involves parallel attempts at reconnection with an imagined Chinese population. Religions can contribute to Chinese cultural nationalism in various ways. One incurs different types of religious resources to achieve reconnection so that imagined resemblance can be engendered or reproduced.

Amid the atmosphere of China rising, cultural nationalism contributes to political nationalism only indirectly, where the agents attain psychological determination from their religious conviction to pursue state or ethnic nationalism. Cultural nationalism hinders political nationalism because culture is necessarily cross-boundary in the Chinese case of multiple religions, and thus, does not fit with any territorial identity. Religious resources that serve the imagination of reconnection in the multi-religious context of China vary in their implications for behavioral consequence. In this manner, post-Chineseness reinforces the image of ethnic and Sinic Chinese nationalism but actually neutralizes its development, embraces cyclical dialectics, and restrains any steady contribution from religion.

Notes

1 This may result in longing for territory (Brophy 2016).
2 Cosmopolitan Christianity is named as cultural Christians in certain literature (Zhuo 2015; Leung 2003) to highlight cross-cultural characteristics.
3 This chapter will not answer the question of whether Confucianism is ultimately a religion or not. It treats Confucianism as faith in filial piety practiced primarily through the ritual of ancestral as well as heavenly worship. Such rituals enable the imagination of common ancestors of all Chinese.
4 Barmé interestingly translates the English notion "new Sinology" to "post-Sinology" (*houhanxue*) in Chinese.

References

Ahmad, Anwar. 2015. 'Religious Leaders: UAE an Exemplary Model of Multi-faith Cooperation,' *The National*, 19 March, available at: www.thenational.ae/uae/religious-leaders-uae-an-exemplary-model-of-multi-faith-cooperation (accessed 12 October 2016).

Barmé, Geremie R. 2005. 'New Sinology,' *Chinese Studies Association of Australia Newsletter* 31, available at: http://ciw.anu.edu.au/new_sinology/index.php (accessed 13 October 2016).

Baugus, Bruce P. 2014. *China's Reforming Churches*. Grand Rapids, MI. Reformation Heritage Books.

Benn, James A. 2007. *Burning for the Buddha: Self-Immolation in Chinese Buddhism*. Honolulu: University of Hawaii Press.

Bovingdon, Gardner. 2010. *The Uyghurs: Strangers in Their Own Land*. New York: Columbia University Press.

Brophy, David. 2016. *Uyghur Nation: Reform and Revolution on the Russia-China Frontier*. Cambridge: Harvard University Press.

Cagle, Megan. 2016. 'Faith and Community Leaders Launch National Refugees Welcome Initiative,' May 21, available at: http://cwsglobal.org/faith-and-community-leaders-launch-national-refugees-welcome-initiative/ (accessed 11 October 2016).

Carlson, Allen. 2009. 'A Flawed Perspective: The Limitations Inherent Within the Study of Chinese Nationalism,' *Nation and Nationalism*, 15(1): 20–35.

Chan, Joseph. 2001. 'Territorial Boundaries and Confucianism,' in David Miller and Sohail H. Hashmi (eds.), *Boundaries and Justice: Diverse Ethical Perspectives*. Princeton, NJ: Princeton University Press, pp. 89–111.

Chang, Pi-chun. 2009. *An Examination on Chinese Alternative Discourses: Cross-Cultural Perspectives on Chinese Nationalism, Postmodernism, and Neo-Confucianism*. Saarbrücken: VDM Verlag.

Chau, Adam. 2008. *Miraculous Response: Doing Popular Religion in Contemporary China*. Stanford, CA: Stanford University Press.

Ching Hai. 2011. *I Have Come to Take You Home*. Taipei: The Supreme Master Ching Hai International Association Publishing.
Cismas, Ioana. 2014. *Religious Actors and International Law*. New York: Oxford University Press.
Clayton, Cathryn H. 2010. *Sovereignty at the Edge: Macau and the Question of Chineseness*. Cambridge, MA: Harvard University Asia Center.
Coe, Shoki. 1980. 'Contextualization as the Way Toward Reform,' in Douglas J. Elwood (ed.), *Asian Christian Theology: Emerging Themes*. Philadelphia: The Westminster Press, pp. 48–55.
———. 1993. *Recollections and Reflections*. Ed. Boris Anderson. Washington, DC: Formosan Christians for Self-Determination.
Crook, John H. 2012. *World Crisis and Buddhist Humanism*. Kindle ed. Wayne, NJ: New Age Books.
Domes, Jürgen. 1990. 'The China Watch: Fr. Ladanyi and His Friends,' *CNA*, Special Commemorative Issue, November.
Entwistle, Phil. 2016. 'Faith in China: Religious Belief and National Narratives Amongst Young, Urban Chinese Protestants,' *National and Nationalism*, 22(2): 347–370.
Faries, Nathan. 2010. *The "Inscrutably Chinese" Church: How Narratives and Nationalism Continue to Divide Christianity*. Plymouth: Lexington Books.
Formicola, Jo Renee, and Hubert Morken (eds.) 2001. *Religious Leaders and Faith-based Politics: Ten Profiles*. Lanham: Rowman & Littlefield.
Fulton, Brent. 2015. *China's Urban Christians: A Light That Cannot Be Hidden*. Eugene, OR: Pickwick Publications.
Goldstein, Melvyn C. 1998. *Buddhism in Contemporary Tibet: Religious Revival and Cultural Identity*. Berkeley: University of California Press.
Granoff, Phyllis, and Shinohara, Koichi (eds.) 2005. *Images in Asian Religions: Texts and Contexts*. Vancouver: UBC Press.
Guruge, Ananda. 2005. *Buddhist Answers to Current Issues: Studies in Socially Engaged Humanistic Buddhism*. Bloomington: Author House.
Han, Christina Hee Yeon. 2011. *Territory of the Sages: Neo-Confucian Discourse of Wuyi Nine Bends Jingjie*. A Thesis Submitted in Conformity with the Requirements for the Degree of Doctor of Philosophy Graduate Department of East Asian Studies University of Toronto.
Harris, Ian. 2013. *Buddhism in a Dark Age: Cambodian Monks Under Pol Pot*. Honolulu: University of Hawaii Press.
Hartig, Falk. 2012. 'Cultural Diplomacy with Chinese Characteristics: The Case of Confucius Institutes in Australia,' *Communication, Politics & Culture*, 45(2): 256–276.
Hau, Caroline S. 2014. *The Chinese Question: Ethnicity, Nation and Region in and Beyond the Philippines*. Kyoto: Kyoto University Press.
Heyndrickx, Jeroom. 2005. 'From China-Watchers to Partners in China Mission,' *Tripod*, 25(138): 49–60.
Hirono, Miwa. 2008. *Civilizing Missions: International Religious Agencies in China*. New York: Palgrave Macmillan.
Hsu, Cho-yun. 1991. 'Applying Confucian Ethics to. International Relations,' *Ethics and International Affairs*, 5(1): 15–31.
Hsu, Victor Wan Chi. 2016. 'A Sobering Retrospective of the Canberra Assembly 25 Years Ago,' available at: https://blog.oikoumene.org/posts/a-sobering-retrospective-of-the-canberra-assembly-25-years-ago (accessed February 2015).
Huang, Chun-chieh. 2015. *East Asian Confucianism*. Taipei: National Taiwan University Press.

Israeli, Raphael. 2007. *Islam in China: Religion, Ethnicity, Culture, and Politics*. Plymouth: Lexington Press.
Ivanhoe, Philip J. 2016. *Three Streams: Confucian Reflections on Learning and the Moral Heart-Mind in China, Korea and Japan*. Oxford: Oxford University Press.
Johnson, Ian. 2017. *The Souls of China: The Return of Religion After Mao*. New York: Patheon.
Kang, Jie. 2016. *House Church Christianity in China: From Rural Preacers to City Pastors*. New York: Palgrave Macmillan.
Katz, Paul. 2014. *Religion in China and Its Modern Fate*. Waltham, MA: Brandeis University Press.
Katz, Paul, and Murray Rubenstein (eds.) 2003. *Religion and the Formation of Taiwanese Identities*. New York: Palgrave Macmillan.
Katzenstein, Peter L. (ed.) 2012. *Sinicization and the Rise of China: Civilizational Processes Beyond East and West*. Oxon: Routledge.
Keenan, Barry C. 2011. *Neo-Confucian Self-Cultivation*. Honolulu: University of Hawaii Press.
Kluver, Randolf. 2014. 'The Sage as Strategy: Nodes, Networks, and the Quest for Geopolitical Power in the Confucius Institute,' *Communication, Culture & Critique*, 7: 192–209.
Kuehn, Julia, Louie, Kam, and Pomfret, David M. (eds.) 2014. *Diasporic Chineseness After the Rise of China: Communities and Cultural Production*. Vancouver: UBC Press.
Kyounghan, Bae. 2009. 'Chiang Kai-shek and Christianity: Religious Life Reflected from His Diary,' *Journal of Modern Chinese History*, 3(1): 1–10.
Leung, Ka Lun. 2003. 'Cultural Christians and Christianity in China,' Trans. Stacy Mosher. *China Rights Forum*, 4: 28–31.
Li, Hsi Chang, Mirmirani, Sam, and Ilacqua, Joseph A. 2009. 'Confucius Institutes: Distributed Leadership and Knowledge Sharing in a Worldwide Network,' *The Learning Organization*, 16(6): 469–482.
Lian, Xi. 2010. *Redeemed by Fire: The Rise of Popular Christianity in Modern China*. New Haven: Yale University Press.
Lim, Benjamin, and Blanchard, Ben. 2013. 'Xi Jinping Hopes Traditional Faiths Can Fill Moral Void in China: Sources. World News September 29,' *Reuters*, available at: www.reuters.com/article/us-china-politics-vacuum-idUSBRE98S0GS20130929 (accessed 14 October 2016).
Liu, Yu. 2015. *Harmonious Disagreement: Matteo Ricci and His Closest Chinese Friends*. New York: Peter Lang.
Louie, Andrea. 2004. *Chineseness Across Borders: Renegotiating Chinese Identities in China and the United States*. Durham, NC: Duke University Press.
Madsen, Richard. 1998. *China's Catholics: Tragedy and Hope in an Emerging Civil Society*. Berkeley: University of California Press.
Makeham, John. 2008. *Lost Soul: "Confucianism" in Contemporary Chinese Discourse*. Cambridge, MA: Harvard University Press.
Marsh, Christopher. 2011. *Religion and the State in Russia and China: Suppression, Survival, and Revival*. New York: Bloomsbury Academics.
Morrissey, Todd. 2008. *Jesuits in Hong Kong, South China and Beyond: Irish Jesuit Mission*. Hong Kong: Xavier Publishing Association Company Limited.
Pittman, Don A. 2001. *Toward a Modern Chinese Buddhism: Taixu's Reforms*. Honolulu: University of Hawaii Press.
Roetz, Heiner. 1993. *Confucian Ethics of the Axial Age: A Reconstruction Under the Aspect of the Breakthrough Toward Postconventional Thinking*. Albany: State University of New York Press.

Rošker, Jana. 2016. *The Rebirth of the Moral Self: The Second Generation of Modern Confucians and Their Modernization Discourses*. Honolulu: University of Hawaii Press.

Sen, Tensen. 2003. *Buddhism, Diplomacy, and Trade*. Honolulu: University of Hawaii Press.

Shan, Mark C. 2012. *Beware of Patriotic Heresy in the Church in China: Drawing on the Historical Lessons of the Nazis' Volk Church to Analyze the Zhao Xiao Phenomenon*. Boston: CreateSpace Independent Publishing Platform.

Sheperd, Robert J. 2013. *Faith in Heritage: Displacement, Development, and Religious Tourism in Contemporary China*. Oxon: Routledge.

Shih, Chih-yu. 2014. 'Introduction: Humanity and Pragmatism Transcending Borders,' *East Asia*, 31(2): 93–101.

―――― (ed.) 2015. *Re-producing Chineseness in Southeast Asia: Scholarship and Identity in Comparative Perspectives*. Oxon: Routledge.

Yang, Mayfair Mei-hui. 2008. 'Goddess Across the Taiwan Strait: Matrifocal Ritual Space, Nation-State, and Satellite Television Footprints,' in Mayfair Mei-hui Yang (ed.), *Chinese Religiosities: Afflictions of Modernity and State Formation*. Berkeley: University of California Press, pp. 323–348.

Stark, Rodney, and Wang, Xiuhua. 2015. *A Star in the East: The Rise of Christianity in China*. West Conshohocken, PA.: Templeton Press.

Sutton, Donald S. 2003. *Steps of Perfection: Exorcistic Performers and Chinese Religion in Twentieth-Century Taiwan*. Cambridge, MA: Harvard University Asia Center.

Tan, Chung. 2015. *Himalaya Calling: The Origins of China and India. Hackensack*. Hackensack, NJ: World Century Publication Corporation.

Tang, Siufu. 2016. *Self-Realization Through Confucian Learning: A Contemporary Reconstruction of Xunzi's Ethics*. Albany: State University of New York Press.

Taylor, Jay. 2011. *The Generalissimo: Chiang Kai-shek and the Struggle for Modern China*. Cambridge: Belknap Press.

Taylor, Rodney L. 1990. *The Religious Dimensions of Confucianism*. Albany: State University of New York Press.

Terrill, Ross (ed.) 2016. *Xi Jinping's China Renaissance: Historical Mission and Great Power Strategy*. New York: CT Times Books.

Tikhonov, Vladimir, and Brekke, Torkel. 2013. *Buddhism and Violence: Militarism and Buddhism in Modern Asia*. Oxon: Routledge.

Truman, Robert. 2011. *Why the Dalai Lama Matters: His Act of Truth as the Solution for China, Tibet and the World*. New York: Atria Books.

Van der Veer, Peter. 2013. *The Modern Spirit of Asia: The Spiritual and the Secular in China and India*. Princeton, NJ: Princeton University Press.

Walton, Matthew J., and Hayward, Susan. 2014. *Contesting Buddhist Narratives: Democratization, Nationalism, and Communal Violence in Myanmar*. Honolulu: East-West Center.

Wang, Cheng-mian. 2014. 'Chiang Kai-shek's Faith in Christianity: The Trial of the Stilwell Incident,' *Journal of Modern Chinese History*, 8(2): 194–209.

Wang, Gungwu. 2000. *The Chinese Overseas: From Earthbound China to the Quest for Autonomy*. Cambridge, MA: Harvard University Press.

Wheeler, Anita. 2015. 'Communicating China to the World: Confucius Institutes and China's Strategic Narratives Politics,' *Journal of Asian and African Studies*, 35: 245–258.

Wittgenstein, Ludwig. 1986. *Philosophical Investigation*. Trans. G. E. M. Anscombe. Oxford: Basil Blackwell Ltd.

Woeser, Tsering. 2016. *Tibet on Fire: Self-Immolations Against Chinese Rule*. Trans. Kevin Carrico. London: Verso.

Yang, Fenggang. 2011. *Religion in China: Survival and Revival Under Communist Rule*. New York: Oxford University Press.
Yao, Xinzhong, and Zhao, Yanxia. 2010. *Chinese Religion: A Contextual Approach*. New York: Bloomsbury Academics.
Yeh, Wen-hsin (ed.) 2000. *Cross-Cultural Readings of Chineseness: Narratives, Images, and Interpretations of the 1990s*. Berkeley: The Institute of East Asian Studies, University of California.
Yu, Dan Smyer. 2014. *The Spread of Tibetan Buddhism in China: Charisma, Money, Enlightenment*. Oxon: Routledge.
Yu, Jimmy. 2012. *Sanctity and Self-Inflicted Violence in Chinese Religions, 1500–1700*. New York: Oxford University Press.
Yu, Xue. 2011. *Buddhism, War, and Nationalism: Chinese Monks in the Struggle Against Japanese Agreesion 1931–1945*. Oxon: Routledge.
Yukong, Zhao. 2013. *The Chinese Secrets for Success*. New York: Morgan James Publishing.
Zhang, Fenzhi. 2015. *Xi Jinping: How to Read Confucius and Other Chinese Classical Thinkers*. New York: CT Times Books.
Zhuo, Xinping. 2015. 'Discussion on "Cultural Christians" in China,' in Stephen Uhalley, Jr. and Xiaoxin Wu (eds.), *China and Christianity: Burdened Past, Hopeful Future*. Oxon: Routledge, pp. 283–300.
Zubrzycki, Geneviéve. 2006. *The Crosses of Auschwitz: Nationalism and Religion in Post-Communist Poland*. Chicago: Chicago University Press.

Conclusion

Takashi Kibe and Giorgio Shani

Nationalism is conventionally understood to be a modern secular ideology constitutive of the modern international system of territorialized nation-states with its origins in the French Revolution. The Revolution with its slogans of *Liberté, égalité, fraternité* based on Enlightenment ideals ushered in a brave new world of modernity which sought to replace the religious cosmologies and feudal structures found in pre-modern, traditional societies. In this view, "'religion' and 'nationalism' figure as two terms in the conventional distinction between tradition and modernity, and in an evolutionary framework that sees an inevitable movement – whether liberating or destructive – from the one to the other" (Smith 2003: 9).

The chapters in this volume have attempted to examine the relationship between religion and nationalism with reference to Asia. In so doing, they have challenged conventional accounts of nationalism as they have developed in the West as well as critically interrogated the distinction drawn between the "religious" and the "secular." They have done so by bringing into question an understanding of modernity as originating in the West and disseminated throughout the rest of the globe through secular nationalism. The concluding chapter has a twofold task. One task is to examine the *legacies* and *possibilities* opened up by an examination of the role which religion has played and continues to play in the construction of Asian nationalisms; another task is to give our answers to the three questions posed in the introduction. As to the first task, we will review modernist theories of nationalism before examining how the various contributors to this volume have challenged conventional accounts of the relationship between religion, nationalism and modernity, followed by an exploration of the possibility of going beyond nationalism in the region. We will then conclude with our answers to the three questions.

Legacies

Theories of nationalism

Modernist accounts view nations and nationalism as intrinsically *modern* phenomena, by-products of capitalism, industrialization, urbanization, rationalization, and the formation of modern statehood. They are best captured in Ernest Gellner's

Conclusion 187

famous dictum that nationalism is *not* the awakening of nations to self-consciousness but invents them where they do not exist (Gellner 1983). This inverts the traditional view which, following Weber, regards the existence of a nation to be a precondition for the establishment of the state.[1] For Gellner, this cultural distinctiveness upon which the state's claim to sovereignty resides is a product of a process of deliberately designed cultural consolidation by nationalist elites which replaced the multiple and incongruent "low" cultures of traditional agrarian societies with a single, homogenous, codified, and literate "high" culture which defines and delimits membership of a nation community. The modern "nation," therefore, is seen to be built upon *invented traditions* (Hobsbawm 1983).[2]

For Benedict Anderson, the nation is a similarly novel political community which replaced the earlier communities of faith which preceded it. Anderson considers the nation to be "an imagined political community – and imagined as both inherently *limited* and *sovereign*" (Anderson 1991: 5). The nation is *imagined* because "the members of even the smallest nation will never know most of their fellow-members, meet them, or even hear of them, yet in the minds of each lives the image of their communion." The nation is imagined as *limited* because "even the largest of them encompassing perhaps a billion living human beings, has finite, if elastic boundaries, beyond which lie other nations" (Anderson 1991: 6–7). Three cultural preconditions existed in order for nations to be imagined. Firstly, the replacement of "sacred silent languages" (Anderson 1991: 14) that offered privileged access to ontological truths with vernacular "print languages" as the principal media through which to imagine the community. Secondly, the decline of the dynastic principle based upon the legitimacy of a sovereign deriving from divinity and its replacement by the principle of popular sovereignty. Finally, following Walter Benjamin, the replacement of "messianic time" – where past and future coexist- in an instantaneous present with a "homogeneous, empty time" marked by temporal coincidence and measured by clock and calendar (Anderson 1991: 24).

The origins of nations and nationalism, for Anderson, lie in "the convergence of capitalism and print technology on the fatal diversity of the human language" (Anderson 1991: 46). Print capitalism, for Anderson, refers to the creation of mechanically reproduced secular "print languages" capable of dissemination through the market. These "print languages" laid the basis for national consciousness first in Europe then elsewhere by creating fixed, unified fields of communication below sacred language and above the spoken regional vernaculars. Books and newspapers written in these "print languages" were the first mass-market commodities in capitalism, designed for consumption in the new "domestic" market. Speakers of regional dialects within a particular territory became capable of understanding one another through articles in newspapers, journals, and books, even though they might find it difficult or even impossible to comprehend each other in conversation. In the process, they became aware of the hundreds or thousands, or even millions, of people who could read their language. These fellow readers, to whom they are connected in print, formed, for Anderson, "the embryo of the nationally imagined community" (Anderson 1991: 44).

For Anderson, the nationally imagined community is an explicitly *secular* political community, one made possible by the eclipse of the cosmopolitan framings of "universal" religious communities. Although he acknowledges that nationalism has not completely "superseded" religion, it can only be understood by being aligned with the "large cultural systems that preceded it, out of which – as well as against which – it came into being" (Anderson 1991: 12). Yet the nation still retained the emotive, atavistic power of the larger religious communities which it replaced. What else can explain its hold on the "imagination" of those prepared not only to kill but also die in the name of a "secular" nation? As Anthony D. Smith presciently notes, the "passion evoked by nationalism, the powerful commitments felt by so many people to their own national identities, could not be explained in conventional economic and political terms." "Only religion," Smith asserts, "with its powerful symbolism and collective ritual, could inspire such fervor" (Smith 2003: vii).

For A. D. Smith, the nation draws upon the myths and symbols of pre-existing religious communities which it never clearly succeeded in replacing. The nation is, for Smith, "best regarded as a *sacred communion* of the people, devoted to the cult of authenticity and the ideals of national autonomy, unity and identity in a historic homeland" (Smith 2003: 254 italics mine). The term "sacred communion," with its explicit Christian imagery and connotations, is deployed by Smith to denote an *ethnic* community, bound by the belief in shared ancestry and kinship, with a public *cult* that unites adherents into a single moral community of the faithful with common rights and duties (Smith 2003: 32–33).

Smith appears to draw on Elie Kedourie's understanding of nationalism as "the secular heir of Christian millennialism and proclaims the same apocalyptic message" (Kedourie 1971: 12). For Kedourie, nationalism was "a spiritual child of the Enlightenment. As such it was a modern, secular, European and invented ideology. It proclaimed the overthrow of God and the power of man as the measure of all things; and it offered a purely terrestrial and anthropocentric vision of perfection in place of earlier religious and other worldly conceptions" (Smith 2003: 9). This ideology, for Kedourie, was imposed on the post-colonial world by "marginal men" who were the products of Western education but frustrated by the lack of opportunities which colonial modernity provided for its racialized subjects. In short, "the mainspring of nationalism in Asia and Africa" was the same "secular millennialism which had its rise and development in Europe and in which society is subjected to the will of a handful of visionaries" (Kedourie 1971: 106).

Multiple modernities

Most of the contributors to this volume follow Sudipta Kaviraj in rejecting the "crude version of this textbook story of nationalism": a diffusionist account of the origins of nationalism which privileges Europe as the point of origin for the emergence of nationalism and modernity. Asian societies are reduced to consumers of a modernity brought by an alien power and its new form of collective belonging: the nation. This reading of nationalism in the post-colonial world as an *imitation* of Western models of political community robs non-Western subjects of agency which is a point explicitly made in Atsuko Ichijo's chapter. To echo Chatterjee, "if nationalisms in the rest of the world have to choose their imagined community from certain 'modular' forms already made available to them by Europe and the Americas, what do they have left to imagine?" (Chatterjee 1993: 5).

The chapters in this volume are replete with examples of "Asian" nationalisms which have diverged from the modular forms suggested by conventional theories of modernization. Whereas the nationalism – in either its civic or ethnic variants – was an exclusionary political community in the West in the sense that it helped to draw a firm boundary between citizens and foreigners, nationalism in many parts of Asia was more inclusive, helping to forge bonds between the colonized which cut across ethnicity, language, and religion. As illustrated in Sudipta Kaviraj's chapter, Rabindranath Tagore's "critical" stance toward nationalism was based on a rejection of the homogeneity demanded of the nation and the subordination of the nation to the state. This, he believed, reproduced the social imaginary of colonialism which made sovereignty the center of all political activity and collective aspirations. Tagore, instead, turned the nation into a "moral imaginary" which could be used strategically as a ground to criticize nation-states. His critical stance toward anti-colonial nationalism proved prophetic as both the "secular" nationalism of the Indian National Congress (INC) and the "religious" nationalism of the Muslim League subordinated the nation to the state leading to the violence of Partition as illustrated in Giorgio Shani's chapter. The specters of Partition, Shani argues, continue to haunt South Asia today in the emergence of exclusivist nationalist discourses associated with the Bharatiya Janata Party (BJP) in India and Islamist parties in Pakistan and Bangladesh which are wedded to a homogenous *modern* conception of the nation-state.

In many respects, communalism in South Asia mirrors sectarianism in the Middle East. As Fanar Haddad points out in his chapter, a distinction is made between sectarianism and nationalism within the region which reveals a "modernist" bias. Secular national identities are considered modern and therefore "good" as distinct from "pre-modern" transnational sectarian identities which are considered atavistic and, therefore, "bad." However, Haddad argues that both are distinctly *modern* political identities which are closely interrelated. Similarly, Manuel Sapitula's analysis of the role which religion plays in the imagination of the Philippines as a "Catholic Nation" appears to bring into question the secular bias of modernist theories of nationalism.

Turning to East Asia, the agency of state, colonial and anti-colonial elites in the forging of East Asian modernities is explicitly taken up in chapters by Takashi Kibe, Atsuko Ichijo and Jun-Hyeok Kwak. Kibe's chapter illustrates the role played by Inoue and Fukuzawa in the imagination of a modern Japanese national identity in the Meiji period. Although they both may have shared an aspiration for the secular nationalism as practiced in the West, their instrumental use of religion led to the subsequent development of religious nationalism in Japan culminating in the Second World War. The Kyoto School of philosophy was closely associated with the expansion of Japanese militarist nationalism in Asia as Kosuke

Shimizu demonstrates in his chapter but the possibilities it offered for transcending Japanese imperial nationalism were seized on by anti-colonial elites as illustrated by Atsuko Ichijo. Ichijo explicitly references Shmuel Eisenstadt's theory of "multiple modernities" which rejects the teleological assumption of modernization theory in order to examine how colonial intellectuals in Taiwan, Korea, and China subverted imperial discourses in order to define modernity in their own terms. Similarly, Kwak focuses on a colonial intellectual, Ahn Changho. Unlike the colonial intellectuals examined by Ichijo, Changho was a Korean nationalist who rejected Japanese imperial discourses yet sought, like Tagore, to articulate a more inclusive nationalism which could be compatible with universal values. His conception of non-domination, which was embodied in his faith, sought to combine a love of the nation with a love of humanity, thereby avoiding the bellicose nationalism characteristic of Japan and much of the West. Finally, Chih-yu Shih demonstrates in his chapter how discourses of "post-Chineseness" contribute to a reimagining of "China" as a deterritorialized cultural community which can encompass Chinese living in the diaspora as well as the mainland. The Chinese "nation," therefore, does not necessarily need to have a territorial basis as considered axiomatic in conventional modernist theories of nationalism.

The religious/secular dyad

The role played by religion in the imagination of the nation begs the question of what is understood by the concept "religion." The chapters in this volume reveal little definitional clarity. Instead, religion may be seen as a *dynamic* concept, a signifier of the "sacred" that may transcend the boundary between "religion" and "culture." As Kibe's chapter illustrates, Shintoism was initially considered a "non-religion" by Inoue and Fukuzawa but became the legitimizing ideology of the Japanese Empire after its transformation into a state "religion." Arguably, the case of Shintoism has many parallels with contemporary China where Confucianism, as the chapters by Zhibin Xie and Chih-yu Shih illustrate, is a source of (post) Chinese identity which can be co-opted to legitimize state power.

If as Derrida (1998) has claimed, *religio* is a concept which cannot be translated out of the Abrahamic context in which it emerged, then what accounts for its prevalence throughout Asia? For Shani, "religion" accompanied colonialism; it was an alien concept imported into South Asia as part of what Chatterjee (1993) has termed colonial governmentality. To be sure, religion as *faith* predated colonialism since there was always a conception of the "sacred" which coexisted with the "profane" in the cosmological traditions of South Asia. However, Shani argues, following Kaviraj, that colonialism transformed previously "thick" faith traditions into "thin" religious identities; "religion" became a marker of an exclusivist identity which could be instrumentalized by nationalist elites in the process of political mobilization. The role of colonialism in the construction of national identities based on religion is a theme taken up by Sapitula in his examination of Filipino nationalism and Haddad in his analysis of sectarianism in the Middle East. In East Asia, religion has historically played less of a role in the construction of national identities but, as Shih points out in his chapter, it may contribute to a sense of *cultural* nationalism which "is not entirely compatible with statist nationalism embedded in territoriality". Cultural nationalism for Shih refers to the process of reconnection between populations through a shared imagination of similar cultural practices which may include the "the worship of ancestors, Buddha, or earthly Gods." Cultural nationalism, therefore, for Shih appears to have a *sacred* dimension.

But what of the other component of the dyad: the "secular"? Does this concept translate into Asian societies? If so, how do Asian "secularisms" differ from their Western counterparts? Charles Taylor in a recent work considers the concept to have a limited applicability outside of the West. As he demonstrates in his exhaustive study, *A Secular Age* (2007), the "secular" developed as a category within Latin Christendom referring to "profane" time as opposed to "sacred" time which was considered eternal. However, it mutates into a term in another dyad where the "secular" refers to an "immanent" frame to be contrasted with the transcendental. The concept of the "immanent frame" refers to a constellation of interlocking impersonal orders which collectively constitute the "modern": the social, cosmic, and moral. It is characterized by an order in which the "buffered identity of the disciplined individual moves in a constructed social space, where instrumental rationality is a key value and time is pervasively secular" (Taylor 2007: 542). Individual identity is "buffered" in the sense that there is a firm boundary between the "self" and "other". It follows for Taylor that there can be no secularism in societies where the distinction between "self" and "other" – or indeed between humans and other sentient beings – are fluid as in many Asian faith traditions such as Hinduism, Buddhism, and Jainism. Therefore, Taylor considers the "secular" to have "very little application in pre-colonial or pre-contact non-western societies" such as "imperial China or traditional Japan" (Taylor 2016: 25).

Taylor, however, is open to its application in those societies where indigenous beliefs have been profoundly transformed by the colonial encounter. Therefore, he considers it applicable in a societal sense in post-colonial India but not in the Mughal period which, under the reign of the Emperor Akbar, was characterized by inter-communal harmony. However, as Shani points out in his chapter, the Indian version of secularism, *Sarva Dharma Sambhava* ("let all religions flourish"), is radically different from its Western counterpart since it is premised on the belief that religion is a fundamental component of political identity and, therefore, cannot be removed from the public sphere. This differs from Western secularism which is based on the assumption that belief in God is "understood to be one option among others, and frequently not the easiest to embrace" (Taylor 2007: 3).

Nevertheless, the contributors to the volume have found the term "secular" to have analytical purchase in those societies which were not directly colonized by the West. For Kibe, the "secular" in Meiji Japan was considered a "non-religious" space which was actively carved out by modernizing elites. He refers to this process as a form of "non-religion" making. If religion-making refers to the way in which religion is conceptualized and institutionalized, within a globalized discourse of world religions (Dressler and Mandair 2011), then "non-religion" making, for Kibe, refers to the way in which cultural traditions which were previously considered "religious" are "secularized." Once they are *de-religionized*, they are no longer seen as an impediment to modernization, and therefore can be co-opted by state elites to legitimize the rule of the state and its modernizing project. Similar processes appear to be at work in China as can be seen implicitly the chapters by Xie and Shih respectively and explicitly in the Chinese Communist Party (CCP)'s rehabilitation of Confucianism in the aftermath of the Cultural Revolution to the extent that it can be seen as a state ideology alongside Marxism in much the same way as Shintoism was – and continues to be – in Japan.

Possibilities

The foregoing discussion on "legacies" that emerge from the chapters of this volume leads us to our next task about "possibilities." What are possible trajectories that develop out of, and perhaps transform, current configurations of nationalism and religion? What are future shapes of secularism? What kind of imaginaries are likely to, or necessary to, guide these configurations? To be sure, it is no easy task to identify those "possibilities." We would like to limit ourselves to three topics: (1) discursive possibilities about religion and nationalism, (2) future trajectories of secularism, and (3) alternative imaginaries.

Discursive possibilities about religion and nationalism

As our discussion on "legacies" suggests, relationships between nationalism and religion are inherently not static but diverse and dynamic in character; they depend heavily on how we draw a line of demarcation between religion and the secular as well as between national and non-national. This line is not given a priori but *discursively* informed and hence open to alterations. Configurations thus depend on what is defined as national and particularly on whether this definition includes religion or not.

At this juncture, the question about what is religion is crucial. Indeed contributors of this volume emphasize multiple aspects of religion: religion as doctrine or identity (Haddad), "thick" or "thin" religion (Kaviraj in Shani), religion as faith or practice (Kibe). Even if such definitional problem is to be solved, there are multiple ways to connect these "religious" elements to nationalism, since, as Shih in this volume demonstrates, this act of connecting inevitably involves processes of reimagining and rediscovering, thereby making connections between religion and nationalism diverse and hence unfixed.

In this context, it is an interesting and vexing question as to whether Confucianism can be considered a religion.[3] Indeed, van der Veer (2014, 2016) and Ichijo in this volume prefer to use spirituality – the very concept that enables us to treat Confucianism as on a par with Buddhism, as Nguyen's study on Vietnam shows (2018). However, it is unclear the extent to which spirituality can escape the same definitional ambiguities haunting that of religion.

Future trajectories of secularism

What possible future trajectories does this volume suggest? Two are clear. One is positive in the sense of affirming secularism; the other is critical. The positive trajectory consists in pursuing the political principle of secularism to the full, thereby attempting to guarantee religious freedom from politics and politicized religion as well as political freedom from religious influence. This trajectory is suggested in Hua's and Xie's chapters on China. Both contributors highlight the need to guarantee religious freedom, while emphasizing the ideal of social harmony and cooperation. In this trajectory, secularism is thus understood as a goal which we should endeavor to approach as closely as possible.

The second trajectory takes a critical stance toward secularism for three reasons. First, secularism is not an effective principle that can fix configurations between religion and nationalism in an ideal way; rather it impacts them, decisively depending in different notion of what is religion and what is national. This situation happens, for example, when the state decides to *de-religionize*, that is, to regard as secular what is otherwise considered religion (see Kibe's chapter in this volume). A case in point is Shinto in modern Japan, as depicted in Kibe's chapter: it was de-religionized to serve the purpose of nation-building. This kind of transformation in religious and national configurations happened to China, when a Chinese popular religion called *nuo* started to receive official recognition and support, after it was interpreted not as religion but as culture (Li 2011: 1308). It goes without saying that such a transformation equally happens when a religion is regarded as a threat to security and hence securitized[4] – a case in which secularism has no say.

Second, secularism does not function properly where the distinction between religion and the secular is difficult to make. Shani's chapter is explicit in making this point. According to Shani, in South Asia it is difficult to separate religious and secular nationalism given the shared colonial legacy and the memory of Partition; the result is that secularism aligned with the nation-state model has been unable to contain communal forces in the region. Kibe's chapter, which considers the ambiguous status of popular religion in modern Japan, points to a similar difficulty, although it does not refute secularism.

Third, secularism is no panacea to solve complicated issues of religion and nationalism. This point is clearly made by Sapitula's chapter. According to Sapitula, Catholic-based nationalism in the Philippines is a problematic form of religious nationalism that runs counter to actually existing religious diversity. This means that despite the embraced secularist principle of strict separation between church and state, Roman Catholicism, the majority religion, can exert a significant influence in shaping the Filipino national identity, thereby marginalizing religious minorities. At stake here is a question about to what extent nationalism is inclusive, thereby preventing exclusion and marginalization of minorities from emerging – for example, this is a move made in Indonesian nationalist discourse to make inclusive measures toward minority groups within Muslims (Schäfer 2018). All of this boils down to a vital question: Is secularism led by substantive normative criteria for inclusion and against exclusion? Irrespective of whether we embrace secularism, this question is likely to affect future possibilities of secularism.

Alternative imaginaries

What kind of alternative imaginaries are presented in this volume, which touch on configurations of religion and nationalism and offer a corrective to deficits of secularism? First of all, some chapters point to alternative imaginaries that make religious pluralism possible. For example, Kaviraj's notion of "critical nationalism" is a case in point. According to this notion, the nation is not simply political imaginary but also a *moral* imaginary of collective belonging. This imaginary has a critical function to remind us of "the state's imperfections, of the state's inevitable exclusions and its unevenness of the real experience of collective life." Drawing on Tagore's novel *Gora*, Kaviraj depicts this imaginary as something in which a "complete 'outsider' can be accepted with completeness." This resonates with the Indian notion of *Sarva Dharma Sambhava* ("let all religions flourish"), as referred to in Shani's chapter. This is the notion which Shani explains "could have been the basis for a unified state at the time of independence" – an idea which "does not attempt to banish religion from the public sphere but sees it as an integral part of politics." In a similar vein, Sapitula argues for the need of such new imaginary about national belonging. In his chapter on the Philippines, Sapitula requires "a deeper reflection on further possibilities of the dynamics of religion and nationalism," which "entails due recognition of alternative trajectories of modern transition and the plural bases of national identity." Roughly speaking, the gist of imaginaries of this type is to conceptualize national identity in a way to make it not only compatible with but also supportive of pluralism. At this juncture, one may wonder how religion can contribute to making a political and moral imaginary. Kwak's chapter on Ahn Changho illustrates how this can happen. His answer is that it happens by offering a religiously informed normative sensitivity. Ahn is an interesting case, in which Christianity helps him develop an imaginary of cosmopolitan patriotism, without claiming to be a constitutive national identity marker; it is open to religious diversity.

Transnational imaginaries are presented in this volume. For example, Shani refers to regional integration in South Asia, which involves "a reimagining of relations between the different political communities which make up the subcontinent along post-secular lines"; Shih presents a variety of cosmopolitan forms of Chinese, Buddhist, Christian, and Confucian identities. These are new transnational imaginaries. These imaginaries should be critically examined in the light of the lessons from the older, notorious transnational imaginaries, such as the Japanese wartime slogan "Greater East Asian Co-prosperity Sphere," as considered by Ichijo and Shimizu. Shimizu shows us a problem with this older imaginary, by arguing that although it is necessary to go beyond nationalism, we should not replace the nation-state model with a supranational, regional model only to fall into the hands of a superpower. Another problem with this imaginary is that it was premised on the homogenous notion of a nation as an ethnic community. These considerations suggest a question about how transnational imaginaries can avoid degenerating into an ideology that allows domination by a superpower at regional level and stifles pluralism at national level. In this context, Kwak's chapter on Ahn Changho is suggestive. Ahn's thought of cosmopolitan patriotism, as construed by Kwak, involves both domestic and transnational dimensions, since it is "the divine reciprocal duty of nations and presenting his vision of national independence as a means of realizing the ideal of non-domination." What we need here is a notion bridging domestic and regional dimensions; a global imaginary which challenges the ethnocentrism of the nationalist discourse at national level thus enabling pluralism to flourish.

Responses to the three questions

Having explored the legacies and possibilities emerging from the chapters of this volume, we are now in a position to give our responses to the questions we have raised: (1) What are characteristic configurations of religion and nationalism in Asian countries respectively? (2) What are differences and commonalities in diverse configurations of nationalism and religion in Asian contexts? (3) Is the nation-state model, coupled with secularism, suitable for the region?

What are characteristic configurations of religion and nationalism in Asian countries respectively?

In the volume, there is no single picture emerging from the chapters. First, both secular and religious types of nationalism can be observed throughout the region. In some cases, nationalism is religiously based. For example, Shani's chapter illustrates how religion in South Asia remains intertwined with nationalism as a result of the colonial legacy, thus posing a challenge to the secular view of nationalism; Sapitula's chapter on the Philippines shows another case of religiously based nationalism, that is, of the Philippines as a "Catholic Nation." For Haddad, sectarianism cannot be divorced from nationalism, further complicating the distinction between secular and religious nationalism in the Middle East. An interesting case is of secular nationalism is China. As Hua's and Xie's chapters on China show, religious freedom is still an actual issue for minority faith groups in secular states. Second, whether the trajectory of nationalism is either secular or religious is an open question, depending on various factors. For instance, Shih's chapter on post-Chineseness shows that different trajectories of national identity formation can emerge, depending on cultural resources which include religion. Kibe illustrates how dynamically fluid the demarcation between secular and religious nationalisms has been in Japanese political modernity in relation to Shintoism while Shimizu focuses on the role Buddhism played in the transition to Empire as well as in opposition to it.

What are differences and commonalities in diverse configurations of nationalism and religion in Asian contexts?

The previous observation immediately leads to the second question. On the one hand, differences in the configurations are profound, since there are both religious and secular nationalisms in the region. Those differences are impacted significantly by "path dependencies," as Künkler and Madeley rightly emphasize (2018: 422). Furthermore, it is difficult to clearly distinguish between secular and religious nationalism. For example, can the Hindutva-based nationalism advocated by the ruling Bharatiya Janata Party in India be seen as religious or secular? Is Shinto-based nationalism in Japan a type of religious or secular nationalism? On the other hand, all of this suggests that it is difficult to pinpoint commonalities in the configurations of the relationship between nationalism and religion – a conceptual fluidity. But one commonality emerging from the cases discussed in this book is clear: *it is a dynamic nature of the relationship between nationalism and religion.* As the chapters by Haddad, Kibe, Shani, and Shih suggest, the relationship between nationalism and religion is inherently dynamic and open to transformation.

Is the nation-state model, coupled with secularism, suitable for the region?

As the foregoing discussion suggests, we need a context-sensitive approach to respond to this question, given the different configurations presented in the chapters. Most chapters in the volume do not provide answers as much as challenges to tackle since most states in the region are still searching for an appropriate configuration of religion and nationalism. Three challenges emerge from this volume. First, a simple application of political secularism in the form of the separation of religion and the state is not viable given the public, and therefore political, nature of religion. Second, we need to go beyond a naive embrace of political secularism in order to conceptualize more substantial normative criteria to safeguard religious diversity and minorities from exclusion and marginalization. Third, we require alternative imaginaries to critically examine nationalism and secularism and to bridge both domestic and regional dimensions. Returning to Tagore's rejection of the *exclusiveness* of modern conceptions of the nation-state and his insistence that any such imaginary be based on "human" values may be a good place to start exploring the possibilities opened up for imagining a world beyond nationalism.

Notes

1 Weber had previously defined "a nation as a community of sentiment which would adequately manifest itself in a state of its own," having previously defined the state in terms of its monopolization of the legitimate use of force over a particular territory (Weber 1991: 117).
2 The term "invented traditions" is used in a broad sense to "mean a set of practices, normally governed by overtly or tacitly accepted rules and of a ritual and symbolic nature,

which seek to inculcate certain values and norms by behavior by repetition, which automatically implies continuity with the past" (Hobsbawm 1983: 1). It occurs "when a rapid transformation of society weakens and destroys the social patterns for which 'old' traditions had been designed, producing new ones to which they were not applicable, or when such old traditions and their institutional carriers . . . no longer prove sufficiently adaptable and flexible, or are otherwise eliminated" (Hobsbawm 1983: 4–5).
3 van der Veer (2016:120) considers Confucianism to be a "political cosmology."
4 Securitization may be understood as an extreme form of politicization, whereby an issue comes to be either politicized or placed above politics. Following Buzan et al., "security" denotes the move which takes politics beyond "the established rules of the game and frames the issue either as a special kind of politics or as above politics" (Buzan, Waever, and de Wilde 1998: 23). A securitized issue is something which is of vital importance to the national interest as defined by the state and which, therefore, cannot be subject to the same critical scrutiny by the media, politicians, and citizens as other issues deemed less important. It is treated as an existential threat requiring emergency measures and justifying "exceptional" responses by the state. In this sense, a securitized issue can be seen as de-politicized in that it is no longer seen as part of public discourse but is articulated in technical terms (Edkins 1999: 10).

References

Anderson, Benedict. 1991. *Imagined Communities: Reflections on the Origin and Spread of Nationalism*. 2nd edn. London: Verso.
Buzan, Barry, Waever, Ole, and de Wilde, Jaap. 1998. *Security: A New Framework of Analysis*. Boulder, CO: Lynne Rienner.
Chatterjee, Partha. 1993. *The Nation and it Fragments: Colonial and Postcolonial Histories*. Princeton, NJ: Princeton University Press.
Derrida, Jacques. 1998. 'Faith and Knowledge: The Two Sources of "Religion" and the Limits of Reason Alone,' in Jacques Derrida and Gianni Vattimo Derrida (eds.), *Religion*. Princeton, NJ: Princeton University Press, pp. 1–79.
Dressler, Marcus, and Mandair, Arvind Pal S. (eds.) 2011. *Secularism and Religion-Making*. New York: Oxford University Press.
Edkins, Jenny. 1999. *Poststructuralism and International Relations: Bringing the Political Back in*. Boulder, CO and London: Lynne Rienner.
Gellner, Ernest. 1983. *Nations and Nationalism*. Oxford: Blackwell.
Hobsbawm, Eric J. 1983. 'Introduction: Inventing Traditions,' in Eric J. Hobsbawm and Terence Ranger (eds.), *The Invention of Tradition*. Cambridge: Cambridge University Press, pp. 1–15.
Kedourie, Elie. 1971. *Nationalism in Asia and Africa*. Ed. Elie Kedourie. London: Weidenfield and Nicholson.
Künkler, Mirjam, and Madeley, John. 2018. *A Secular Age Beyond the West*. Cambridge: Cambridge University Press.
Lan, Li. 2011. 'The Changing Role of the Popular Religion of *Nuo* in Modern Chinese Politics,' *Modern Asian Studies*, 45(5): 1289–1311.
Nguyen, Phi-Vân 2018. 'A Secular State for a Religious Nation: The Republic of Vietnam and Religious Nationalism, 1946–1963,' *Journal of Asian Studies*, 77(3): 741–771.
Schäfer, Saskia 2018. 'Ahmadis or Indonesians? The Polarization of Post-Reform Public Debates on Islam and Orthodoxy,' *Critical Asian Studies*, 50(1): 16–36.
Smith, Anthony D. 2003. *Chosen Peoples*. Oxford: Oxford University Press.

Taylor, Charles. 2007. *A Secular Age*. Cambridge, MA: Harvard University Press.
———. 2016. 'Can Secularism Travel?' in Akeel Bilgrami (ed.), *Beyond the Secular West*. New York: Columbia University Press, pp. 1–28.
van der Veer, Peter. 2014. *The Modern Spirit of Asia: The Spiritual and the Secular in China and India*. Princeton, NJ: Princeton University Press.
———. 2016. 'Is Confucianism Secular?' in Akeel Bilgrami (ed.), *Beyond the Secular West*. New York: Columbia University Press, pp. 117–135.
Weber, Max. 1991. *From Max Weber*. Trans. and eds. H. H. Gerth and C. Wright Mills. London and New York: Routledge.

Index

Ahn Changho 9, 124–139, 194–195
Anderson, Benedict 2, 4, 36, 57, 109, 124, 186–188
Asad, Talal 1–2, 4–5, 86
Asia 1–10; *see also* East Asia; South Asia; Southeast Asia
Augustine, Saint 10, 124, 154–155, 158–165

Bangladesh 6–7, 24, 33, 39, 42, 189
Bharatiya Janata Party (BJP) 33, 37, 42, 44n15, 189, 196
Bengal: Bengali 1–2, 13, 15, 20, 23, 26, 29–30, 38–39; West Bengal 36
Buddhism 2–3, 10, 58, 81, 86, 94–108, 164, 168–186, 191–192, 195; Buddhist 2, 7, 8, 10, 33, 41, 83, 194

Casanova, José 1, 4, 48
Catholicism 47–62; Catholic 7, 10, 145, 154–159, 161–166, 189, 193, 195; Catholic nation 57–58, 189, 195; *see also* Christianity
Chatterjee, Partha 29n2, 34, 121n2, 189, 190
China 2, 3, 6, 8–10, 14, 101–102, 108–110, 114–115, 117–119, 139–154, 154–168, 168–186, 190–193, 195; People's Republic of 3, 6, 139–154, 164, 176–177; Post-Chinese 10, 168–186, 190, 195; Republic of China 3, 6, 164, 168, 179; *see also* Taiwan
Christianity 1, 3, 9, 10, 48, 90n3, 127–129, 133, 135, 136n2, 139–149, 154–157, 160–165; *see also* Catholicism; Protestant, Protestantism
colonialism 20, 27, 34–35, 42, 52, 56, 189–190; anti-colonialism 2, 14, 27; British 20, 27, 34–35, 42; colonial governmentality 34–35, 190; Japanese (*see* imperialism, Japanese); post-colonialism 6, 7, 33–36, 41, 43, 188, 191; Spanish 52, 56; US 52; *see also* empire
Confucian 9, 10, 82, 118–119, 132, 135, 140–141, 143–145, 148–149; Confucianism 2, 3, 10, 135, 140–141, 145, 168–186; Confucius 164

Daoism 2, 3, 99, 104
Derrida, Jacques 190
Donatism 10, 154–168

East Asia 1, 2, 3, 6, 8, 9, 94–106, 108–120; East Asia League 9, 108, 118–120; East Asian Community 9, 108–109, 111, 115–118, 120; Great(er) East Asian Co-prosperity Sphere 2, 8, 9, 94–108, 116, 194
Eisenstadt, Shmuel. N. 5, 8, 108, 190; *see also* multiple modernities
empire 8, 9, 10, 14, 29n1, 95, 96, 108, 110, 113–119, 154–166, 176, 190, 195; British 14 (*see also* colonialism); Japanese 8, 9, 94–108, 108–120, 128; Qing 176; Roman 10, 154–166; Spanish Empire (*see* colonialism); *see also* imperialism

Fukuzawa Yukichi 8, 79–94

Gandhi, Indira 38, 39
Gandhi, Mohandas. K (Mahatma) 19, 23, 26, 28, 37, 127
Gandhi, Rajiv 38
Gellner, Ernest 4, 109, 186–188
Greater East Asian Co-Prosperity Sphere 94, 106, 116, 194

Index

Hindu 2, 4, 7, 15–18, 20, 24–26, 28, 30, 32–33, 35–38, 40, 42, 44n5; Hinduism 7, 35, 42, 58, 191; Hindu nationalism 4, 7, 26, 33, 37, 42, 44n5; the Hindus 7, 15, 17, 24, 35–38, 40, 42; *Hindutva* 33, 37, 196 (*see also* Savarkar, V. D.); religion 16

imperialism 5, 7, 9, 13, 16, 68, 95–97, 101, 108–124, 127–129, 134, 135, 173, 176, 196; British (*see* colonialism); Japanese 9, 101, 108–124, 127–129, 134, 135, 136n2; Western Imperialism 68, 111, 173
India 2–4, 6–7, 11, 13–32; Indian 3, 13–29, 32–44; Indian National Congress (INC) 16, 36, 38, 189; from secular to religious nationalism 36–38
Inoue Kowashi 8, 79–94
International Relations (IR) 3, 97, 121n3
Iraq 6, 8, 62–79;
Islam 7, 8, 33, 35–36, 40, 42, 58, 62–75; Islamic 4, 39, 67–68, 70, 73–74; Political Islam 7; Shia Islam 8, 35, 65, 67–69, 71–74; Sunni Islam 8, 35, 40, 65–69, 71–74; *see also* Muslim

Japan 1, 3, 4, 6, 8–9, 11, 79–94, 108–124; *see also* modernity, Japanese modernity
Jinja Honcho (Association of Shinto Shrines) 4
Jinnah, Muhammad Ali 4, 36, 38–39, 42
Juergensymeyer, Mark 4, 80–81

Korea 6, 9, 95, 100, 116–122, 124–139; South 6, 104
Kyoto School 8, 9, 94, 96–98, 100–105, 108, 111–115, 119, 189

Liang Qichao 2
legacies 5, 10, 186–192

Marxism 118, 120, 151n4, 168, 192
Mazzini, Giuseppe 9, 15, 133
Meiji 2, 3, 8, 79–85, 87–88, 90, 189, 191; restoration 2–3, 80, 101
Middle East 8, 62–70, 190, 195
Modi, Narendra 37, 42
modernity 4–5, 9, 14, 19, 21–22, 27, 174, 186, 188, 190; Asian modernity 10; East Asian modernity 3; Japanese modernity 79–80, 88, 108–124, 129, 195; Korean modernity 135; multiple modernities 5, 8, 188–190; modernization 4, 186–188; political modernity 8; secular modernity 57; Western modernity 19, 28, 135, 180; *see also* nationalism, nationalism and modernity
Muslim 4, 7–8, 16–18, 25–26, 28, 32–33, 35–40, 42, 58, 75n2, 189, 193

Nandy, Ashis 23, 27, 35
nation 4–5, 7–9, 13–15, 18–21, 23–29, 36–38, 40, 42, 44n5, 47–48, 53, 56–57, 75n4, 79, 95, 97, 99–100, 102, 116–117, 127–128, 130, 132–133, 135, 149, 151n1, 168, 170, 175–176, 187–190, 194–196; nation-state 1, 3–7, 11, 14, 20, 27, 31n42, 33, 36, 42–43, 62, 65–70, 73–75, 88–90, 95, 102, 106, 120, 125, 132, 148, 176, 186, 189, 193–196
nationalism 1, 3–11, 13–29, 32–44, 47–50, 52–54, 56–58, 62, 64, 66–67, 69–75, 79–89, 95, 106, 108–111, 111, 115–116, 118–121, 124, 126, 134, 139, 158, 168–169, 171, 173–174, 177–181, 186–188, 190–196; anti-colonial nationalism 26, 189; critical nationalism 13–32, 194; cultural nationalism 10, 33, 168–171, 176, 178, 180, 191; ethno-nationalism 3, 71, 134, 180; nationalism and modernity 6, 11, 27; political nationalism 168, 171, 176–177, 179–180; religious nationalism 3–4, 7, 32–33, 36–38, 40, 48, 52, 56–58, 75, 79–80, 88–90, 124–125, 128, 135, 168, 189; secular nationalism 1, 11n1, 33, 36–38, 40, 79–80, 82, 86, 125, 186, 189, 193, 196; theories of nationalism 186–188; ultranationalism 79, 87, 89
Nehru, Jawaharlal 3, 4, 28, 36–37
Nishihongwanji 8, 94, 96, 98–105

Okakura Tenshin 2
Okawa Shumei 2, 111
Orientalism 2, 10

Pakistan 3–4, 6–7, 32, 33, 35–36, 38–42, 44n10, 189; East Pakistan 33, 39, 42; West Pakistan 38
Pan-Asianism 2, 120n1
Partition 7, 32–33, 35–36, 39, 42–43, 189
patriotism 1, 53, 57, 73, 178; cosmopolitan patriotism 124–135, 194–195
Philippines 6, 7, 47–62, 189, 193–195; Filipino 47–62

Index

Protestant 10, 50–51, 57, 60, 65, 126, 138–139, 146, 155, 164–165; Protestantism 164; *see also* Christianity
possibilities 6, 10, 192–196

religion 1–11, 32–47, 190–192, 196; colonial construction of 34–35; Hindu religion 16; native religion 99; non-religion 8, 84, 87–88; political religion 11n1; politicized religion 125; popular religion 6, 50, 86, 193; public religion 48; religion as doctrine vs religion as identity 67; religion-making 86, 191; religious-secular dyad 190–192; state religion 39, 79, 81; thick and thin 39, 190, 192
republicanism 49; republican 9, 49, 131–132
Rushdie, Salman 32

Savarkar, V. D. 26, 37
sectarianism 62–79, 189–190; sectarian 7–8, 40, 42, 159, 163
secularism 1, 5, 7, 42–43, 51, 66, 87–90, 106, 190–192; future trajectories 193–194; *see also* nationalism

Shintoism 2–4, 8, 79–94, 99, 190, 192; Shinto 8, 79–94, 193, 195–196
Smith, A. D. 11n1, 70, 124, 186–188
South Asia 1, 6–7, 32–47; South Asian Association of Regional Cooperation (SAARC) 43
Southeast Asia 1, 6, 11, 178–179
Sri Lanka 6–7, 32, 34, 40–42

Tagore, Rabindranath 1–2, 6, 11, 13–32, 43, 189–190, 194, 196
Taiwan 3, 9, 100, 104, 108, 113–115, 119–120, 168, 174–175, 177, 190
Taylor, Charles 11n2, 29n17, 191

Veer, Peter van der 5, 11, 192, 197n3

West 1, 8, 10, 25, 34, 56, 94–96, 102, 110, 113, 115, 117, 120, 175, 177, 186, 190–191; Western imperialism 111, 119, 173; Western modernity 2, 20, 28; post-Western 106, 109, 121n3, 180